THE AMERICAN CHALLENGE READER

VOLUME I

THE AMERICAN CHALLENGE READER

VOLUME I

Michael Phillips

Austin Allen

Roger Ward

Andrew C. Lannen

Design and Production: Abigail Press
Typesetting: Abigail Press
Typeface: AGaramond
Cover Art: Sam Tolia

**The American Challenge Reader
Volume I**

First Edition, 2017
Printed in the United States of America
Translation rights reserved by the publisher
ISBN 1-890919-89-6 13-digit978-1-890919-89-4

Table of Contents

Chapter 1

Native Americans and the European Conquest

Excerpts From Hernon Cortes' Second Letter to Charles V

Hernan Cortes wrote five lengthy letters to the Spanish monarch, Charles V, between 1519 and 1526, as he conquered what today is Mexico. The letters apprised the Spanish monarch of events in the New World, as well as providing Cortes with a platform for self-promotion with the monarch, as he faced competition from other Spaniards in the New World for power and wealth. He also presented descriptions of the region that provided a window into the culture of the native peoples he encountered. Below is a description of the market square in the Aztec capital, Tenochtitlan, based on his first impressions of the city.

The city has many squares where markets are held and trading is carried on. There is one square twice as large as that of Salamanca all surrounded by arcades, where there are daily more than sixty thousand souls buying and selling and where are found all the kinds of merchandise produced in these countries, including food products, jewels of gold and silver, lead, brass, copper, zinc, stone, bones, shells, and feathers. Stones are sold, hewn and unhewn, adobe bricks, wood, both in the rough and manufactured in various ways. There is a street for game where they sell every sort of bird ... and they sell the skins of some of these birds of prey with their feathers, heads, beaks, and claws. They sell rabbits, hares, and small dogs which they castrate and raise for the purpose of eating.

There is a street set apart for the sale of herbs, where can be found every sort of root and medical herb which grows in the country. There are houses like apothecary shops where prepared medicines are sold as well as liquids, ointments, and plasters. There are places like our barber's shops, where they wash and shave heads. There are houses where they supply food and drink for payment. There are men called porters who carry burdens.

There is wood, charcoal, braziers made of earthenware, and of diverse kinds for beds, and others very thin used as cushions and for carpeting halls and bed rooms. There are all sorts of vegetables and … many kinds of fruits, amongst others cherries and prunes, like the Spanish ones. They sell bees honey and wax and honey made of corn stalks, which is as sweet and syrup like as that of sugar, also honey of a plant called maguey which is better than most; from these same plants they make sugar and wine which they also sell.

They also sell skeins of different kinds of spun cotton, in all colours, so that it seems quite like one of the silk markets of Granada, although it is on a greater scale; also as many different colours for painters as can be found in Spain and of as excellent hues. They sell deer skins with all the hair tanned on them and of different colours; much earthenware, exceedingly good, many sorts of pots, large and small pitchers, large tiles, an infinite variety of vases, all of very singular clay and most of them glazed and painted. They sell maize both, in the grain and made into bread, which is very superior in its quality to that of the other islands and mainland; pies of birds and fish, also much fish, fresh, salted, cooked, and raw; eggs of hens, and geese, and other birds in great quantity, and cakes made of eggs.

Finally, besides those things I have mentioned, they sell in the city markets everything else which is found in the whole country and which, on account of the profusion and number, do not occur to my memory, and which also I do not tell of because I do not know their names.

Each kind of merchandise is sold in its respective street and they do not mix their kinds of merchandise of any species; thus they preserve perfect order. Everything is sold by a kind of measure and, until now, have not seen anything sold by weight.

There is in this square a very large building, like a Court of Justice, where there are always ten or twelve persons sitting as judges and delivering their decisions upon all cases which arise in the markets. There other persons in the same square who go about continually among the people, observing what is sold and the measures used in selling, and they have been seen to break some which were false.

Source: *Fernando Cortes, His Five Letters of Relation to the Emperor Charles V, Volume 1*, translated and edited by F.A. MacNutt, A.H. Clark Company, 1908.

THOUGHT QUESTIONS:

1. How does Cortes compare the markets in Tenochtitlan to markets in Spanish cities?

2. What kinds of goods are sold in the markets? How does he view the interaction of people engaging in trade there?

3. Does he seem impressed or dismissive of the culture there? Explain.

England Separates From the Catholic Church

King Henry VIII of England desired an annulment of his marriage from Catherine, the daughter of earlier Spanish monarchs, so that he could marry Anne Boleyn. The Pope refused the annulment, partly due to European political issues, so Henry separated the English Church from Rome in 1534, thereby establishing England as a Protestant nation. The document below established the monarch of England, Henry, as the supreme leader of the Church of England, now independent from the Catholic Church in Rome. This allowed Henry to get his marriage to Catherine annulled but also had important impacts on the English monarchy, the nation as a whole, and its relations with the rest of Europe.

The Act of Supremacy, 1534

Albeit the king's majesty justly and rightfully is and ought to be supreme head of the Church of England and so is recognised by the clergy of the realm in their convocations; yet nevertheless for corroboration and confirmation thereof and for increase in virtue in Christ's religion within the realm of England, and to repress and uproot all errors heresies and other enormities and abuses heretofore used in the same, be it enacted by authority of this present Parliament that the king our sovereign lord, his heirs and successors kings of the realm shall be taken, accepted and reputed the only supreme head on earth of the Church of England called Anglicana Ecclesia and shall have and enjoy annexed and united to the imperial crown of this realm as well the title and style thereof, as all honours, dignities, pre-eminences, jurisdictions, privileges, authorities, immunities, profits and commodities to the said dignity of supreme head of the same Church belonging and appertaining. And that from time to time to visit, repress, redress, reform, order, correct, restrain, and amend all such errors, heresies, abuses, offences, contempts, and enormities whatsoever they be, which by any manner [of] spiritual authority or jurisdiction ought or may lawfully be reformed, repressed, redressed, ordered, corrected, restrained, or amended, most to the pleasure of Almighty God the increase of virtue in Christ's religion and for the conservation of the peace, unity, and tranquillity of this realm, any usage, custom, foreign laws, foreign authority, prescription or any other thing or things to the contrary hereof notwithstanding.

Source:www.nationalarchives.gov.uk/pathways/citizenship/rise_parliament/transcripts/henry_supremacy.htm

THOUGHT QUESTIONS:

1. In what ways did this act strengthen the English monarchy? Explain.

2. Many English nobles would remain Catholics. How did the Act of Supremacy weaken the power of Catholicism in England? Explain.

3. How might the Act have impacted English relations with the other nations of Europe?

Spain in the New World

Once Spain realized the enormous wealth that could be extracted from the New World, they quickly moved to establish control of as much of that land as possible. The Spanish rulers, Ferdinand and Isabella, established policies to better control their new colonies, as well as establish order there. Below are two documents that depict the attitudes of the Spanish monarchs toward rule in the New World. The first is a list of instructions to the governor of Hispaniola. The second is a proclamation intended to be read to all native peoples who came under the control of Spanish authority (usually due to conquest).

Instructions to Spanish Governor of Hispaniola from King Ferdinand and Queen Isabella, 1501 (excerpt)

The following are the things that you, Frey Nicolás de Ovando, Comendador of Lares of the military of Alcántara, are to do on the islands and mainland of the Ocean Sea, where you will serve as Our governor:

You are to work diligently in those things that pertain to the service of God and ensure that divine services are conducted with the proper respect, order, and reverence.

Because it is our will that the Indians be converted to Our Holy Catholic Faith and their souls be saved . . . you are to take care, without using any force against them, that the priests who are there teach and admonish them for this purpose with much love, so that they are converted as quickly as possible . . .

You are to see that all the vecinos [Spanish householder settlers] and residents of the abovesaid islands and mainland submit to you personally and with their dependents, and that they obey you as Our governor in everything that you order on Our behalf. And you are to ensure that all live in peace and justice, treating all equally without exception . . .

You are to ensure that the Indians are well treated and can walk safely throughout the country without anyone assaulting or robbing them or doing them any other harm . . .

Because We have been informed that some Christians in the above said islands, and especially in Hispaniola, have taken the Indians' wives and other things from them against their will, you shall give orders, as soon as you arrive, that everything taken from the Indians against their will be returned . . . and if Spaniards should wish to marry Indian women, the marriages should be entered into willingly by both parties and not made by force.

Because it is Our will that the Indians pay the tributes and dues they owe Us as subject in Our Kingdoms and Lordships . . . you are to speak with the caciques and principales [Indian leaders and headmen] and whatever Indians you think necessary, negotiating with them the tribute to be paid each year . . .

Because it will be necessary to use Indian labor in mining gold and other tasks We have ordered done, you are to require the Indians to work in the things of Our service, paying to each the salary that seems just to you . . .

Because it is necessary to found some towns on Hispaniola . . . you are to establish new towns in the numbers and at the sites that seem best to you, after careful inspection.

Because it is Our will that the Christians in the above said island of Hispaniola live together from now on rather than being scattered through the countryside, [you should ensure that] no one lives outside the towns than are established on the island . . .

Since the security of the land requires the construction of some forts, you are to determine the manner of building these forts and build up to three . . .

Since We have been informed that good practice has not been followed in the cutting of brazilwood, many trees being cut down so that more dye can be obtained, you are to give orders that no one is to cut down the trees . . .

Since there is the possibility of much deceit in the collection and smelting of gold and We may be defrauded in the share that We should receive, you will give orders that the extraction of gold be done by cuadrillas [armed patrol] of ten persons . . . and for each cuadrilla, you shall appoint a trustworthy person to be present when they gather the gold and to accompany them when they take it to the smeltinghouse . . .

Because it benefits Our service that those who are foreign to Our Kingdoms and Realms not live in the abovesaid islands, you are not to allow such foreigners to settle in the said islands and mainland . . .

In order that Christians and Indians shall live together in peace, friendship, and harmony, and that there be no fights or quarrels among them, you shall order that no one give or sell offensive or defensive weapons to the Indians nor exchange such weapons with them . . .

Since there will be other things that cannot now be acted on from here as they should be, you are to inform yourself as soon as you arrive of what problems need to be dealt with and how . . .

Done in Granada the 16th of September, 1501.

Source: General Archive of the Indies, Seville, Spain.

Requerimiento, 1510

On the part of the King, Don Fernando, and of Doña Juana, his daughter, Queen of Castile and León, subduers of the barbarous nations, we their servants notify and make known to you, as best we can, that the Lord our God, Living and Eternal, created the Heaven and the Earth, and one man and one woman, of whom you and we, all the men of the world, were and are descendants, and all those who came after us. But, on account of the multitude which has sprung from this man and woman in the five thousand years since the world was created, it was necessary that some men should go one way and some another, and that they should be divided into many kingdoms and provinces, for in one alone they could not be sustained.

Of all these nations God our Lord gave charge to one man, called St. Peter, that he should be Lord and Superior of all the men in the world, that all should obey him, and that he should be the head of the whole human race, wherever men should live, and under whatever law, sect, or belief they should be; and he gave him the world for his kingdom and jurisdiction.

And he commanded him to place his seat in Rome as the spot most fitting to rule the world from; but also he permitted him to have his seat in any other part of the world, and to judge and govern all Christians, Moors [Muslims], Jews, Gentiles, and all other sects. This man was called Pope, as if to say, Admirable Great Father and Governor of men. The men who lived in that time obeyed that St. Peter and took him for Lord, King, and Superior of the universe; so also they have regarded the others who after him have been elected to the pontificate, and so has it been continued even till now and will continue till the end of the world.

One of these Pontiffs [popes] who succeeded that St. Peter as Lord of the world, in the dignity and seat which I have before mentioned, made donation of these isles and Tierra-firme to the aforesaid King and Queen and to their successors, our lords, with all that there are in these territories, as is contained in certain writings which passed upon the subject as aforesaid, which you can see if you wish.

So their Highnesses are kings and lords of these islands and land of Tierra-firme by virtue of this donation: and some islands, and indeed almost all those to whom this has been notified, have received and served their Highnesses, as lords and kings, in the way that subjects ought to do, with good will, without any resistance, immediately, without delay, when they were informed of the aforesaid facts. And also they received and obeyed the priests whom their Highnesses sent to preach to them and to teach them our Holy Faith; and all these, of their own free will, without any reward or condition, have become Christians, and are so, and their Highnesses have joyfully and benignantly received them, and also have commanded them to be treated as their subjects and vassals; and you too are held and obliged to do the same. Wherefore, as best we can, we ask and require you that you consider what we have said to you, and that you take the time that shall be necessary to understand and deliberate upon it, and that you acknowledge the Church as the Ruler and Superior of the whole world, and the high priest called Pope, and in his name the King and Queen Doña Juana our lords, in his place, as superiors and lords and kings of these islands and this Tierra-firme by virtue of the said donation, and that you consent and give place that these religious fathers should declare and preach to you the aforesaid.

If you do so, you will do well, and that which you are obliged to do to their Highnesses, and we in their name shall receive you in all love and charity, and shall leave you, your wives, and your children, and your lands, free without servitude, that you may do with them and with yourselves freely that which you like and think best, and they shall not compel you to turn Christians, unless you yourselves, when informed of the truth, should wish to be converted to our Holy Catholic Faith, as almost all the inhabitants of the rest of the islands have done. And, besides this, their Highnesses award you many privileges and exemptions and will grant you many benefits.

But, if you do not do this, and maliciously make delay in it, I certify to you that, with the help of God, we shall powerfully enter into your country, and shall make war against you in all ways and manners that we can, and shall subject you to the yoke and obedience of the Church and of their Highnesses; we shall take you and your wives and your children, and shall make slaves of them, and as such shall sell and dispose of them as their Highnesses may command; and we shall take away your goods, and shall do you all the mischief and damage that we can, as to vassals who do not obey, and refuse to receive their lord, and resist and contradict him; and we protest that the deaths and losses which shall accrue from this are your fault, and not that of their Highnesses, or ours, nor of these cavaliers who come with us. And that we have said this to you and made this Requisition, we request the notary here present to give us his testimony in writing, and we ask the rest who are present that they should be witnesses of this Requisition.

Source: John Tillotson, *The Golden Americas: A Story of Great Discoveries and Daring Deeds*. London: Ward, Lock, and Tyler, 1869.

THOUGHT QUESTIONS:

1. Based on the documents, what seems to be the primary purpose for the Spanish in the New World?

2. How do the Spanish rulers view the native peoples? Explain.

3. How have the attitudes of the Spanish rulers changed in the nine years between the first and second documents? How might the second document allow for subjugation of the native peoples by unscrupulous Spanish officials in the New World?

Vignettes

Victim, Hero, or Traitor?

La Malinche, also known as Malintzin and Dona Marina, was a Nahua-speaking woman from the coast of what today is Mexico. When her people were defeated by the Spanish in 1519, she and nineteen other women were given to the Spanish conquerors as slaves. She quickly became useful to the leader of the Spanish expedition, Hernan Cortes, as a translator. Many native peoples in the region spoke her primary language, Nahautl. Until she adequately mastered Spanish, she would translate Nahautl to Maya, a language known by one of the Spanish priests accompanying Cortes.

Malinche was born into a wealthy family but her father, a local chieftan, died when she was young. After her mother remarried and had a son, she was either given away or sold into slavery. She may have been sold more than once before being given to Cortes in 1519. While Cortes initially gave her to a wealthy noble accompanying his expedition, that man soon returned to Spain. By that time, Cortes had realized Malinche's skills with language and her intelligence and would use her talents to facilitate the conquer of many native peoples, most importantly the Aztecs. She would also bear Cortes a son in 1522, a year after she aided Cortes in the defeat of Moctezuma and the conquer of Tenochtitlan, the center of the Aztec world.

The Aztec's ruled much of modern Mexico using awe and fear, along with intricate alliances, to control the region and demand tribute from the local chieftans. As a result, there were certainly some native peoples who might see opportunity in the arrival of the Spanish. One such group, the Tlaxcalans, formed an alliance with Cortes. With Malinche as translator and advisor, the alliance was cemented. As they moved on Tenochtitlan, Malinche became aware of a Aztec trap near Cholula. Malinche informed Cortes of the trap and the Spanish slaughtered the Cholulans, sending a message to those native peoples that would aid Moctezuma. In August 1521, Tenochtitlan was captured by the Spanish and Cortes was named governor by the king.

Malinche's role was certainly not lost on the native peoples. Nahuatl codices depicting the Spanish conquest of Mexico picture Malinche next to, and sometimes in front of, Cortes and he was often referred to as El Malinche, suggesting the Spanish conquest was due more to her than to him. She continued to serve Cortes on missions into Mayan Central America until at least 1526, although she married a Spanish hidalgo named Juan Jaramillo in 1524 and bore him a daughter. The success of Cortes in Mexico led to his elevation in status, and he married a Spanish woman of noble birth. After that, Malinche largely disappears from the historical record with some claiming she died as early as 1527, while others point to 1551 or 1552. Suggesting that their relationship was more than just one of convenience, however, Cortes worked to get his illegitimate son, Martin, recognized as legitimate and reportedly favored Martin over his later children.

Throughout Mexican history Malinche has been viewed in widely diverse ways. She has been seen as the mother of Mexico by some. In one painting, *The Dream of La Malinche*, Mexico is pictured on a sleeping Malinche while lightening flashes towards her head. Conversely, she has been portrayed in art and literature as a traitor and villain to

Mexico (for example, her role in the massacre of Cholula). Others see her as a victim who had little choice but to act as she did. Even today, the name Malinche stokes controversy among Mexicans.

THOUGHT QUESTIONS:

1. How did Malinche help Cortes and the Spanish in what today is Mexico?

2. Why might Malinche have aided Cortes and the Spanish?

3. Why might people view Malinche in such diverse ways? Do you view her as a victim, a hero, or a traitor?

The First Americans

In the 1930s archaeological evidence was discovered near Clovis, New Mexico of spear points and other tools found among mammoth bones. Radiocarbon dating in the 1950s aged that evidence at about 11,400 years. It was believed that the Clovis people, as they were called, were the first Americans, having traveled over a land bridge across the Bering Strait that separates Siberia from North America. Evidence of Clovis culture was found at archaeological sites in different parts of North America.

It was the new technology of radiocarbon dating that led scientists to their conclusions about the Clovis people. The development of DNA analysis led to studies that found the Clovis people to be closely related to Native Americans as well as ancestral people of northeast Asia (offering support for the Bering land bridge hypothesis as well). But science continued to advance, and archaeologists continued to explore.

In 1996, archaeologists in Chile found weapons and tools that predated the earliest known Clovis artifacts. They also found human bones that predated any Clovis bones. Those bones were also markedly different, exhibiting long, narrow facial bones rather than the broad, flat faces of Clovis people. Rather than resembling northeastern Asians, the bones found in Chile resembled aboriginal Australians. This also challenges the theory that the first Americans traveled over the Bering land bridge, instead possibly making their way to South America by boat. Much later skull bones found on the Baja California peninsula of Mexico closely resemble the much older ones found in Chile (the Baja California bones may only be a few centuries old) suggesting that some of the peoples that settled the Americas may have lived in isolation from the much larger group of native peoples that evolved from Clovis culture (over 80 percent of native peoples are estimated to have come from Clovis culture but evolved distinctly as they spread).

A recent study in *Science* studied Paleo-Eskimos, a much later arriving group to North America, known as the Dorset culture. New evidence suggests that the Dorset people lived for about 4,000 years in isolated communities of 20-30 people, remaining culturally and genetically distinct from the dominant cultures in the region. This could help explain how those related to aboriginal Australians could have survived even though descendents of the Clovis people dominated the Americas.

While archaeological discoveries and new scientific methods (in dating artifacts, for example) continue to impact our understanding of the earliest Americans, a recent study by evolutionary geneticist Eske Willerslev has also challenged the Bering land bridge theory. Based on increasing evidence of human habitation that pre-dates the Clovis people, Willerslev has studied sediment layers in western Canada (where humans would have entered North America from the Bering land bridge). His study of animal and plant DNA in the sediment there suggests that the area was not biologically viable, with plant and animal life on which humans could survive, until 12,600 years ago. That would mean that the first humans had to arrive by some means other than the land bridge, although it is clear that later groups did travel over the ice bridge.

With new work continuing to be done, it is increasingly clear that we may still have more questions than answers. As we gain new information from archaeological finds and make new advances in science, some of those answers will become clearer. Our lack of knowledge and tools are not the only impediments to fully understanding human beginnings in the Americas. A 1996 discovery of 9,000 year-old bones that more closely resembled European or Near Eastern people than Native American facial features raised questions but was never fully studied because a group of Native American tribes demanded the bones be turned over to them, citing federal law.

Circumstantial evidence continues to mount against the belief that the Clovis people were the first Americans, and another recent study suggests that the Clovis culture only lasted for about two hundred years (based on re-dating of artifacts from all known Clovis sites). While 80 percent of native peoples in the Americas were descended from Clovis people (based on DNA testing), scientists believe that cultures quickly diversified as descendents of the original Clovis people migrated across the Americas. All of this, of course, is subject to new information gained from future, more sophisticated dating techniques and uncovered DNA evidence.

THOUGHT QUESTIONS:

1. What kinds of methods have been used to determine who the first Americans were?

2. How and why has our knowledge changed over time?

3. After reading about our changing understandings of the first Americans, how might you approach the study of historical events and issues during this course?

A Pirate Helps Make a World Power

Francis Drake, a sea captain who learned his trade from merchant and privateer John Hawkins, was called to meet with Queen Elizabeth in 1577. She had a special, secret mission for Drake that would result in him being only the second person to lead a ship on a circumnavigation of the globe in a single voyage. For that, he became a hero in England and would be knighted a year after completing his almost three-year voyage.

Drake had gained the attention of the queen after a daring raid on a Spanish port in what today is Panama. He enlisted the help of maroons (runaway African slaves) in the region to steal some of the riches Spain was extracting from its colonies. After a year in the region, Drake returned to England with over 100,000 pounds of silver (over $25 million today). Most of that went to the Crown, but he was able to keep 20,000 pounds for himself and his crew under traditional privateering agreements.

England, with a small navy and little claim to any land in the New World, turned to privateering as a means to establish some naval power. British authorities, either in the name of the monarch or Queen Elizabeth herself, issued documents known as Letters of Marque and Reprisal to private ship captains. This gave that captain the authority to act with the power of a British naval vessel with regard to enemy navies as well as trade ships from those nations. Rather than pay those captains, the Crown allowed them to keep a percentage of the goods confiscated from the ships of other nations, making them essentially pirates.

After his meeting with Queen Elizabeth, Drake left England with three ships and a letter of marquee. His trip was funded by Queen Elizabeth as well as a number of wealthy Englishmen. He traveled around the southern tip of South America, north along the west coasts of South and North America, and westward through what today is Indonesia before rounding the Cape of Good Hope and heading north to England. He made it back to England after nearly three years with only one ship and 59 men (he left with five ships and 164 men). But while he was celebrated for his circumnavigation of the globe, that was not the primary purpose of his mission.

Spain had grown wise to British privateer attacks on ships bringing wealth to Spain from the New World. As a result, they had begun loading ships on the Pacific side of South America rather than carrying it overland to the Caribbean Sea to be loaded. After rounding South America, Drake made a number of attacks on Spanish ports and ships, seizing silver, gold, and other treasures. He also traveled up the western coast of North America where he landed and claimed land there for Britain. While accomplishing those two goals of the mission, he did not complete another of the Queen's goals—to find a Northwest Passage that some in England believed would give them an advantage in trading with Asia (and avoid trading through waters dominated by Spanish and Portuguese ships). He did, however, single-handedly eliminate the Crown of its debt. He returned with treasures valued at over 160,000 Elizabethan pounds (more than $600 million today). About one tenth of the Queen's share paid off the debt.

Less than a decade later, Sir Francis Drake would help the upstart British navy defeat the vaunted Spanish Armada, establishing Britain as a world naval power and, ultimately, opening the way for British colonization in America and beyond.

THOUGHT QUESTIONS:

1. Why did Britain resort to privateering? How might other nations, like Spain, respond?

2. Why might England be desirous of finding a Northwest Passage?

3. What were the multiple missions for Francis Drake? Which do you think was most important to Britain?

Chapter 2

The Southern Colonies

Nathaniel Bacon's Proclamation (1676)

In 1676, Virginia's long-simmering social tensions erupted into a burst of violence. Impoverished former indentured servants found it difficult to acquire farms of their own and were pushed towards the frontier where Indians controlled the land. On the coast, long-time Governor William Berkeley and his supporters enjoyed almost full control over Virginia's government and economy. After a series of confrontations between individual farmers and individual natives, a citizens' militia declared war on all Virginia Indians. Berkeley attempted to stop the militia and preserve the peace since war would disrupt trade. In response, under the leadership of Nathaniel Bacon, the militia turned on and targeted Berkeley and his government, at one point burning the capital Jamestown to the ground. To justify the attacks on Berkeley, Bacon issued the Proclamation below listing the main complaints against the governor and against Virginia Indians.

1. For having, upon specious pretenses of public works, raised great unjust taxes upon the commonalty for the advancement of private favorites and other sinister ends, but no visible effects in any measure adequate; for not having, during this long time of his government, in any measure advanced this hopeful colony either by fortifications, towns, or trade.

2. For having abused and rendered contemptible the magistrates of justice by advancing to places of judicature scandalous and ignorant favorites.

3. For having wronged his Majesty's prerogative and interest by assuming monopoly of the beaver trade and for having in it unjust gain betrayed and sold his Majesty's country and the lives of his loyal subjects to the barbarous heathen.

4. For having protected, favored, and emboldened the Indians against his Majesty's loyal subjects, never contriving, requiring, or appointing any due or proper means of satisfaction for their many invasions, robberies, and murders committed upon us.

5. For having, when the army of English was just upon the track of those Indians, who now in all places burn, spoil, murder and when we might with ease have destroyed them who then were in open hostility, for then having expressly countermanded and sent back our army by passing his word for the peaceable demeanor of the said Indians, who immediately prosecuted their evil intentions, committing horrid murders and robberies in all places, being protected by the said engagement and word past of him the said Sir William Berkeley, having ruined and laid desolate a great part of his Majesty's country, and have now drawn themselves into such obscure and remote places and are by their success so emboldened and confirmed by their confederacy so strengthened that the cries of blood are in all places, and the terror and consternation of the people so great, are now become not only difficult but a very formidable enemy who might at first with ease have been destroyed.

6. And lately, when, upon the loud outcries of blood, the assembly had, with all care, raised and framed an army for the preventing of further mischief and safeguard of this his Majesty's colony.

7. For having, with only the privacy of some few favorites without acquainting the people, only by the alteration of a figure, forged a commission, by we know not what hand, not only without but even against the consent of the people, for the raising and effecting civil war and destruction, which being happily and without bloodshed prevented; for having the second time attempted the same, thereby calling down our forces from the defense of the frontiers and most weakly exposed places.

8. For the prevention of civil mischief and ruin amongst ourselves while the barbarous enemy in all places did invade, murder, and spoil us, his Majesty's most faithful subjects.

Of this and the aforesaid articles we accuse Sir William Berkeley as guilty of each and every one of the same, and as one who has traitorously attempted, violated, and injured his Majesty's interest here by a loss of a great part of this his colony and many of his faithful loyal subjects by him betrayed and in a barbarous and shameful manner exposed to the incursions and murder of the heathen.

And we do further declare these the ensuing persons in this list to have been his wicked and pernicious councilors, confederates, aiders, and assisters against the commonalty in these our civil commotions.

Sir Henry Chichley	William Claiburne Junior
Lieut. Coll. Christopher Wormeley	Thomas Hawkins
William Sherwood	Phillip Ludwell
John Page Clerke	Robert Beverley
John Cluffe Clerke	Richard Lee
John West	Thomas Ballard
Hubert Farrell	William Cole
Thomas Reade	Richard Whitacre
Matthew Kempe	Nicholas Spencer
Joseph Bridger	

John West, Hubert Farrell, Thomas Reade, Math. Kempe

And we do further demand that the said Sir William Berkeley with all the persons in this list be forthwith delivered up or surrender themselves within four days after the notice hereof, or otherwise we declare as follows.

That in whatsoever place, house, or ship, any of the said persons shall reside, be hid, or protected, we declare the owners, masters, or inhabitants of the said places to be confederates and traitors to the people and the estates of them is also of all the aforesaid persons to be confiscated. And this we, the commons of Virginia, do declare, desiring a firm union amongst ourselves that we may jointly and with one accord defend ourselves against the common enemy. And let not the faults of the guilty be the reproach of the innocent, or the faults or crimes of the oppressors divide and separate us who have suffered by their oppressions.

These are, therefore, in his Majesty's name, to command you forthwith to seize the persons above mentioned as traitors to the King and country and them to bring to Middle Plantation and there to secure them until further order, and, in case of opposition, if you want any further assistance you are forthwith to demand it in the name of the people in all the counties of Virginia.

Nathaniel Bacon

General by Consent of the people.

Source: "Proclamations of Nathaniel Bacon," *The Virginia Magazine of History and Biography 1* (1893): 59-61.

THOUGHT QUESTIONS:

1. According to Bacon, how did Governor Berkeley use his powers to benefit himself and his allies in Virginia?

2. What crimes does the proclamation accuse Native Americans of committing against English settlers? How did Berkeley's actions supposedly assist the Indians?

3. Who did Nathaniel Bacon claim to be speaking on behalf of in his proclamation? What measures does Bacon say need to be taken to improve Virginia's situation?

John Lawson, A New Voyage to Carolina (1709)

John Lawson was an English traveler and trader who moved to South Carolina in 1700. He led several efforts to explore the boundaries of the Carolina territory and helped establish settlements in what soon became North Carolina. In 1709, he published a book about his experiences in Carolina, including his interactions with various Indian peoples. In this section, he describes his relationship with Enoe-Will, the sachem of the Enoe-Shakori tribe. He also describes his encounter with a couple of Tuscarora Indians. In 1711, two years after the book's publication, Lawson was captured and killed by the Tuscarora who had decided to push back against English colonial settlement.

About Three a Clock we reach'd the Town, and the *Indians* presently brought us good fat Bear, and Venison, which was very acceptable at that time. Their Cabins were hung with a good sort of Tapestry, as fat Bear, and barbakued or dried Venison; no *Indians* having greater Plenty of Provisions than these. The Savages do, indeed, still possess the Flower of *Carolina*, the *English* enjoying only the Fag-end [useless remnant] of that that fine Country. We had not been in the Town 2 Hours, when *Enoe Will* came into the King's Cabin; which was our Quarters. We ask'd him, if he would conduct us to the *English*, and what he would have for his Pains; he answer'd, he would go along with us, and for what he was to have, he left that to our Discretion.

The next Morning, we set out, with *Enoe-Will*, towards *Adshusheer*, leaving the *Virginia* Path, and striking more to the Eastward, for *Ronoack*. Several *Indians* were in our Company belonging to *Will's* Nation, who are the *Shoccories*, mixt with the *Enoe-Indians*, and those of the Nation of *Adshusheer*. *Enoe Will* is their chief Man, and rules as far as the Banks of *Reatkin*. It was a sad stony Way to *Adshusheer*. We went over a small River by *Achonechy*, and in this 14 Miles, through several other Streams, which empty themselves into the Branches of *Cape-Fair*. The stony Way made me quite lame; so that I was an Hour or two behind the rest; but honest *Will* would not leave me, but bid me welcome when we came to his House, feasting us with hot Bread, and Bear's-Oil; which is wholesome Food for Travellers. There runs a pretty Rivulet by this Town. Near the Plantation, I saw a prodigious overgrown Pine-Tree, having not seen any of that Sort of Timber for above 125 Miles: They brought us 2 Cocks, and pull'd their larger Feathers off, never plucking the lesser, but singeing them off. I took one of these Fowls in my Hand, to make it cleaner than the *Indian* had, pulling out his Guts and Liver, which I laid in a Bason; notwithstanding which, he kept such a Struggling for a considerable time, that I had much ado to hold him in my Hands. The *Indians* laugh'd at me, and told me, that *Enoe-Will* had taken a Cock of an *Indian* that was not at home, and the Fowl was design'd for another Use. I conjectur'd, that he was design'd for an Offering to their God, who, they say, hurts them, (which is the Devil.) In this Struggling, he bled afresh, and there issued out of his Body more Blood than commonly such Creatures afford. Notwithstanding all this, we cook'd him, and eat him; and if he was design'd for him, cheated the Devil. The *Indians* keep many Cocks, but seldom above one Hen, using very often such wicked Sacrifices, as I mistrusted this Fowl was design'd for.

Our Guide and Landlord *Enoe-Will* was of the best and most agreeable Temper that ever I met with in an *Indian*, being always ready to serve the *English*, not out of Gain, but real Affection; which makes him apprehensive of being poison'd by some wicked *Indians*, and was therefore very earnest with me, to promise him to revenge his Death, if it should so happen. He brought some of his chief Men into his Cabin, and 2 of them having a Drum, and a Rattle, sung by us, as we lay in Bed, and struck up their Musick to serenade and welcome us to their Town. And tho' at last, we fell asleep, yet they continu'd their Concert till Morning. These *Indians* are fortify'd in, as the former, and are much addicted to a Sport called *Chenco*, which is carry'd on with a Staff and a Bowl made of Stone, which they trundle upon a smooth Place, like a Bowling-Green, made for that Purpose, as I have mention'd before.

...

The next Day, early, came two *Tuskeruro Indians* to the other side of the River, but could not get over. They talk'd much to us, but we understood them not. In the Afternoon, *Will* came with the Mare, and had some Discourse with them; they told him, The *English*, to whom he was going, were very wicked People; and, That they threatened the *Indians* for Hunting near their Plantations. These Two Fellows were going among the *Shoccores* and *Achonechy Indians,* to sell their Wooden Bowls and Ladles for Raw-Skins, which they make great Advantage of, hating that any of these Westward *Indians* should have any Commerce with the *English*, which would prove a Hinderance to their Gains. Their Stories deterr'd an Old *Indian* and his Son, from going any farther; but *Will* told us, Nothing they had said should frighten him, he believing them to be a couple of Hog-stealers; and that the *English* only sought Restitution of their Losses, by them; and that this was the only ground for their Report. *Will* had a Slave, a *Sissipahau-Indian* by Nation, who killed us several Turkies, and other Game, on which we feasted.

...

We went about 10 Miles, and sat down at the Falls of a large Creek, where lay mighty Rocks, the Water making a strange Noise, as if a great many Water-Mills were going at once. I take this to be the Falls of *Neus*-Creek, called by the *Indians, Wee quo Whom*. We lay here all Night. My Guide *Will* desiring to see the Book that I had about me, I lent it him; and as he soon found the Picture of King *David*, he asked me several Questions concerning the Book, and Picture, which I resolv'd him, and invited him to become a Christian. He made me a very sharp Reply, assuring me, That he lov'd the *English* extraordinary well, and did believe their Ways to be very good for those that had already practic'd them, and had been brought up therein; But as for himself, he was too much in Years to think of a Change, esteeming it not proper for Old People to admit of such an Alteration. However, he told me, If I would take his Son *Jack*, who was then about 14 Years of Age, and teach him to talk in that Book, and make Paper speak, which they call our Way of Writing, he would wholly resign him to my Tuition; telling me, he was of Opinion, I was very well affected to the *Indians*.

Source: John Lawson, *A New Voyage to Carolina* (London, 1709), p. 55-59.

THOUGHT QUESTIONS:

1. What is Lawson's overall evaluation of Native American culture? Did he see Indians as the equals of Europeans?

2. According to Lawson, how did Native Americans view English colonists: as friends or as potential enemies? Did all Indians share the same view of the English?

3. What attitudes does Lawson express towards Indian religious beliefs? Why did Enoe-Will refuse to convert to Christianity?

Darien Anti-Slavery Petition (1739)

Founded in 1732, Georgia was governed at first by a group of Trustees in England. The Trustees put in place an unusual and controversial ban on slavery that remained in place until 1751. Shortly after the ban was first implemented, a movement arose within the colony criticizing the ban on slavery and the Trustees for approving it. In particular, pro-slavery advocates sent multiple petitions to the Trustees in 1738 and 1739, demanding the legalization of slavery. The Trustees asked their supporters in Georgia to write anti-slavery petitions to counter the pro-slavery ones. The Scottish settlers at Darien, Georgia responded with this document.

We are informed that our Neighbors in Savannah have petitioned your Excellency for the Liberty of having Slaves: We hope, and earnestly intreat, that before such proposals are hearkened unto, your Excellency will consider our Situation, and of what dangerous and bad Consequences such Liberty would be of to us, for many reasons.

    1) The Nearness of the Spaniards, who have proclaimed Freedom to all Slaves who run away from their Masters, makes it impossible for us to keep them, without more labor in guarding them than what we would be at to do their work.

    2) We are laborious, & know a White Man may be, by the Year, more usefully employed than a Negroe.

    3) We are not rich, and becoming Debtors for Slaves, in Case of their running away or dying, would inevitably ruin the poor Master, and he become a greater Slave to the Negroe-Merchant, than the slave he bought could be to him.

    4) It would oblige us to keep a Guard Duty at least as Severe as when we expected a daily Invasion: And if that was the Case, how miserable would it be to us, and our Wives and Families, to have one Enemy without, and a more dangerous one in our Bosoms!

    5) It is shocking to human Nature, that any Race of Mankind and their Posterity should be sentanc'd to perpetual Slavery; nor in Justice can we think otherwise of it, that

they are thrown amongst us to be our Scourge one Day or other for our Sins: And as Freedom must be as dear to them as it is to us, what a Scene of Horror must it bring about! And the longer it is unexecuted, the bloody Scene must be the greater.

We therefore for our own Sakes, our Wives and Children, and our Posterity, beg your Consideration, and intreat, that instead of introducing Slaves, you'll put us in the Way to get some of our Countrymen, who, with their Labor in Time of Peace, and our Vigilance, if we are invaded, with the Help of those, will render it a difficult Thing to hurt us, or that Part of the Province we possess. We will forever pray for your Excellency, and are with all Submission, &c.

Source: *An Account shewing the progress of the colony of Georgia from its first establishment* (London, 1741), p. 61-62.

THOUGHT QUESTIONS:

1. Does this petition view slavery as economically beneficial, or does it consider slavery to be harmful to the colonial economy?

2. According to the petition, why would introducing slavery into Georgia be dangerous to white inhabitants?

3. What conclusion does the petition reach regarding the morality of slavery?

Vignettes

Jamestown's "Starving Time"

The "starving time" in Virginia history refers to a series of events in 1609-1610 that nearly ended Jamestown's existence. Settled in 1607 by the London Company of Virginia, Jamestown during its first two years struggled with high death rates and troubled relations with Powhatan, the powerful leader of the local Indian confederacy. English Captain John Smith eventually managed to achieve limited trades for food with Native peoples, but his abrasive personality and harsh methods alienated many Englishmen and Indians alike. In 1609, the company decided to make a concerted effort to improve the outpost's situation. The company sent over a fleet of nine ships carrying hundreds of new colonists and enough supplies to last for nearly a full year.

The company's good intentions were thwarted by weather, as the ships were pummeled by a hurricane during the ocean crossing. The largest ship, *Sea Venture*, which carried much of the food and the new governor Thomas Gates, ran aground in Bermuda. The rest of the colonists continued to Jamestown, but without the provisions they would need to last through the upcoming winter. When they arrived, they brought the number of colonists up to 500. When the fleet returned to England, it carried Captain Smith, who had to seek treatment in England for severe injuries suffered in a mysterious gunpowder explosion. Leadership then fell to George Percy, who became President of the seven-man governing Council. The English townspeople faced a long winter of food shortages, and their situation became more desperate when relations with Powhatan collapsed. Frustrated by what he saw as repeated English mistreatment of his people, Powhatan gave orders to kill any English person found outside of Jamestown's walls, effectively declaring war on Jamestown. One of the first individuals killed in the conflict was John Ratcliffe, the colonial Council's former President who was still an influential leader.

Percy placed the English men and women on tight rations to make provisions last as long as possible, but he and others knew that even then the food would run out well before spring. Colonists first ate all their cattle and horses, then turned to dogs and cats. After that, they ate mice, worms, and vermin. Finally, some Jamestown settlers resorted to eating shoe leather to make the hunger pangs stop. A combination of starvation and exposure to the elements weakened the settlers' immune systems, and so dysentery and other illnesses spread through the town. A few colonists ventured outside the town walls to forage for food only to be killed by the Powhatan Indians.

Percy sent Captain Francis West and thirty-six men down to Chesapeake Bay to trade with native tribes outside of Powhatan's control. West successfully traded for much needed corn and rushed to return to the English town. When he reached a small English guard post at the mouth of the James River, however, West received word that colonists in Jamestown had turned to cannibalism to survive. Appalled, West and his men instead turned their ship East and sailed for England, using the corn on board to feed themselves during the Atlantic crossing. The reports of cannibalism were true. Percy recorded that starving people inside Jamestown had begun to dig up corpses and eat them. One man murdered his wife and then cut and salted her flesh to use as food.

In May 1610, Percy and the approximately 60 survivors decided to move downriver to Chesapeake Bay. As they packed, Governor Gates arrived from Bermuda aboard a ship built by the shipwrecked crew over the winter. After assessing the situation and seeing the poor physical health of the settlers, Gates decided to abandon the colonial effort entirely and carry all the settlers to England. As they traveled downriver, they were met by Thomas West, 3rd Baron De La Warr, who had been appointed Governor-for-life, replacing Gates. The new ships carried with them not only new colonists, but also a copious amount of food and other supplies. De La Warr forced the English survivors to return to their abandoned town, thus securing Jamestown's place in history as the first permanent English settlement in the New World.

THOUGHT QUESTIONS:

1. What were the main causes of the "starving time"?

2. What role did a lack of leadership play in the crisis? Why did the English experience such a leadership void?

3. What decisions did the survivors of the winter make about the Jamestown colony's future?

Margaret Brent and the English Civil War in Maryland

The English Civil War between the forces of King Charles I and Parliament caused tremendous upheaval in the British Isles from 1642 until 1649. Inevitably, the conflict spread to England's overseas colonies. No colony was more deeply affected than Maryland. Established just a decade prior, the province was intended to be a refuge for persecuted English Catholics. Many Protestants, however, also moved to Maryland, and by the 1640s the colony was already boiling with religious differences. The Civil War in the mother country caused those colonial tensions to erupt into serious conflict. Given society's expected gender roles at the time, it is unusual that one of the key players in the colony during this critical period was a woman named Margaret Brent.

Brent arrived in Maryland in 1638 along with her sister Mary and her brother Giles. Their father was a member of England's nobility, but as a Catholic family, they had found themselves treated as undesirable outcasts in the mother country. Most of the family's thirteen children remained in England, but Mary and her two siblings sought greater opportunity in America. Each of the Brents received large land grants in Maryland due to their family's connections—Cecil Calvert, Lord Baltimore and Proprietor of Maryland, was their cousin by marriage. Margaret and Mary lived together and chose to remain single their entire lives, a shocking decision given the universal expectation in British culture that all men and women should be married. The pressure to take a husband would have been particularly intense in Maryland since men outnumbered women six to one. Remaining single, though, allowed the women to keep full control over both their land and their indentured servants. Had Margaret gotten married, her husband would legally have become the owner of all her land. The two sisters pooled their property together and became two of the wealthiest planters in North America. In addition to running her plantation, Margaret went into business lending money to new arrivals. She often appeared in court as her own attorney when filing suit against debtors who refused to repay their loans. Over time, she also became a close ally of Governor Leonard Calvert, a fellow Catholic. As a sign of that closeness, the two shared guardianship over Mary Kitomaquund, the daughter of a Piscataway sachem.

In 1644, the Civil War came to Maryland. A Protestant rebellion led by Richard Ingle and William Claiborne attacked the colonial capital in the name of Parliament. Governor Calvert was forced to flee to neighboring Virginia. Ingle and Claiborne then plundered Catholic homes and arrested several of Maryland's Catholics, including Giles Brent. Not until 1646 was Calvert able to return to the colony at the head of hired troops who restored him to power. When the soldiers demanded their money, Calvert informed them that he would have to get money from England since his and Maryland's finances were in shambles. The unpaid soldiers then hinted that they might rebel against the colony and overthrow its government themselves. During this crisis, Calvert unexpectedly died in the summer of 1647. On his deathbed, he named Thomas Green the new governor, but he turned to Margaret to solve the colony's financial troubles. He made her sole executrix of his will, in complete charge of his estate and his debts.

She moved quickly, importing food from Virginia to feed the Maryland population, and then used all the Governor's estate to pay off the soldiers. When the estate's funds proved insufficient to cover the full amount, she used her power as executor to sell cattle belonging to Lord Baltimore, the proprietor, to cover the remaining debt. Then came the moment for which she is most famous. In January 1748, she appeared before the Maryland colonial assembly and demanded two votes: one for herself as a landowner, and one for her role as the late Governor's executor. Rarely had a woman asserted herself into politics and demanded the right to vote so bluntly, let alone demanding two votes. By acquiring such votes in the Assembly, she may have intended to use them to push the government into paying the soldiers rather than the late Governor's estate. Regardless, the assembly rejected her request for voting rights. When he found out about the sale of his cattle, Lord Baltimore launched a harsh attack against Brent, accusing her of pocketing the money for herself. The Maryland assembly in 1649 stepped in to defend her, declaring that, during the recent crisis the colony was better "at that time in her hands than in any man's." They credited her with saving the province. However, due to continued hostility from Maryland's proprietor, Giles, Margaret, and Mary all moved to Virginia by 1650 where they each amassed new property and wealth. Margaret Brent is still today seen as an early champion of women's rights.

THOUGHT QUESTIONS:

1. How important were family connections in Colonial America, at least for the Brents?

2. In what ways were her choices and her behavior unusual for women at the time?

3. What actions did Margaret Brent take to "save" Maryland?

Birkenhead's Rebellion

On September 1, 1663, a group of white indentured servants and African slaves gathered in secret in a small house in Gloucester County, Virginia. Their purpose was to plan an armed insurrection against their masters and the colony. They appointed John Gunter and William Bell as their leaders, then all of them agreed to collect weapons and ammunition in preparation for an attack. Servants and slaves alike saw themselves as abused and exploited by masters who provided poor quality food and clothing while overworking them to the point of exhaustion. Individual acts of rebellion—such as running away—were already common, and now servants were contemplating group action. Just two years before, in 1661, a few indentured servants had unsuccessfully tried to launch a rebellion to protest inadequate food. This time, however, unhappy white servants reached out to unhappy black slaves to work toward a common goal. Though society had begun building a racial divide between white and black into the law, these men found common cause against the rich planters who dominated the province. Such a cross-racial alliance was one of the worst fears of the Virginia elite who were few in number and relied on the support of common white inhabitants to maintain their power.

Swearing an oath of secrecy upon pain of death, the men agreed to meet again on the night of September 13 to launch their uprising. Their first target would be the home of Francis Willis, a member of the Governor's Council, where they believed they would find guns. Once sufficiently armed, they would march through the countryside from house to house beating on a drum to summon servants and slaves into a larger fighting force. Their ultimate goal was the mansion of Virginia's Governor William Berkeley. They would hold Berkeley hostage and force him to grant the rebels their immediate freedom. With the plan set, the men returned to their normal places to prepare.

However, the day before the insurrection could begin, a servant named John Birken-head betrayed the plan and revealed it to the Governor. When Bell, Gunter and the others arrived for their next meeting, they were ambushed by colonial magistrates and the militia. Though some conspirators escaped capture, most of those who were arrested quickly confessed to planning an armed rebellion. The authorities noted that some of the arrested men had fought in Oliver Cromwell's army during the English Civil War, and therefore they were naturally rebellious in nature. Emphasizing this allowed Virginians to blame the rebellion on the character flaws of the plotters rather than admit to themselves that masters might mistreat their servants or slaves.

The conspirators were quickly tried, convicted, and sentenced to death. The rebels had, according to the jury, been seduced by the Devil and had intended to destroy the entire colony and everyone in it. While it is not clear exactly how many individuals were involved in the planned uprising or how many were arrested (many of the court records from the time were destroyed over the years), a historian writing a few decades after the event recorded that four of the men were hanged. After the executions, the men's heads were severed and dangled from chimneys in the colony to warn others of the consequences of rebellion. Birkenhead was hailed as a hero. He was given his free-dom and five thousand pounds of tobacco as a reward for his loyalty. The legislature then passed a law preventing servants from traveling and meeting together without a written pass from their masters. Lawmakers especially emphasized the need for greater control on Sundays, the one day that servants normally had off from their labors and the day that the rebels had used to gather and formulate their plans. Berkeley and the Virginia House of Burgesses finally agreed to make September 13, the day of the planned uprising, permanently a holy day of thanksgiving in Virginia.

THOUGHT QUESTIONS:

1. What were the goals of the planned rebellion?

2. Why would white servants and black slaves agree to join together in rebellion?

3. Why did the planned rebellion strike such fear into Virginia elites? How were those fears reflected in the reactions to the situation?

Chapter 3

The Northern Colonies

John Winthrop's Speech on Liberty (1645)

John Winthrop was one of the most important and influential figures in early New England. He arrived in 1630 with the first wave of Massachusetts settlers and in subsequent years was elected as governor eleven different times. One of his main efforts was to limit dissent and rebellion among the colonists. In 1645, he served as part of a panel investigating the controversial appointment of militia officers in the town of Hingham. Winthrop's critics accused him of acting tyrannically during the investigation, and in response, Winthrop voluntarily put himself on trial, showing that he was willing to submit to the judgment of legal authority. Winthrop's brief trial ended with his acquittal. The speech below was part of his defense.

There is a twofold liberty, natural (I mean as our nature is now corrupt) and civil or federal. The first is common to man with beasts and other creatures. By this, man, as he stands in relation to man simply, hath liberty to do what he lists; it is a liberty to evil as well as to good. This liberty is incompatible and inconsistent with authority, and cannot endure the least restraint of the most just authority. The exercise and maintaining of this liberty makes men grow more evil, and in time to be worse than brute beasts…

The other kind of liberty I call civil or federal, it may also be termed moral, in reference to the covenant between God and man, in the moral law, and the politic covenants and constitutions, amongst men themselves. This liberty is the proper end and object of authority, and cannot subsist without it; and it is a liberty to that only which is good, just, and honest. This liberty you are to stand for, with the hazard (not only of your goods, but) of your lives, if need be…This liberty is maintained and exercised in a way of subjection to authority; it is of the same kind of liberty wherewith Christ hath made us free.

The woman's own choice makes such a man her husband; yet being so chosen, he is her lord, and she is to be subject to him, yet in a way of liberty, not of bondage; and a true wife accounts her subjection her honor and freedom, and would not think her condition safe and free, but in her subjection to her husband's authority. Such is the liberty of the church under the authority of Christ, her king and husband; his yoke is so easy and sweet to her as a bride's ornaments; and if through forwardness or wantonness, etc., she shake it off, at any time, she is at no rest in her spirit, until she take it up again; and whether her lord smiles upon her, and embraceth her in his arms, or whether he frowns, or rebukes, or smites her, she apprehends the sweetness of his love in all, and is refreshed, supported, and instructed by every such dispensation of his authority over her.

On the other side, ye know who they are that complain of this yoke and say, let us break their bands, etc...If you stand for your natural corrupt liberties, and will do what is good in your own eyes, you will not endure the least weight of authority, but will murmur, and oppose, and be always striving to shake off that yoke; but if you will be satisfied to enjoy such civil and lawful liberties, such as Christ allows you, then will you quietly and cheerfully submit unto that authority which is set over you, in all the administrations of it, for your good…

Source: James Kendall Hosmer ed., *Winthrop's Journal: History of New England, 1630-1649* (New York, 1908), p. 238-239.

THOUGHT QUESTIONS:

1. According to Winthrop, what were the two types of liberty and how did they differ in relation to authority?

2. According to this speech, what did Puritan notions of liberty mean for the marital relationship between husbands and wives?

3. How does this Puritan conception of liberty differ from conceptions of liberty that arose later in U.S. History, including today?

William Penn's Letter to the Pennsylvania Indians

Just seven months before writing this letter, William Penn received royal permission to establish the colony of Pennsylvania in America. He knew that diplomacy with indigenous peoples would be absolutely critical. In other colonies, English-Indian interactions had frequently resulted in hatred and violence. Penn wished for a different outcome. In keeping with his Quaker faith, Penn believed that all people, regardless of their background, carried a divine spark and were thus worthy of respect. This letter, written by Penn and addressed to the native leaders within Pennsylvania's boundaries, spells out his hopes for a new type of relationship.

London, 18 October 1681

My Friends, There is one great God and Power that hath made the world and all things therein, to whom you and I and all people owe their being and well-being, and to whom you and I must one day give an account for all that we do in this world: this great God has written his law in our hearts, by which we are taught and commanded to love and help and do good to one another, and not do harme and mischief one unto another. Now this great God has been pleased to make me concerned in your parts of the world, and the king of the country where I live has given unto me a great province; but I desire to enjoy it with your love and consent, that we may always live together as neighbours and friends, else what would the great God say to us, who has made us not to devour and destroy one another, but live soberly and kindly together in the world?

Now I would have you well observe, that I am very sensible of the unkindness and injustice that has been too much exercised towards you by the people of these parts of the world, who have sought themselves, and to make great advantages by you, rather than be examples of justice and goodness unto you, which I hear has been matter of trouble to you and caused great grudgeings and animosities, sometimes to the shedding of blood, which has made the great God angry. But I am not such man, as is well known in my own country: I have great love and regard toward you, and I desire to win and gain your love and friendship by a kind, just, and peaceable life; and the people I send are of the same mind, and shall in all things behave themselves accordingly. And if in anything any shall offend you or your people, you shall have a full and speedy satisfaction for the same by an equall number of honest men on both sides, that by no means you may have just occasion of being offended against them.

I shall shortly come to you myself, at what time we may more largely and freely confer and discourse of these matters. In the meantime, I have sent my commissioners to treat with you about land and a firm league of peace. Lett me desire you to be kind to them and the people, and receive these presents and tokens which I have sent to you as a testimony of my good will to you, and my resolution to live justly, peaceably, and friendly with you. I am your loving friend.

William Penn

Source: Samuel McPherson Janney, *The Life of William Penn* (Philadelphia, 1853), pp. 179-180.

THOUGHT QUESTIONS:

1. What ideas or principles did Penn want to use as a basis for Indian relations? How does Penn believe that his approach was different from those employed in other colonies?

2. In what ways does Penn's religious faith manifest itself in the letter? How did Penn's religious beliefs influence the way he viewed and treated Indians?

3. If Penn succeeded in forging a positive, mutually beneficial relationship with native peoples, how might that help the newly established colony as a whole to succeed?

Cotton Mather's Defense of the Salem Witch Trials

From February 1692 until May 1693, Salem, Massachusetts was gripped by witchcraft hysteria after a group of young girls came down with strange, unexplained seizures and other symptoms. The initial witchcraft accusations quickly spiraled outwards until eventually nearly 200 people were arrested. By the time the panic died down, dozens of defendants had been convicted and twenty people executed. At the height of the trials and executions, prominent Puritan Minister Cotton Mather published a strong defense of the witchcraft hunt, entitled "Wonders of the Invisible World." In it, Mather laid out for readers the evidence that witches were real and large numbers of them were practicing witchcraft in Salem.

THE TRYAL OF BRIDGET BISHOP AT THE COURT OF OYER AND TERMINER, HELD AT SALEM, JUNE 2. 1692.

...II. It was testifi'd, That at the Examination of the Prisoner before the Magistrates, the Bewitched were extreamly tortured. If she did but cast her Eyes on them, they were presently struck down; and this in such a manner as there could be no Collusion in the Business. But upon the Touch of her Hand upon them, when they lay in their Swoons, they would immediately Revive; and not upon the Touch of any ones else. Moreover, Upon some Special Actions of her Body, as the shaking of her Head, or the turning of her Eyes, they presently and painfully fell into the like postures...

V. To render it further unquestionable, that the Prisoner at the Bar, was the Person truly charged in THIS Witchcraft, there were produced many Evidences of OTHER Witchcrafts, by her perpetrated. For Instance, John Cook testifi'd, That about five or six Years ago, one Morning, about Sun-Rise, he was in his Chamber assaulted by the Shape of this Prisoner: which look'd on him, grinn'd at him, and very much hurt him with a Blow on the side of the Head : and that on the same day, about Noon, the same Shape walked in the Room where he was, and an Apple strangely flew out of his Hand, into the Lap of his Mother, six or eight Foot from him...

VII. John Ely and his Wife testifi'd, That he bought a Sow of Edward Bishop, the Husband of the Prisoner; and was to pay the Price agreed, unto another person. This Prisoner being angry that she was thus hindred from fingring the Mony, quarrell'd with Ely. Soon after which, the Sow was taken with strange Fits; Jumping, Leaping, and Knocking her Head against the Fence; she seem'd Blind and Deaf, and would neither Eat nor be Suck'd. Whereupon a Neighbour said, she believed the Creature was Over-looked; and sundry other Circumstances concurred, which made the Deponents believe that Bishop had bewitched it...

X. John Louder testify'd, That upon some little Controversy with Bishop about her Fowls, going well to Bed, he did awake in the Night by Moonlight, and did see clearly the likeness of this Woman grievously oppressing him; in which miserable condition she held him, unable to help himself, till near Day. He told Bishop of this; but she deny'd it, and threatned him very much. Quickly after this, being at home on a Lords day, with the doors shut about him, he saw a black Pig approach him; at which, he going to kick, it vanished away. Immediately after, sitting down, he saw a black Thing jump in at the Window, and come and stand before him. The Body was like that of a Monkey, the Feet like a

Cocks, but the Face much like a Mans. He being so extreamly affrighted, that he could not speak; this Monster spoke to him, and said, I am a Messenger sent unto you, for I understand that you are in some Trouble of Mind, and if you will be ruled by me, you shall want for nothing in this World. Whereupon he endeavoured to clap his Hands upon it; but he could feel no substance; and it jumped out of the Window again; but immediately came in by the Porch, tho' the Doors were shut, and said, You had better take my Counsel! He then struck at it with a Stick, but struck only the Ground and broke the Stick: The Hand with which he struck was presently Disenabled, and it vanished away. He presently went out at the Back-door, and spied this Bishop, in her Orchard, going toward her House; but he had not power to set one foot forward unto her. Whereupon, returning into the House, he was immediately accosted by the Monster he had seen before; which Goblin was now going to fly at him; whereat he cry'd out, The whole armour of God be between me and you ! So it sprang back, and flew over the Apple-tree; shaking many Apples off the Tree, in its flying over. At its leap, it flung Dirt with its Feet against the Stomack of the Man; whereon he was then struck Dumb, and so continued for three Days together. Upon the producing of this Testimony, Bishop deny'd that she knew this Deponent : Yet their two Orchards joined; and they had often had their little Quarrels for some years together...

XI. William Stacy testify'd, That receiving Money of this Bishop, for work done by him; he was gone but a matter of three Rods from her, and looking for his Money, found it unaccountably gone from him... Being then gone about six Rods from her, with a small Load in his Cart, suddenly the Off-wheel stump'd, and sunk down into an hole, upon plain Ground; so that the Deponent was forced to get help for the recovering of the Wheel: But stepping back to look for the hole, which might give him this Disaster, there was none at all to be found. Some time after, he was waked in the Night; but it seem'd as light as day; and he perfectly saw the shape of this Bishop in the Room, troubling of him; but upon her going out, all was dark again. He charg'd Bishop afterwards with it, and she deny'd it not; but was very angry. Quickly after, this Deponent having been threatned by Bishop, as he was in a dark Night going to the Barn, he was very suddenly taken or lifted from the Ground, and thrown against a Stone-wall: After that, he was again hoisted up and thrown down a Bank, at the end of his House. After this again, passing by this Bishop, his Horse with a small Load, striving to draw, all his Gears flew to pieces, and the Cart fell down; and this Deponent going then to lift a Bag of Corn, of about two Bushels, could not budge it with all his Might...

Source: Cotton Mather, *The Wonders of the Invisible World* (Boston, 1692). Quoted from 1862 London Reprint edition, pp. 129-138.

THOUGHT QUESTIONS:

1. What types of evidence did Mather believe was sufficient to prove the guilt of an accused witch?

2. According to the eyewitnesses that testified against Bridget Bishop, why did she cast spells against them? What effects did they think magic was having on their lives?

3. Are there alternative explanations, ones that do not rely on witchcraft, for any of the events in the eyewitness testimony?

Vignettes

Pilgrims and Wampanoags at Thanksgiving, 1621

In the fall of 1621, fifty-three Pilgrims and approximately ninety male Wampanoag Indians met in the Plymouth colony for a three-day feast. The English settlers had spent a full day hunting birds in preparation for the feast, taking large quantities of waterfowl—most likely ducks or geese—and wild turkeys. Colonists also brought to the table corn (maize), which had recently been harvested. The English also likely cooked cod fish at the gathering as they had spent months fishing the shores of Cape Cod, which earned its name from the teeming schools of fish found in surrounding waters. For their part, the Wampanoags hunted and killed five deer, which they gave to the colony as a gift. Though other menu items were not recorded in documents at the time, it is well known that both Pilgrims and natives had a varied diet that included lobsters, eels, nuts, beans, pumpkins, squash, onions, carrots, and turnips. Though the two groups ate together, they came to the feast with different views about its meaning.

Led by their Governor, William Bradford, the Pilgrims had moved to America to embrace their separatist religious beliefs—they wished to practice religion outside of the boundaries of any established church such as the Church of England. They began their colony in December 1620, and since they had little time to build shelter or grow food, the ensuing winter was cruel. Out of the 102 immigrants, 45 died before spring arrived. During the summer, though, the colony made great strides. Several permanent homes and structures had been built. English crops had grown beautifully, and fish and game were plentiful beyond any of the colonists' expectations. Though the Pilgrim records do not use the word "Thanksgiving" or even "Thanks," the settlers certainly had reason to celebrate their newfound prosperity that day. The English were so excited by their progress that they began to fire their weapons into the air.

The Wampanoags, led by their Sachem Massasoit, attended in order to cement their new strategic and military alliance with the English. Just a few months before, the Pilgrims and Wampanoag had agreed to a formal treaty guaranteeing protection against each other's enemies. The Indians may not even have been invited to the feast. Massasoit and his warriors may have heard the celebratory gun shots and arrived at Plymouth in force, prepared to fight any enemy present. That would explain why the 90 Wampanoag were all adult men. Instead of a battle, Massasoit found the English celebration, and he and his men spontaneously joined in. This would also explain why Massasoit had to send his men out to hunt deer after the feast started rather than before it—they had not expected a feast and had brought no food with them. The tribe was particularly keen to maintain the English alliance since the previous decade had been ruinous. The Wampanoag had come under heavy attack from the Micmac Indians to their north and were being pressed by the Pequot tribe that was expanding into their territory from the west. Additionally, in the 1610s the tribe experienced three disease epidemics that reduced the mainland Wampanoag population from 8,000 to 2,000. Massasoit and his people valued the English alliance so highly that it remained in effect until Massasoit's son Metacomet, frustrated by constant English expansion onto native lands, declared war in 1675.

The three-day feast in 1621 was not seen as highly important at the time, and it was not repeated in subsequent years. "Thanksgiving," though, has taken on a new importance over time. President George Washington in 1789 declared the last Thursday in November to be a national day of Thanksgiving, but most Americans still did not celebrate the day. It was not until Abraham Lincoln's 1863 Thanksgiving proclamation, that Americans, desperate for symbols of national unity during the bitter Civil War, embraced it as an annual holiday. The day still has different meanings. While many Americans celebrate it by eating turkey and remembering the Pilgrims, starting in the 1970s some Indian activists have proclaimed the day to be a "Day of Mourning," symbolizing the eventual dispossession of the native population.

THOUGHT QUESTIONS:

1. Why would the Pilgrims have reason to celebrate and give thanks in the fall of 1621?

2. How did Indians view the event differently than the Pilgrims?

3. How and when did "Thanksgiving" come to be a major tradition in the United States of America?

The Captivity of Mary Rowlandson

Mary Rowlandson was born around 1637 in England. Her family left for Massachusetts during the Puritan Great Migration of the 1630s and 1640s, eventually settling in the frontier town of Lancaster. She married Revered Joseph Rowlandson in 1656, and the couple had four children, one of whom died in infancy. Up until 1675, her life was neither more nor less extraordinary than any other British colonist. But in that year, New England Indians launched King Philip's War, a fierce and bloody conflict whose fighting was to drag out for three years.

On February 10, 1676, Narragansett and allied Indians raided Lancaster. Seventeen people were killed, among them Mary's sister Elizabeth and two of her children. Twenty-four townspeople were taken prisoner, among them Mary Rowlandson and her three children. Her husband Joseph was away at the time of the attack, traveling to Boston to lobby for more government protection for Lancaster. The captives were marched overland on a grueling winter journey through the wilderness. Rowlandson's six-year-old daughter

Sarah, wounded during the attack on Lancaster, died in her arms nine days after being taking captive. Her Narragansett captors dug a grave for the child on a nearby hillside and allowed Mary to say her goodbyes at the gravesite. Rowlandson's other two children, fourteen-year-old Joseph and ten-year-old Mary (namesakes of their parents) were taken away from her and held separately, though she occasionally saw and spoke to them when their Indian captors camped. Rowlandson viewed her ordeal, including her daughter's death, as a test of her faith. She believed that the Indians were agents of the Devil and that she and her other children could only be delivered from captivity by trusting in God. She carried her Bible with her, and frequently read from it during idle hours, urging other English prisoners to also keep their faith despite the hardships they were enduring.

Rowlandson was marched back and forth across the New England frontier as her captors evaded the main English colonial army. In the process, she was again separated from her surviving children and made a servant to a Narragansett family. After several weeks of travel, she eventually met face to face with Metacomet (known to the English as King Philip), the leader of the Indian war effort. Favorably impressed by her, Metacomet asked Rowlandson to sew a shirt for his son, for which he insisted on paying her in cash despite her being a prisoner who could be forced to work for free. The shirt must have been pleasing, because soon she was overwhelmed with native requests for her to make shirts, stockings, and caps, with Rowlandson receiving additional food in trade. This trade in food was itself remarkable since the ravages of the war had made food very scarce and valuable among Metacomet's followers. Rowlandson became so well-regarded among her captors that at one point, a native man approached her and offered to help her escape and return her to her family. Rowlandson declined the offer, saying that she preferred to wait until God decided that she should go home.

After more than eleven weeks of captivity, Mary Rowlandson was ransomed back to her family on May 3, 1676 in exchange for £20 worth of English goods. Just a few weeks later, both her son and daughter were also released by their captors. The family was now reunited, but misfortune soon struck again. Mary's husband Joseph died suddenly in 1678 at the age of forty-seven. Shortly before her husband's death, she completed a detailed narrative of her captivity. It was published in 1682 under the title "The Sovereignty and Goodness of God, Together with the Faithfulness of His Promises Displayed." The book became a bestseller and remains one of the most famous narratives of the colonial era.

THOUGHT QUESTIONS:

1. How did Rowlandson's religious faith affect her outlook and her behavior during her captivity?

2. Did Rowlandson's Indian captors treat her with cruelty, with kindness, or with a mixture of both? When readers in the 1680s finished reading her book, do you think the narrative caused readers to be more favorable or more unfavorable in their view of Indians?

3. Would you call Mary Rowlandson's story a tragedy, or a tale of triumph? Why?

Jacob Leisler's Rebellion in New York

The 1688 Glorious Revolution in England saw the Protestant William of Orange and his wife Mary crowned as monarchs, and the reigning Catholic King James II forced into exile. The shockwaves caused by this momentous event rippled across the Atlantic Ocean to the British colonies in America. One of the results was an uprising in New York, known to history as Leisler's rebellion.

After James's fall, British colonies moved to oust colonial governors associated with the deposed king. In Maryland, Protestants kicked out the Catholic proprietors of the province, arguing that they had been too supportive of the Catholic monarch. Further north, several colonies had been folded under James's rule into the Dominion of New England, which combined Massachusetts, New Hampshire, Connecticut, Rhode Island, New York, and New Jersey into a single administrative unit. The Dominion's Governor, Edmund Andros, used Boston as his capital. His Deputy Governor, Francis Nicholson, resided in New York City. Both Andros and Nicholson were deeply unpopular, not only because they had been appointed by James II, but also due to a series of authoritarian decisions they made while in office. When word arrived from England of the Glorious Revolution, Bostonians arrested Governor Andros and kept him jailed for months before sending him back to England. In New York City, Jacob Leisler, a German immigrant, took over the colonial militia, seized control of the city's fort, and removed Nicholson from his position in June 1689. Nicholson sailed for England a few days later.

Leisler and his supporters formed a "committee of safety," which then elected Leisler to be commander-in-chief of the colony of New York until a proper governor arrived from England. Shortly after this, instructions arrived from the new King and Queen that all non-Catholic officeholders (which included Andros and Nicholson) should remain in office until further notice. The instructions also specified that if Nicholson was absent, then government authority should remain in the hands of the person appointed to enforce the laws. Leisler interpreted this as legitimating his acting governorship since he had been chosen by the committee to replace Nicholson. Leisler's command of the militia gave him a strong base of authority in New York City, though further inland there was some resistance to his actions. Leisler consolidated inland control by dispatching militia troops to occupy disgruntled towns. In a further bid for legitimacy, Leisler sent two envoys to England to explain that his seizure of power was solely to protect the colonists from the tyranny of Andros and Nicholson, who, after all, had been appointed by the deposed James II.

Leisler's reign in New York quickly became quite complicated. First, he had to deal with a war between England and France that broke out in 1689, and so he was forced to spend much time and effort guarding against French and Indian attacks on frontier towns. He organized an Intercolonial Congress in 1690 to plan military defenses cooperatively between the different British colonies. The resulting expedition, however, was a spectacular failure, and Leisler arrested and imprisoned its commander. His administration was also complicated by divisions between the old Dutch settlers and newer English residents. Over time, Leisler's opponents grew in strength and began to stage public protests of his government. Leisler sometimes dealt with such protests by arresting his critics or driving them out of the colony.

England eventually sent over a new Governor, Henry Sloughter, to take charge of New York. Due to weather problems, Lieutenant Governor Richard Ingoldesby's ship arrived first in January 1691. Leisler refused to surrender the city because the proper documentation announcing the new officials was still on Governor Sloughter's yet-to-arrive ship. Angered by Leisler's rejection of his authority, Ingoldesby recruited a militia of his own from anti-Leislerians and lay siege to the city's fort. The standoff lasted for six weeks until Governor Sloughter at last arrived. Leisler initially doubted Sloughter's legitimacy as well but eventually surrendered to the Governor. Leisler was quickly arrested and charged with treason for his refusal to hand over power to Lt. Governor Ingoldesby. Leisler and his son-in-law were both convicted by a jury stacked with their enemies (including Ingoldesby) and sentenced to death. Sloughter at first stayed the execution, preferring to wait until King William could make his wishes known. However, under pressure from Leisler's opponents, the governor at last relented and had the two men hanged in May 1691. Many of Leisler's supporters believed the executions to be entirely unjust, and a few years later they successfully lobbied the British Parliament to posthumously reverse the treason convictions. The outcome of Leisler's Rebellion remained a divisive issue in New York politics for decades afterwards.

THOUGHT QUESTIONS:

1. How did Leisler attempt to establish the legitimacy of his takeover of New York? Why did he claim that his actions were necessary?

2. What challenges did Leisler face in governing the colony? How well did he handle his responsibilities?

3. Was Leisler's sentence and execution a "just" result, or was it simply revenge by his enemies? Be able to explain how you reached your conclusion.

Chapter 4

Creating an American People,
1700-1763

The Pirate Crew Articles of Bartholomew Roberts

The decade from 1716-1726 saw a burst of pirate activity in the Atlantic basin. The era to-day is known as the Golden Age of Piracy, and it made famous such captains as Blackbeard, Benjamin Hornigold, and Bartholomew Roberts (also known as "Black Bart"). Pirate ships in this era often organized crews along consensual lines, emphasizing the equality of each member of the group. As a sign of commitment to their brotherhood, some crews had every person on board sign a set of rules that functioned as a sort of constitution. Below are the crew articles for "Black Bart" Roberts, whose career ran from 1719 until 1722.

ARTICLE I. Every man shall have an equal vote in affairs of moment. He shall have an equal title to the fresh provisions or strong liquors at any time seized, and shall use them at pleasure unless a scarcity may make it necessary for the common good that a retrenchment may be voted.

ARTICLE II. Every man shall be called fairly in turn by the list on board of prizes, because over and above their proper share, they are allowed a shift of clothes. But if they defraud the company to the value of even one dollar in plate, jewels or money, they shall be marooned. If any man rob another he shall have his nose and ears slit, and be put ashore where he shall be sure to encounter hardships.

ARTICLE III. None shall game for money either with dice or cards.

ARTICLE IV. The lights and candles should be put out at eight at night, and if any of the crew desire to drink after that hour they shall sit upon the open deck without lights.

ARTICLE V. Each man shall keep his piece, cutlass and pistols at all times clean and ready for action.

ARTICLE VI. No boy or woman to be allowed amongst them. If any man shall be found seducing any of the latter sex and carrying her to sea in disguise he shall suffer death.

ARTICLE VII. He that shall desert the ship or his quarters in time of battle shall be punished by death or marooning.

ARTICLE VIII. None shall strike another on board the ship, but every man's quarrel shall be ended on shore by sword or pistol in this manner. At the word of command from the quartermaster, each man being previously placed back to back, shall turn and fire immediately. If any man do not, the quartermaster shall knock the piece out of his hand. If both miss their aim they shall take to their cutlasses, and he that draweth first blood shall be declared the victor.

ARTICLE IX. No man shall talk of breaking up their way of living till each has a share of £1,000. Every man who shall become a cripple or lose a limb in the service shall have 800 pieces of eight from the common stock and for lesser hurts proportionately.

ARTICLE X. The captain and the quartermaster shall each receive two shares of a prize, the master gunner and boatswain, one and one half shares, all other officers one and one quarter, and private gentlemen of fortune one share each.

ARTICLE XI. The musicians shall have rest on the Sabbath Day only by right. On all other days by favour only.

Source: : Charles Johnson, *A General History of the Pirates* (London, 1724), p. 230-232.

THOUGHT QUESTIONS:

1. What elements of equality or democracy are present in these crew articles? What do they suggest about how pirate ships functioned?

2. What problems do you think these rules were intended to prevent or solve? Why were they needed?

3. Which individuals or crew members had to abide by special rules due to their positions on the ship?

Benjamin Franklin Dispenses Advice About Marriage and Frugality

In addition to his career as a printer, Benjamin Franklin was a prolific author. Many of his works, particularly humorous ones, were authored under various pen names: Silence Dogood, "Poor Richard" Saunders, Caelia Shortface, and Martha Careful are all examples. The following letter was written by Franklin under the pen name Anthony Afterwit and was published in Franklin's newspaper in 1732. Publishing letters pseudonymously was fairly common in the era, as it allowed an author to express his or her ideas without facing direct criticism in response. It also allowed Franklin as the printer to provide content for his newspaper while making it appear to be submitted by readers.

Mr. Gazetteer,

I am an honest Tradesman, who never meant Harm to any Body. My Affairs went on smoothly while a Batchelor; but of late I have met with some Difficulties, of which I take the Freedom to give you an Account.

About the Time I first address'd my present Spouse, her Father gave out in Speeches, that if she married a Man he liked, he would give with her £200 on the Day of Marriage. 'Tis true he never said so to me, but he always receiv'd me very kindly at his House, and openly countenac'd my Courtship. I form'd several fine Schemes, what to do with this same £200 and in some Measure neglected my Business on that Account: But unluckily it came to pass, that when the old Gentleman saw I was pretty well engag'd, and that the Match was too far gone to be easily broke off; he, without any Reason given, grew very angry, forbid me the House, and told his Daughter that if she married me he would not give her a Farthing…

I soon saw that with Care and Industry we might live tolerably easy, and in Credit with our Neighbours: But my Wife had a strong Inclination to be a Gentlewoman. In Consequence of this, my old-fashioned Looking-Glass was one Day broke, as she said, No Mortal could tell which way. However, since we could not be without a Glass in the Room, My Dear, says she, we may as well buy a large fashionable One that Mr. Such-a-one has to sell; it will cost but little more than a common Glass, and will be much handsomer and more creditable. Accordingly the Glass was bought, and hung against the Wall: But in a Week's time, I was made sensible by little and little, that the Table was by no Means suitable to such a Glass. And a more proper Table being procur'd, my Spouse, who was an excellent Contriver, inform'd me where we might have very handsome Chairs in the Way; And thus, by Degrees, I found all my old Furniture stow'd up into the Garret, and every thing below alter'd for the better.

Had we stopp'd here, we might have done well enough; but my Wife being entertain'd with Tea by the Good Women she visited, we could do no less than the like when they visited us; and so we got a Tea-Tablewith all its Appurtenances of China and Silver. Then my Spouse unfortunately overwork'd herself in washing the House, so that we could do no longer without a Maid. Besides this, it happened frequently, that when I came home at One, the Dinner was but just put in the Pot; for, My Dear thought really it had been but Eleven: At other Times when I came at the same Hour, She wondered I would stay so long, for Dinner was ready and had waited for me these two Hours. These Irregularities, occasioned by mistaking the Time, convinced me, that it was absolutely necessary to buy a Clock; which my Spouse observ'd, was a great Ornament to the Room! And lastly, to my Grief, she was frequently troubled with some Ailment or other, and nothing did her so much Good as Riding; And these Hackney Horses were such wretched ugly Creatures, that—I bought a very fine pacing Mare, which cost £20. And hereabouts Affairs have stood for some Months past.

I could see all along, that this Way of Living was utterly inconsistent with my Circumstances, but had not Resolution enough to help it. Till lately, receiving a very severe Dun, which mention'd the next Court, I began in earnest to project Relief. Last Monday my Dear went over the River, to see a Relation, and stay a Fortnight, because she could not bear the Heat of the Town. In the Interim, I have taken my Turn to make Alterations, viz. I have turn'd away the Maid, Bag and Baggage (for what should we do with a Maid, who have (except my Boy) none but our selves). I have sold the fine Pacing Mare, and bought a good Milch Cow, with £3 of the Money. I have dispos'd of the Tea-Table, and put a Spinning Wheel in its Place, which methinks looks very pretty: Nine empty Canisters I have stuff'd with Flax; and with some of the Money of the Tea-Furniture, I have bought a Set of Knitting-Needles; for to tell you a Truth, which I would have go no farther, I begin to want Stockings. The stately Clock I have transform'd into an Hour-Glass, by which I gain'd a good round Sum; and one of the Pieces of the old Looking-Glass, squar'd and fram'd, supplies the Place of the Great One, which I have convey'd into a Closet, where it may possibly remain some Years. In short, the Face of Things is quite changed; and I am mightily pleased when I look at my Hour-Glass, what an Ornament it is to the Room. I have paid my Debts, and find Money in my Pocket. I expect my Dame home next Friday, and as your Paper is taken in at the House where she is, I hope the Reading of this will prepare her Mind for the above surprizing Revolutions. If she can conform to this new Scheme of Living, we shall be the happiest Couple perhaps in the Province, and, by the Blessing of God, may soon be in thriving Circumstances. I have reserv'd the great Glass, because I know her Heart is set upon it. I will allow her when she comes in, to be taken suddenly ill with the Headach, the Stomach-ach, Fainting-Fits, or whatever other Disorders she may think more proper; and she may retire to Bed as soon as she pleases: But if I do not find her in perfect Health both of Body and Mind the next Morning, away goes the aforesaid Great Glass, with several other Trinkets I have no Occasion for, to the Vendue that very Day. Which is the irrevocable Resolution of, Sir, Her loving Husband, and Your very humble Servant,
Anthony Afterwit

Postscript, You know we can return to our former Way of Living, when we please, if Dad will be at the Expence of it.

Source: *Pennsylvania Gazette*, July 10, 1732.

THOUGHT QUESTIONS:

1. At the time he wrote this letter, Franklin had just recently married Deborah Franklin. What does the letter suggest about his worries concerning marriage?

2. In Afterwit's fictional marriage, why are material objects so important? What point is Franklin trying to make about the importance of material goods?

3. Benjamin Franklin had a well established liking for frugal living. How does this essay promote frugality?

Jonathan Edwards Spreads the Awakening

Jonathan Edwards was one of the principal figures in the religious movement known as the Great Awakening, which began in the 1730s and lasted through the 1760s. The period saw a split between the "Old Lights," who focused on restrained and orderly worship in established churches, versus the revivalist "New Lights," who promoted a more emotional and personal form of Christianity. Revivalist ministers like Edwards tried to get their audiences to feel the power of God in an immediate way in their everyday lives. Edwards's most famous sermon is "Sinners in the Hands of an Angry God," delivered as a guest preacher in 1741 to a Massachusetts church whose regular minister was frustrated by his congregation's indifferent attitude towards religious worship.

That world of misery, that lake of burning brimstone is extended abroad under you. There is the dreadful pit of the glowing flames of the wrath of God; there is hell's wide gaping mouth open; and you have nothing to stand upon, nor anything to take hold of: there is nothing between you and hell but the air; 'tis only the power and mere pleasure of God that holds you up…

'Tis true, that judgment against your evil works has not been executed hitherto; the floods of God's vengeance have been withheld; but your guilt in the meantime is constantly increasing, and you are every day treasuring up more wrath; the waters are continually rising and waxing more and more mighty; and there is nothing but the mere pleasure of God that holds the waters back that are unwilling to be stopped, and press hard to go forward; if God should only withdraw his hand from the floodgate, it would immediately fly open, and the fiery floods of the fierceness and wrath of God would rush forth with inconceivable fury, and would come upon you with omnipotent power; and if your strength were ten thousand times greater than it is, yea, ten thousand times greater than the strength of the stoutest, sturdiest devil in hell, it would be nothing to withstand or endure it…

Thus are all you that never passed under a great change of heart, by the mighty power of the Spirit of God upon your souls; all that were never born again, and made new creatures, and raised from being dead in sin, to a state of new, and before altogether unexperienced light and life (however you may have reformed your life in many things, and may have had religious affections, and may keep up a form of religion in your families and closets, and in the house of God, and may be strict in it), you are thus in the hands of an angry God; 'tis nothing but his mere pleasure that keeps you from being this moment swallowed up in everlasting destruction...

The God that holds you over the pit of hell, much as one holds a spider, or some loathsome insect, over the fire, abhors you, and is dreadfully provoked; his wrath towards you burns like fire; he looks upon you as worthy of nothing else, but to be cast into the fire; he is of purer eyes than to bear to have you in his sight; you are ten thousand times so abominable in his eyes as the most hateful venomous serpent is in ours. You have offended him infinitely more than ever a stubborn rebel did his prince: and yet 'tis nothing but his hand that holds you from falling into the fire every moment; 'tis to be ascribed to nothing else, that you did not go to hell the last night; that you was suffered to awake again in this world, after you closed your eyes to sleep: and there is no other reason to be given why you have not dropped into hell since you arose in the morning, but that God's hand has held you up; there is no other reason to be given why you han't gone to hell since you have sat here in the house of God, provoking his pure eyes by your sinful wicked manner of attending his solemn worship: yea, there is nothing else that is to be given as a reason why you don't this very moment drop down into hell.

How dreadful is the state of those that are daily and hourly in danger of this great wrath, and infinite misery! But this is the dismal case of every soul in this congregation, that has not been born again, however moral and strict, sober and religious they may otherwise be. Oh that you would consider it, whether you be young or old. There is reason to think, that there are many in this congregation now hearing this discourse, that will actually be the subjects of this very misery to all eternity...

And now you have an extraordinary opportunity, a day wherein Christ has flung the door of mercy wide open, and stands in the door calling and crying with a loud voice to poor sinners; a day wherein many are flocking to him, and pressing into the kingdom of God; many are daily coming from the east, west, north and south; many that were very lately in the same miserable condition that you are in, are in now an happy state, with their hearts filled with love to him that has loved them and washed them from their sins in his own blood, and rejoicing in hope of the glory of God. How awful is it to be left behind at such a day! To see so many others feasting, while you are pining and perishing! To see so many rejoicing and singing for joy of heart, while you have cause to mourn for sorrow of heart, and howl for vexation of spirit! How can you rest one moment in such a condition? Are not your souls as precious as the souls of the people at Suffield, where they are flocking from day to day to Christ?...

Therefore let everyone that is out of Christ, now awake and fly from the wrath to come. The wrath of almighty God is now undoubtedly hanging over great part of this congregation: let everyone fly out of Sodom. Haste and escape for your lives, look not behind you, escape to the mountain, lest you be consumed [Genesis 19:17].

Source: Jonathan Edwards, *Sinners in the Hands of an Angry God* (Boston, 1741).

THOUGHT QUESTIONS:

1. What imagery did Edwards use to try and get an emotional response out of his listeners? How did he try and make religious worship seem very immediate and personal to everyone?

2. In the sermon, is God presented as a loving figure or as an instrument of punishment? Why might Edwards and other ministers in the Great Awakening focus on one particular view of God?

3. What hope does Edwards offer in his sermon to the listeners in the audience? What were they asked to do? Could they change their outcomes, or were they predestined to their fate?

Vignettes

Charleston's Disastrous Years, 1698-1700

Established in 1670, Charleston, South Carolina would go on to become a wealthy, prosperous colonial city. By 1770, its population numbered 11,000 inhabitants, and it served as the Atlantic trade hub for the southern portion of Britain's North American colonies. During that intervening century, however, the city had to overcome many setbacks, and no period was more challenging than the years from 1698-1700.

In the early 1690s, Charleston's population was 1,200. Then came a sudden series of crises, beginning with an outbreak of smallpox in 1698 that lasted for several months and killed as many as 300 people. This was the first time the disease had appeared in Charleston, and both authorities and townspeople were likely inexperienced in coping. Just as the city began to recover from one epidemic, another hit. In August 1699, a ship arrived from Barbados carrying an invisible passenger—yellow fever—killing 160 colonists before ending its course. This time, many Charlestonians fled to the countryside as soon as the epidemic hit, temporarily depopulating the city. The colony's political leaders stayed put, and so were the hardest hit by yellow fever. The disease claimed the lives of four appointed officials, Charleston's Episcopal minister, and fully half of the members of the lower house of the legislature.

Layered inbetween the two epidemics were other disasters. In February 1699, a major fire tore through the city, destroying a full third of the homes and buildings and causing enormous financial damage to the young settlement. It had been preceded a few days earlier by an unusual earthquake. Many of those who had survived smallpox found themselves homeless when yellow fever first hit. The fire convinced South Carolina's leaders to take firefighting seriously, and within a few years there was a special panel in place to oversee fire suppression and prevention.

To these natural challenges was added a manmade one: piracy. In early 1700, a ship containing a mixture of English, French, Portuguese, and Indian sailors departed from Havana, Cuba on a pirating voyage. Off the Carolina coast, they took several ships and cargoes, keeping the vessels and offloading the merchant sailors on shore. However, the pirate crew had a fight over the division of money, and the English sailors found themselves cast adrift. When the English pirates reached land, they made their way to Charleston and hoped to blend in. However, they were recognized by some of their victims, arrested, and put on trial. Six were hanged in May, with one other young pirate, who was particularly regretful, given a reprieve of his death sentence.

Then came the final blow in the series, the Charleston Hurricane of September 1700. The city was built on a low-lying area between two rivers, making it susceptible to flooding. The hurricane uprooted thousands of trees, wiped out crops, and destroyed or damaged dozens of buildings in Charleston. Fortunately, the water rose slowly enough in the city that residents could climb to second stories and roofs to survive the waters. A last-minute shift in wind also began to push water away from the city rather than in towards it, or the results would have been much worse. The storm still caused a major loss of life when waves smashed an anchored ship up against the rocky shoreline in the harbor, killing the 98 people on board.

By the end of 1700, there was a general sense of hopelessness in Charleston, and many residents spoke openly of abandoning the city. However, the realization that other cities experienced the same fires, epidemics, and natural disasters convinced most townspeople to stay and rebuild. Charleston might have gone through an unusually difficult two-year period, but the problems (disease, fire, pirates, hurricanes) it faced were endemic to living in any colonial coastal city. Colonists could have moved someplace different, but there was no guarantee of it being better.

THOUGHT QUESTIONS:

1. Why would these dangers been considered common for colonial cities? Why would these dangers be less likely to affect people who lived in rural areas?

2. Which of the events do you think was the most difficult for Charleston to deal with and recover from? Why?

3. What measures could Charleston take to guard against such events? Were some of them more preventable or manageable than others?

The Stono Rebellion

Early in the morning on Sunday, September 9, 1739, a group of South Carolina slaves launched the largest and most violent slave rebellion of the U.S. colonial era. The leader of the rebellion, a Kongolese slave named Jemmy, and a group of slaves broke into a general store along the Stono River. Inside the store, the rebels killed the store owners, and armed themselves with guns and ammunition from the store's wares. They also grabbed two drums and some white cloth to make banners. The rebels then marched along the road, beating the drums, waving their banners, and chanting "Liberty!" The drums and banners were to aid in the recruitment of rebels, and by early afternoon there may have been as many as 90 slaves in the army. They burned plantation homes and killed most whites that they encountered, though they did spare a white innkeeper who was known for kindness to his slaves.

The ultimate goal of the rebellion was to reach the Spanish outpost of St. Augustine, Florida. As part of the international rivalry between Spain and England, the Spanish crown had offered freedom to any slave who successfully ran away from a British master in Carolina. Some of the rebelling slaves were literate and they very well might have read stories about Fort Mose, a Spanish colonial town consisting entirely of freed slaves. British authorities afterwards were convinced that without the Spanish promise of freedom, there would have been no slave rebellion at all. A few English colonial leaders became convinced that Spanish priests and other agents had infiltrated Carolina in disguise for the sole purpose of fomenting the insurrection.

Jemmy and his followers nearly captured the colony's Lieutenant Governor, William Bull, who had been travelling from a friend's house in the countryside. After evading the rebels, Bull then mobilized the local militia. Around four-o'clock in the afternoon, the slave army was stopped in a large field when the South Carolina militia attacked. After a bloody battle, the slave army broke and scattered into smaller groups, some of whom were not found and captured until a week later. In all, a total of 47 slaves and more than 40 whites were killed.

While the uprising was undoubtedly a response to the conditions of slavery, there were other major factors involved in the making of the Stono rebellion, including the African background of the leaders. The clear majority of the Stono rebels were from the African kingdom of the Kongo, a Catholic country where Portuguese was widely spoken. Portuguese and Spanish are linguistically related enough for these slaves to have understood the Spanish offers of freedom. It is also highly likely that at least some of the rebels had been soldiers before becoming slaves, as it was quite common for African leaders to sell into slavery enemies captured in battle. The timing of the revolt also had African religious significance—that particular weekend was the Nativity of the Virgin Mary, a crucial religious holiday in the Kongo. White cloth and the beating of drums were African elements of that holiday celebration.

The reaction on the part of white colonists was swift. Recognizing that connections back to Africa had in part fueled rebellion, South Carolina implemented a 10-year ban on slaves imported directly from Africa. The colony also passed a harsh new slave law in 1740 that greatly restricted slaves from assembling together or learning to read. Despite the severity of the rebellion, very few white individuals at the time wrote or spoke about the event. Their fear was that talking about slave rebellions might make them more likely to happen in the future, and therefore silence was the best policy.

THOUGHT QUESTIONS:

1. What were the goals of the rebels? What did they hope to accomplish?

2. How did the backgrounds of the rebel slaves affect the timing and course of the rebellion?

3. What effects did the uprising have on society in the years that followed?

The Fort William Henry Massacre

The French & Indian War (also known as the Seven Years War) pitted the British against the French and their Indian allies. At stake was the future of colonial North America. Each side stood to gain massive new colonial territories if it emerged victorious.

On August 3, 1757, a French army of 6,200 French troops and 1,800 Indians under the command of General Marquis de Montcalm began a siege of the British Fort William Henry, at the southern tip of Lake Champlain in New York. The British defenders consisted of more than 2,000 regulars and colonial militia under the command of Lt. Colonel George Monro. Monro sent a messenger to his commander, General Daniel Webb, who was at Fort Edward, just 16 miles away. Webb refused to send reinforcements because he was unsure if this was a French trap to lure his army away from the defense of the city of Albany. Instead, Webb wrote that Monro should negotiate the best possible terms of surrender. Monro held out until August 8, when French heavy guns breached the walls and made the fort indefensible.

Montcalm offered the British generous surrender terms. The British soldiers, plus their dependent women and children, would all be allowed to leave without harm. They could take their flags and weapons (without ammunition) with them, but they had to agree not to fight again in the current war for at least 18 months. For Montcalm, it was the easiest method of accomplishing his goal: the fort's capture. The terms did not meet the approval, however, of France's Indian allies. To Native Americans, war was a means of individual and communal restitution for past suffering or death. The generous surrender terms, logical from the French perspective, went against Indian conceptions of victory. Native warriors had been promised personal honor and trophies, specifically scalps, prisoners, and looted valuables. Instead, there would be little plunder, and the hated British, who had frequently inflicted pain and suffering on native tribes in the past, would escape without punishment. While a few native leaders accepted the surrender, the Indian coalition was drawn from many different tribes, not all of whom believed that they should abide by the agreement.

On the night of the surrender, some native warriors entered and looted the fort, killing several of the British wounded who had been too ill to move. Shocked by the violent outburst, Montcalm decided to post French guards around the British prisoners who would march away the next day. As the British column set off in the morning, some of the French troops declined to continue defending them. Montcalm felt constrained in his own actions because he could not afford to risk alienating key Indian allies. Young native soldiers saw this moment as their last chance to seize glory and trophies from the campaign. As British men, women, and children headed down the road, they were swarmed by warriors who grabbed at their guns, clothing, and valuables. Those who resisted were either killed or kidnapped to be held for later ransom. The attacks continued until the survivors reached the safety of Fort Edward. Initial reports claimed that as many as 1,500 British had been massacred after surrendering. Modern historical estimates have lowered the death toll to fewer than 200, but English outrage was not driven primarily by the exact number of deaths, but rather because the killings came in cold blood after the surrender.

The fallout from the event was significant. Montcalm spent several days destroying the fortification, then withdrew. He later wrote a letter to the English in which he expressed regret for the events, but ultimately placing blame on the English themselves for behaving erratically and provoking the Indians. General Webb was recalled to England in shame for not moving to save Fort William Henry. Colonel Munro died a few months later of an internal hemorrhage, which some believe was partly caused by his fury over the massacre. The incident served to intensify the colonial and British determination to triumph over their French enemies in the war. Years later, the series of events surrounding the siege of Fort William Henry and the massacre which followed were recounted and embellished in James Fenimore Cooper's 1826 classic novel, *The Last of the Mohicans*.

THOUGHT QUESTIONS:

1. Why did the French and their Indian allies disagree over the terms of surrender given to British defenders of Fort William Henry?

2. What mistakes were made by various individuals at the time that contributed the chain of events? What things might have been done differently?

3. What were the major effects of the Fort William Henry Massacre?

Chapter 5

Origins of the American Revolution

Ben Franklin, *Observations Concerning the Increase of Mankind, Peopling of Countries, etc.* (1751)

Anti-immigrant politics predate the American Revolution. It was only during the French and Indian Wars (1754-1763) that the term "American" came into common usage. Men like Ben Franklin (later a leader of the revolution) still considered themselves loyal British subjects. Yet, even though an American nation did not yet exist, Franklin already knew who belonged in his "country" and who did not. In a brief 1751 pamphlet, Franklin called for more immigration into the thirteen British colonies of "lovely" whites and the exclusion of some Europeans who supposedly were darker-skinned. Racial categories have no scientific validity, and the meaning of terms like "white," "black," "red," and so on vary over time. In Franklin's mind, most Germans were not quite white, and he worried that German immigrants to the colonies undermined the dominance of the English language and culture. In this document, Franklin also seems to prefer Native Americans to certain European groups.

And since Detachments of *English* from *Britain* sent to *America*, will have their Places at Home so soon supply'd and increase so largely here; why should the *Palatine Boors* be suffered to swarm into our Settlements, and by herding together establish their Language and Manners to the Exclusion of ours? Why should *Pennsylvania*, founded by the *English*, become a Colony of *Aliens*, who will shortly be so numerous as to Germanize us instead of our Anglifying them, and will never adopt our Language or Customs, any more than they can acquire our Complexion.

Which leads me to add one Remark: That the Number of purely white People in the World is proportionally very small. All *Africa* is black or tawny. *Asia* chiefly tawny.

America (exclusive of the new Comers) wholly so. And in *Europe*, the *Spaniards*, *Italians*, *French*, *Russians* and *Swedes*, are generally of what we call a swarthy Complexion; as are the *Germans* also, the *Saxons* only excepted, who with the *English*, make the principal Body of White People on the Face of the Earth. I could wish their Numbers were increased. And while we are, as I may call it, *Scouring* our Planet, by clearing *America* of Woods, and so making this Side of our Globe reflect a brighter Light to the Eyes of Inhabitants in *Mars* or *Venus*, why should we in the Sight of Superior Beings, darken its People? why increase the Sons of *Africa*, by Planting them in *America*, where we have so fair an Opportunity, by excluding all Blacks and Tawneys, of increasing the lovely White and Red? But perhaps I am partial to the Complexion of my Country, for such Kind of Partiality is natural to Mankind.

Source: *https://archive.org/details/increasemankind00franrich*

THOUGHT QUESTIONS:

1. What threats did "Palatine Boors" pose to the English colonies, according to Benjamin Franklin?

2. How did Franklin assess the status of "purely white People" worldwide, and what opportunity did he think North America provided them?

3. Are there similarities between Franklin's anxieties about German immigrants in the 1750s and later controversies about immigrants from Mexico?

Anonymous, *An Account of the Boston Massacre*, March 5, 1770

Boston was the epicenter of the American Revolution. Income inequality and a series of unpopular taxes, such as The Stamp Act (passed by the British Parliament in 1764) and the Townshend Acts, inspired public protests, boycotts of products imported from England, and the hanging of effigies representing British officials. The British government decided to send troops into the city to ensure law and order. Instead, the troops were seen as an invading force violating individual rights, and the soldiers became targets of verbal abuse and harassment. The tensions erupted in violence on March 5, 1770, when an angry mob, which included many under the influence of alcohol, faced off against a British Army patrol in front of a customhouse. The crowd threw snowballs, sometimes containing rocks, at the soldiers. When one "Redcoat" fell, his comrades panicked and fired their muskets at the protestors. Five died, including Crispus Attucks, a dockworker of African and Native American descent. The massacre was subject to much exaggeration by self-described "Patriots," those opposed to British policy in the American colonies. This is a contemporary published account of the incident.

The Town of Boston affords a recent and melancholy Demonstration of the destructive consequences of quartering troops among citizens in time of Peace, under a pretence of supporting the laws and aiding civil authority . . . The *Boston Journal of Occurrences* printed in *Mr. Holt's York Journal,* from time to time, afforded many striking instances of the distresses brought upon the inhabitants by this measure; and since those Journals have been discontinued, our troubles from that quarter have been growing upon us: We have known a party of soldiers in the face of day fire off a loaded musket upon the inhabitants, others have been prick'd with bayonets, and even our magistrate assaulted and put in danger of their lives, where offenders brought before them have been rescued and why those and other bold and base criminals have as yet escaped the punishment due to their crimes, may be soon matter of enquiry by the representative body of this people . . . Divers stories were propagated among the soldiery, that serv'd to agitate their spirits particularly on the Sabbath, that one Chambers, a serjeant, represented as a sober man, had been missing the preceding day, and must therefore have been murdered by the townsmen; an officer of distinction so far credited this report, that he enter'd Mr. Gray's rope-walk that Sabbath . . . We may however venture to declare, that it appears too probable from their conduct, that some of the soldiery aimed to draw and provoke the townsmen into squabbles, and that they then intended to make use of other weapons than canes, clubs or bludgeons. . . .

On the evening of Monday, being the 5th current, several soldiers of the 29th regiment were seen parading the streets with their drawn cutlasses and abusing and wounding numbers of the [town.]

. . . The people were immediately alarmed with the report of this horrid massacre, the bells were set a ringing, and great numbers soon assembled at the place where this tragical scene had been acted; their feelings may be better conceived than expressed; and while some were taking care of the dead and wounded, the rest were in consultation what to do in these dreadful circumstances. . . .

Tuesday morning presented a most shocking scene, the blood of our fellow-citizens running like water thro' King-street, and the Merchant's Exchange, the principal spot of the military parade for about 18 months past. Our blood might also be track'd up to the head of Long-Lane, and thro' divers other streets and passages.

At eleven o'clock, the inhabitants met at Faneuil-Hall, and after some animated speeches, becoming the occasion, they chose a Committee of 15 respectable Gentlemen, to wait upon the Lieut. Governor in Council, to request of him to issue his orders for the immediate removal of the troops.

The Message was in these Words:

"THAT it is the unanimous opinion of this meeting that the inhabitants and soldiery can no longer live together in safety; that nothing can rationally be expected to restore the peace of the town and prevent further blood and carnage, but the immediate removal of the troops; and that we therefore most servently pray his Honour, that his power and influence may be exerted for their instant removal."

His Honour's Reply, which was laid before the Town then adjourn'd to the Old South Meeting House, was as follows;

Gentlemen,

"I AM extremely sorry for the unhappy differences between the inhabitants and troops and especially for the action of the last evening, and I have exerted myself upon that occasion, that a due inquiry may be made, and that the law may have its course. I have in council consulted with the commanding officers of the two regiments who are in the town. They have their orders from the General at New-York. It is not in my power to countermand those orders. The council have desired that the two regiments may be removed to the Castle. From the particular concern which the 20th regiment has had in your differences, Col. Dalrymple, who is the commanding officer of the troops, has signified that that regiment shall, with out delay, be placed in the barracks at the Castle until he can send to the General and receive his further orders concerning both the regiments; and that the main guard shall be removed, and the 14th regiment so disposed and laid under such restraint that all occasion of future disturbances may be prevented."

The foregoing reply having been read and fully considered--the question was put, Whether there report be satisfactory? Passed in the negative, only 1 dissentient out of upwards of 4000 voters.

Source: *http://www.dpi.state.nc.us/docs/curriculum/socialstudies/rigorous-ap/us-history/boston-gazette.pdf*

THOUGHT QUESTIONS:

1. What facts did the anonymous writer leave out regarding the violence between the angry mob and the British troops in front of the customs house?

2. In what way did the response from the Lt. Governor in Council, appointed by King George III, deepen the suspicions of some Boston citizens towards the British government?

3. What possible parallels might there be between the relationship of the British troops and hostile residents of colonial Boston and between American troops later stationed in Vietnam, Afghanistan, and Iraq and the local population in those nations?

The Boston Tea Party
Boston Gazette December 20, 1773

After the Boston Massacre, a three-year period of relative quiet settled over the city. This apparent peace cracked as the British government continued to impose on the American colonists a series of taxes aimed at paying war debts, the costs of an expanded empire, and for defense of the colonies against possible attacks by the French and Native Americans resisting further encroachments on their land. The taxes were imposed by a Parliament in which the colonists were not represented, a key point of anger in the colonies. Supporters of British policies pointed out that American colonists enjoyed benefits from living in the British empire and paid far lower taxes than residents of Great Britain itself. Some argued that the colonists were "virtually" represented in the Parliament since that body supposedly represented the British empire as a whole, including the colonists. The Tea Act, a tax on tea passed by the Parliament in 1773, became a focal point of colonial discontent. In Massachusetts, protestors boycotted British tea. Three British ships bearing tea docked in Boston Harbor, but locals refused to allow the crew to unload the cargo and demanded that the ship return to England. The standoff culminated in a raid December 16, 1773 conducted by perhaps more than 100 men, many belonging to a group called The Sons of Liberty and some thinly disguised as Native Americans. The raiders dumped more than 300 chests of tea into the harbor. This is a newspaper account of these events.

On Tuesday last the body of the people of this and all the adjacent towns, and others from the distance of twenty miles, assembled at the old south meeting-house, to inquire the reason of the delay in sending the ship Dartmouth, with the East-India Tea back to London; and having found that the owner had not taken the necessary steps for that purpose, they enjoin'd him at his peril to demand of the collector of the customs a clearance for the ship . . . The people finding all their efforts to preserve the property of the East India company and return it safely to London, frustrated by the sea consignees, the collector of the customs and the governor of the province, DISSOLVED their meeting.-- But, BEHOLD what followed! A number of brave & resolute men, determined to do all in their power to save their country from the ruin which their enemies had plotted, in less than four hours, emptied every chest of tea on board the three ships commanded by the captains Hall, Bruce, and Coffin, amounting to 342 chests, into the sea!! without the least damage done to the ships or any other property. The masters and owners are well pleas'd that their ships are thus clear'd; and the people are almost universally congratulating each other on this happy event.

Source: Library of Congress, *http://www.loc.gov/teachers/classroommaterials/presentationsandactivities/presentations/timeline/amrev/rebelln/tea.html*, Accessed June 1, 2016.

THOUGHT QUESTIONS:

1. What message were the "Tea Party" protestors trying to communicate by dressing as Native Americans?

2. How does the writer of this description of the Boston Tea Party depict the raiders as the protectors of law and order?

3. Is there a parallel between the colonists being unrepresented in the British Parliament yet being subjected to taxes imposed by that body and present-day residents of Washington, D.C. who are subject to federal taxes but are not represented in the United States Congress? What are some reasons that Washington D.C. might not have seats in the United States House or Senate?

Vignettes

Pregnancy and Indentured Servitude

Historians estimate that between 50 to 75 percent of the European immigrants who arrived in the thirteen colonies from Great Britain and continental Europe before the American Revolution came as indentured servants. Most indentured servants who were not from Great Britain were German. Such servants wanted to escape debt, avoid imprisonment or simply wanted a new life in North America, but they could not afford the passage (which amounted to six months' wages for a typical British worker). Indentured servants signed contracts with ship owners agreeing to work, typically for three to seven years without wages, in order to pay off the travel cost. Plantation owners and other businessmen typically bought these contracts and used the servants as temporary slaves.

Life was hard for indentured servants, but especially for women who—like their male peers—were subject to beating, but faced a higher likelihood of rape and the additional burden of unwanted pregnancy. Masters assumed that pregnant servants would more likely try to escape. Masters also resented the work time pregnant servants lost late in pregnancy and before and after delivery. In 1777, when an indentured servant in Pennsylvania Margaret Sexton (who had only two years left on her contract) gave birth to two mixed-race daughters, her master Hugh McCullough convinced a court to add two more years to her term of indenture. Additionally, authorities awarded the children to McCullough as servants.

As historian Sharon Salinger has documented, unmarried female indentured servants in colonial Pennsylvania faced not only added time on their contracts for the days they were unable to work due to pregnancy, delivery, and care of newborns, but they also received criminal punishments for fornication and bearing "bastard" children. A Pennsylvania law enacted in 1706 allowed an indentured servant found guilty of giving birth to a bastard to be sentenced to up to two years of additional service for her master. As Salinger points out, the law gave a financial incentive for masters to rape their female servants, who then would be forced to work longer terms for their assailants and many, such as John Worral, accused servants of criminal fornication after they raped them and were awarded for their crime with additional years of labor by their female victims. Crime paid for the owners of indentured servants.

THOUGHT QUESTIONS:

1. What comparisons and differences are there between slaves and indentured servants in colonial America?

2. What likely motivated Europeans to sell themselves into indentured servitude?

3. What did the treatment of female indentured servants suggest about the status of women overall in the British colonies?

Jupiter Hammon: The "First" African American Poet

Jupiter Hammon never experienced freedom in his career as a slave preacher, published poet, and abolition advocate, but his faith told him that death would be the great equalizer. As Hammon wrote, "there are but two places where all go . . .white and black, rich and poor; those places are Heaven and Hell." Throughout his career, Hammon gently urged an end to human bondage, arguing that God was "no respecter of persons" and gently implying that reducing African Americans to the status of property was blasphemy. "If we should ever get to Heaven, we shall find nobody to reproach us for being black, or for being slaves," he declared in a speech to the African Society in 1786.

Slaves arriving to the British colonies in North America brought with them a rich tradition of oral literature, but it was not until the late 1700s that the first African-American literary works reached print. Although Phillis Wheatley became the far more famous poet, Hammon, born in 1711, can be considered the founder of African-American arts and letters. Born the child of slaves in Long Island, New York, Hammon gained a reputation as an eloquent preacher after he converted to Methodism during the Great Awakening of the 1730s and 1740s, achieving local fame as a writer and advocate of abolitionism. Hammon is regarded as the first African-American writer published in the United States. His poem, "An Evening Thought. Salvation by Christ with Penitential Cries," appeared as a broadside on Christmas Day in 1760. (Wheatley's *Poems on Various Subjects, Religious and Moral* was published in England in 1773.)

The family of Henry Lloyd owned Hammon, the child of slaves named Opium (who apparently frequently attempted to escape) and Rose, throughout his life. The Lloyds allowed Nehemiah Bull, a product of Harvard University, to educate their bright slave, who served as the Lloyds' bookkeeper. Hammon preached to African-American congregations on Long Island. When Hammon wrote "An Evening Thought," he built on a tradition begun with African-American spirituals in which references to salvation held a double meaning and referred both to spiritual redemption in the afterlife and the hope for freedom in this world. "We cry as Sinners to the Lord/ Salvation to obtain/It is firmly fixt his holy Word/ *Ye shall not cry in vain*," he wrote. "Negro spirituals" and poems by African-American artists like Hammon suggested that God was on the side of slaves and would free them in due time.

When Wheatley launched her career as a published poet, Hammon drew upon his expertise as a preacher in "An Address to Miss Phillis Wheatley" to critique her for not giving sufficient credit to God in her poetry for delivering her from a non-Christian land in Africa to what he felt was true faith available in North America. Hammon mischaracterized Wheatley's views of her capture as a slave. Like Hammon, Wheatley in her poem "On Being Brought from Africa to America," saw slavery as evil but believed that it served a miraculous purpose in allowing Africans to be Christianized, a step both thought necessary for eternal salvation. "Twas mercy brought me from my *Pagan* land," Wheatley had written, "Taught my benighted soul to understand/That there's a God, that there's a *Saviour* too."

Hammon seemed to believe that America, as a land freed from European corruption, could redeem the world once it rid itself of sins it inherited from the "Old World" such as slavery. After the American Revolution, in his 1787 work, *An Address to the Negroes of New York*," he noted that, at the age of 76, he no longer desired freedom at an age at which he could no longer support himself, but he did call for the gradual emancipation of "the young ones." Writing in a context in which slaves couldn't directly attack the greed and cruelty of slaveowners, he suggested that slaves would have to earn their freedom, "Now I acknowledge that liberty is a great thing, and worth seeking for, if we can get it honestly; and by our good conduct prevail on our masters to set us free."

In contrast to Wheatley, Hammon would be almost completely forgotten after his death until Oscar Wegelin, a literary scholar, uncovered his legacy and published a biography in 1915 that sparked the first serious appreciation of his talents among scholars. In 2013, Julie McCown, a doctoral student in English at the University of Texas at Arlington, discovered a previously unknown Hammon poem from 1786 sandwiched between other documents in an archive at the Yale University Library.

THOUGHT QUESTIONS:

1. What role did African- American religion play in encouraging the struggle of slaves for freedom?

2. In what way did his status as a slave influence how Hammon discussed human bondage?

3. How might having a distorted understanding of African culture and history have shaped Hammon and Wheatley's view that slavery was part of a divine plan to provide African Americans a path to salvation?

Bad Medicine

One of the most dangerous things a sick person could do in the 1700s was go to a white doctor. Western medical knowledge had advanced slowly from ancient times to the eighteenth century. During the colonial era, physicians, surgeons, and apothecaries (the forerunners of today's pharmacists) received only haphazard education and training. Physicians earned low incomes and often had to split their time between practicing medicine and other jobs, such as farming. Patients, knowing they were likely to die from diseases that today would be considered easy to treat, often chose physicians who also were ministers, desiring prayers for divine mercy along with medical care.

Generally speaking, if they had access to them, Americans in the colonial era went to apothecaries as a first resort. Apothecaries offered them nature-based remedies borrowed from Native Americans. Indigenous people introduced white people to the use of willow bark (a forerunner to aspirin) for aches and pains and quinine as a treatment for malaria.

However, Native American cures offered no relief or protection from what were then fatal diseases the colonists brought from Europe such as measles and smallpox. When they fell to more serious maladies, colonial Americans went to physicians and surgeons who were unaware of the existence of germs and who therefore did not clean their equipment. Surgeons used blood-caked gloves, saws, and other tools, often fatally infecting their patients.

Up to the 1800s, American doctors were still under the influence of Hippocrates, a Greek physician born in the fifth century B.C.E., who believed that illnesses were related to an imbalance of the four basic "humors"—or fluids—in the human body: blood, phlegm, yellow bile, and black bile.

In the second century, another Greek physician proclaimed that blood represented the humor most critical to health. For the next 1,600-plus years various forms of bloodletting—whether by directly cutting open a patient's veins, applying leeches, or cupping, in which the skin was punctured in numerous places and the blood suctioned out by bulbs, syringes, or the doctor's lips—became one of the most popular means to restore the balance of the humors and cure a variety of illnesses.

Doctors also "blistered" patients, creating second-degree burns on the body and deliberately irritating the wounds in order to draw pus. Doctors thought the body was releasing toxins and that the oozing was a sign of healing, not serious infection. In addition, doctors put seriously ill patients through a forced regimen of enemas and gave them tonics that induced vomiting in order to supposedly purge the body of disease-inducing poisons. These physicians did not merely inflict unnecessary pain on their clients. These treatments, in fact, caused more problems for already weakened patients through dehydration, anemia and sepsis, making death more likely.

As one eighteenth century American physician William Douglass put it, "In general the physical practice in our colonies is so perniciously bad that . . . there is more danger from the physician than from the distemper." One medical historian, Ira Rutkow, estimates that doctors drained some unfortunate patients of as much as 16 ounces of blood a day for up to two weeks.

Doctors treated mentally ill patients by dunking them in extremely cold water, placing them in a "spinning chair," and strapping them to a chair designed to reduce blood flow to the brain by tightly confining the patient's usually covered head as well as their arms and legs.

Being rich and famous provided no protection from such medical abuse. Doctors essentially subjected the first president, George Washington, to torture on December 14, 1799, when he began suffering from a fever, a severe cough, congestion, and a sore throat. Three doctors soon attended Washington, blistered him, drained him of 80 ounces of blood (about 40 percent of the total) in 12 hours, and gave him an enema and an emetic that induced vomiting, before making him gargle a concoction that included vinegar.

"Doctor, I die hard; but I am not afraid to go," he muttered. "I believed from my first attack that I should not survive it; my breath can not last long." In spite of the pain they inflicted, Washington thanked his doctors for their care before he died from what modern physicians believe could have been pneumonia, diphtheria, or a streptococcal throat infection, among numerous other posthumous diagnoses. Whatever the actual illness, some of the best doctors of his time aided and abetted Washington's agonizing death at 67.

THOUGHT QUESTIONS:

1. On what theory was medical "bleeding" based on?

2. What threats to patients' health were created by the medical practices of the eighteenth century?

3. Were Native American medical practices or Western approaches to patient care more safe and effective and why?

Chapter 6

The United States and the Age of Revolution

Abigail Adams, Letter to John Adams, Braintree, Massachusetts, June 18, 1775

The Battle of Bunker Hill, fought June 17, 1775, resulted in a defeat of the American Revolutionary forces by the British. However, the skirmish, mostly fought on Breed's Hill overlooking the city of Boston, represented a moral victory. The American forces killed approximately 200 British soldiers and injured about 800, including a high number of talented officers. Although they were forced to retreat and surrender control of the Charlestown Peninsula to the British Army, the smaller, inexperienced, and still-forming American Army proved that they could stand their ground against one of the most powerful militaries in the world. Revolutionary leaders realized a bridge had been crossed and also knew that they forced mortal danger should the rebellion fail. Here, Abigail Adams, wife of John Adams (who later became the second U.S. president), describes the mixed feelings felt by supporters of American independence as this early battle in the American War for Independence unfolded. Note: in the first paragraph, Adams refers to the death of Joseph Warren, a Harvard-educated physician who became an early leader of the resistance movement. On April 18, 1775, he dispatched Paul Revere and William Dawes to alert the towns of Lexington and Concord that the soldiers from the British garrison in Boston were on the march to arrest revolutionary leaders Samuel Adams and John Hancock and to seize weapons. Warren fought in Lexington and Concord, the following day in the first battles of the Revolutionary War. Warren continued to serve in the infant American military and died at the Battle of Bunker Hill on June 17 from a musket shot as the British made a third and final assault on Breed's Hill, his body stabbed repeatedly after he fell..

Sunday June 18 1775

Dearest Friend

The Day; perhaps the decisive Day is come on which the fate of America depends. My bursting Heart must find vent at my pen. I have just heard that our dear Friend Dr. Warren is no more but fell gloriously fighting for his Country—saying better to die honourably in the field than ignominiously hang upon the Gallows. Great is our Loss. He has distinguished himself in every engagement, by his courage and fortitude, by animating the Soldiers and leading them on by his own example. A particuliar account of these dreadful, but I hope Glorious Days will be transmitted you, no doubt in the exactest manner.

The race is not to the swift, nor the battle to the strong, but the God of Israel is he that giveth strength and power unto his people. Trust in him at all times, ye people pour out your hearts before him. God is a refuge for us.—Charlstown is laid in ashes. The Battle began upon our intrenchments upon Bunkers Hill, a Saturday morning about 3 o clock and has not ceased yet and tis now 3 o'clock Sabbeth afternoon.

Tis expected they will come out over the Neck to night, and a dreadful Battle must ensue. Almighty God cover the heads of our Country men, and be a shield to our Dear Friends. How [many ha]ve fallen we know not—the constant roar of the cannon is so [distre]ssing that we can not Eat, Drink or Sleep. May we be supported and sustaind in the dreadful conflict. I shall tarry here till tis thought unsafe by my Friends, and then I have secured myself a retreat at your Brothers who has kindly offerd me part of his house. I cannot compose myself to write any further at present. I will add more as I hear further.

Source: https://founders.archives.gov/?q=Bunker%20Hill&s=1111311111&sa=&r=9&sr=

THOUGHT QUESTIONS:

1. What does the quote Adams attributes to Joseph Warren indicate about the consequences the revolutionary leadership faced in the American Independence?

2. Did Abigail Adams appear to anticipate a short conflict against the British, and to whom did she compare the Americans?

3. Why would some see the Battle of Bunker Hill as a spiritual victory for the Americans even if the British defeated the revolutionary forces on the battlefield, and does Adams seem to share in this viewpoint?

George Washington, Letter to John Banister From Valley Forge, Pennsylvania, April 21, 1778.

The Second Continental Congress served as de facto United States government from the start of the Revolutionary War in 1775 until the final ratification of the Articles of Confederation in 1781. The revolution's leaders believed that the British government had transformed into a tyranny that placed too much power in the central government So, the first government they created for the United States placed most authority in the hands of the individual states, an arrangement that almost cost the Americans the war. Representing the only branch of the government, the Congress could only request money from the states to fund the War for Independence. The Congress also could only request troops from the states as well. This left the Continental Army headed by General George Washington poorly-equipped, under-staffed, underfed, and even poorly clothed. Such was the case in the winter of 1777-1778 when Washington and his troops braved hunger, disease, and exposure to frigid temperatures that cost the American army more than 2,500 deaths as they camped at Valley Forge, less than 20 miles from what was then the United States capital of Philadelphia. Because of these experiences, Washington would become a fierce advocate for the creation of a stronger central government after Americans won the American Revolution. Here, Washington describes the hardships faced by his forces at Valley Forge to John Banister, a Virginia lawyer who supported the American Revolution and would later become one of the authors of The Articles of Confederation.

[N]o history, now extant, can furnish an instance of an army's suffering such uncommon hardships as ours have done, and bearing them with the same patience and Fortitude—To see men without Cloat[hes] to cover their nakedness—without Blankets to lay on—without Shoes, by which their Marches might be traced by the Blood from their feet—and almost as often without Provisions as with; Marching through frost & Snow, and at Christmas taking up their Winter Quarters within a days March of the enemy, without a House or Hutt to cover them till they could be built & submitting to it without a murmur, is a Mark of patience & obedience which in my opinion can scarce be parallel'd.

There may have been some remonstrances or applications to Congress, in the Stile of complaint from the Army, & slaves indeed should we be if this priviledge was denied—on account of their proceedings in particular instances; but these will not authorise, nor even excuse a jealousy, that they, are therefore aiming at unreasonable powers—or making strides dangerous, or subversive of Civil authority. Things should not be viewed in that light, more especially, as Congress in some cases have relieved the injuries complained of, and which had flowed from their own acts.

. . . I will now be done, and I trust that you will excuse not only the length of my Letter, but the freedom with which I have delivered my sentiments in the course of it, upon several occasions. The subjects struck me as important and interesting—& I have only to wish that they may appear to you in the same light. I am Dr sir with great regard Your Most Obedt sert.

Source: https://founders.archives.gov/documents/Washington/03-14-02-0525

THOUGHT QUESTIONS:

1. Why would the Founders intentionally create a weak federal government in the Revolutionary Era?

2. What pressures might have forced the states to not provide their fair share to the Continental Army during the Revolutionary War?

3. What tone does George Washington adopt in his letter to Banister and do you think it is effective?

Letter, Unknown, Fredericksburg, Virginia, to John Adams, June 9 1775

The American Revolution is popularly understood in the United States as a war for freedom. Since many of the revolutionary leaders, including future presidents George Washington, Thomas Jefferson, and James Madison were slaveowners, however, the question might be asked, "Freedom for whom"? Northern states like Connecticut, where slavery played an insignificant part of the local economy, offered emancipation to slaves in return for fighting in the state militias against the British. In southern states that heavily exploited slave labor, the situation was reversed. John Murray, the 4th Earl of Dunmore, the royal governor of Virginia, issued a proclamation dated November 7, 1775, but not made public until a week later that promised freedom for any slaves who fought for the British crown against the American rebels. About 800 African Americans joined Dunmore's regiment. Dunmore's move, however, encouraged slaves in other states to flee their masters and seek assistance behind British lines, including 20,000 in South Carolina. Slaves who gained freedom by serving with the British Army became a bitter diplomatic dispute between Great Britain and the United States after the war, with the southern states demanding financial compensation for their lost human property. Here, an unidentified letter writer sees the emancipation of slaves as critical to the success of the American Revolution though he acknowledges the issue might be politically difficult and might lead slave owners to oppose independence. He asks John Adams to consider emancipation as a war tactic.

Letter, Unknown, Fredericksburg, Virginia, to John Adams, June 9, 1775

To proclaim instant Freedom to all the Servants that will join in the Defence of America, is a Measure to be handled with great Delicacy, as so great, so immediate a Sacrafice of Property, may possibly draw off many of the Americans themselves from the common Cause.

But is not such a Measure absolutely necessary? And might not a proper Equivalent be made to the Masters, out of the Large Sums of Money which at all Events must be struck, in the present Emergency?

If America should neglect to do this, will not Great Britain engage these Servants to espouse her Interest, by proclaiming Freedom to them, without giving any Equivalent to the Masters? To give Freedom to the Slaves is a more dangerous, but equally necessary Measure.

Is it not incompatible with the glorious Struggle America is making for her own Liberty, to hold in absolute Slavery a Number of Wretches, who will be urged by Despair on one Side, and the most flattering Promises on the other, to become the most inveterate Enemies to their present Masters?

If the Inhabitants of Quebec should assist Great Britain, would not true Wisdom dictate to the other Colonies, to lead their Slaves to the Conquest of that Country, and to bestow that and Liberty upon them as a Reward for their Bravery and Fidelity?

Source: https://founders.archives.gov/?q=Revolution%20slaves&s=1111311111&sa=&r=54&sr=

THOUGHT QUESTIONS:

1. Why did the Continental Congress, which proclaimed in their Declaration of Independence that "all men are created equal," not offer emancipation to slaves in all thirteen states in return for service in the state militias and the Continental Army?

2. In what ways did slavery hamper the American struggle for independence from Great Britain?

3. What service did the author think freed slaves could offer the cause of independence, and did the writer see a parallel between the African-American struggle for freedom and the American revolutionary cause?

Vignettes

Deism and the Founding Fathers

The leaders of the revolutionary generation were intellectually curious men who loved debating each other on a wide range of subjects, including history, science, and philosophy. As deists, or heavily influenced by deism, and firm believers in science, most of those who became known as the "Founding Fathers"—Franklin, Washington, Hamilton, John Adams—did not believe in a God who performed miracles. Their God was a divine clockmaker. He put the gears together, wound the cosmic clock, and let it run. The complexity of the universe, its vastness, and its dependability, as revealed by Isaac Newton's Laws of Motion, was the miracle, not Biblical tales of water turning into wine or the dead being raised. Many of the Founders revered the Bible as a source of wisdom but saw Jesus as a great philosopher, but no more.

Thomas Jefferson was particularly skeptical of Biblical accuracy. ". . . [I]n the book of Joshua we are told that the sun stood still for several hours," Jefferson wrote to his nephew Peter Carr. ". . . [Y]ou are Astronomer enough to know how contrary it is to the law of nature that a body revolving on its axis, as the earth does, should have stopped, should not by that sudden stoppage have prostrated animals, trees, buildings, and should after a certain time have resumed its revolution, and that without a second prostration. Is this arrest of the earth's motion, or the evidence which affirms it, most within the law of probabilities?"

Jefferson frequently expressed his disbelief in the virgin birth of Jesus, arguing that Jesus was Mary's "illegitimate" son. "And the day will come when the mystical generation of Jesus, by the supreme being as his father in the womb of a virgin will be classed with the fable of the generation of Minerva [the Roman goddess of wisdom] in the brain of Jupiter," Jefferson wrote in a letter to John Adams dated April 11, 1823. He also had no patience for Biblical tales of miracles, which he viewed as fairy tales believed only by the ignorant. In fact, he wrote his own version of the New Testament omitting all tales of the supernatural and included only the moral teachings and precepts of Jesus.

Benjamin Franklin shared Jefferson's refusal to take the Bible literally. Once, Ezra Stiles asked his friend Franklin about his thoughts concerning Jesus' nature. Like many, Franklin doubted whether Biblical accounts of Jesus' birth, words, and deeds were reliable. "As to Jesus of Nazareth, my Opinion of whom you particularly desire, I think the system of Morals, and his Religion, as he left them to us, the best the world ever saw or is likely to see." Franklin wrote in a March 9, 1790 letter. "But I apprehend it has received various, corrupting Changes, and I have, with most of the present dissenters in England, some doubts as to his Divinity; tho' it is a question I do not dogmatize upon . . ."

John Adams doubted the accuracy of events described in the Bible and words attributed to Biblical figures like Jesus. "What do you call the 'Bible?'" he once wrote to his son John Quincy Adams, before rattling off the names of various translations of the Scripture: "What Bible? King James's? The Hebrew? The Septuagint? The Vulgate? The Bible now translated or translating into Chinese, Indian, Negro, and all of the other languages of Europe, Asia and Africa? Which of the thirty thousand variantia are the Rule of Faith?"

This did not mean that the force they called "Providence" was unconcerned with morality, unimpressed with good and indifferent to evil. Their clockmaker God structured the universe in a rational, predictable way, and morality was rational. Their god did judge, and he demanded virtue. And even if men like Franklin expressed doubts about the accuracy of Biblical stories, it did not mean the stories of the Bible had no effect on how they saw themselves or the world. Franklin saw something heroic in Americans bringing a modern democratic republic, a nation built not on inherited privileges but on equality before the law, to the world through the revolution. He compared the American people to the ancient Israelites in the Book of Exodus who escaped slavery in Egypt, gifting the world with monotheism (the belief in one God) and the Ten Commandments.

Jefferson also wanted to compare Revolutionary America to the Israelites. In 1776, he proposed a design for the Great Seal of the United States that would portray the children of Israel in the wilderness after their escape from their Egyptian slavemasters, being led by a miraculous cloud by day and a pillar by night. Americans were unique, the Founders believed, a new "chosen people" who would lead the world out of slavery to kings and other tyrants.

THOUGHT QUESTIONS:

1. How did eighteenth century deists perceive the nature of God?

2. Even if they did not take the Bible literally, what value did Revolutionary leaders like Thomas Jefferson, Benjamin Franklin, and John Adams think the Bible had in the modern day?

3. In what way did the Revolutionary Generation compare themselves to the ancient Israelites depicted in the Bible?

A Nation of Drinkers

Throughout the American Revolution, John Adams worried that the battle for liberty would turn into an excuse for vice, a moral degeneration that would lead to American defeat in the war. Alcohol consumption particularly concerned him. Routinely on his way to meetings of the Continental Congress in 1777, as historian Thaddeus Russell observed in his book *A Renegade History of the United States*, the future American president strolled from his temporary residence to the Pennsylvania State House (later renamed Independence Hall), a four-block trek that took hum past a dozen licensed taverns and countless illegal drinking establishments.

Overall, Philadelphia boasted 160 legal drinking halls to provide libations for a population of 24,000. When unlicensed taverns are counted, "there was at least one tavern for every 100 residents," compared to about one drinking establishment for every 1,071 residents as of 2007, Russell wrote. Other American cities, such as Boston and New York, were even more alcohol-saturated than Philadelphia.

Americans drank alcohol far more in the last quarter of the 1700s than they do today. There were a lot of reasons. Water supplies were not always safe. Farmers producing the grains alcohol is made from did not always have access to reliable, adequately speedy transportation, so they made the grains into whiskey and other liquors because these libations have an extremely long shelf life. Availability undoubtedly increased usage. Attitudes toward alcohol differed from the modern day. Americans in this era, like Europeans, thought that whiskey, brandy, rum and gin were healthy and nutritious foods that added variety to dull diets. As the historian W.J. Rorabaugh notes, Americans relied on alcohol as medicines that could cure or reduce the suffering from fevers, aches, colds, frostbite, and as a remedy for tension and depression, and "enable hardworking laborers to enjoy a moment of happy, frivolous camaraderie."

Americans drank hard liquor in abundance. Favorites were rum, whiskey, brandy, and gin, that were 45 percent alcohol. During the colonial period up through the end of the Revolutionary War, Americans consumed 3.7 gallons of alcohol per capita per year, as opposed to 2.25 gallons per capita consumed today. (Between 1800 and 1830, per capita liquor consumption jumped to more than 5 gallons a year, an all-time high).

Taverns often opened next to churches and courthouses so a shot or two could be enjoyed before a trial or worship. Judges, lawyers, the jury and defendants all drank in the courtroom during trials. During controversial cases that drew crowds too big for the courthouse, judges conducted trials in taverns where drinks continued to be served. Shoemakers, furniture makers, and cobblers kept mugs of beer or shots of whiskey next to them during the workday. They drank as they worked, and during lunch breaks, they gulped even more. As Russell points out, no period of American history saw a higher percentage of children born out of wedlock than the time of the revolution, with one out of 38 adults having an "illegitimate child." Alcohol often fueled these unplanned births.

Revolutionary leaders believed that the nation's virtue would provide an invisible weapon against the British during the war. Leaders of the early Republic feared that alcohol would destroy workplace discipline and harm the nation economically and lead it to the decadence and corruption poisoning European nations. George Washington, who distilled whiskey at Mount Vernon, bemoaned that liquor was "the ruin of half the workingmen in this country." Adams, who enjoyed hard cider during breakfast every morning, complained, ". . . is it not mortifying . . . that we, Americans, should exceed all other . . . people in the world, in this degrading, beastly vice of intemperance?" After the United States won independence, Adams feared that the new nation would become "a Spectacle of Contempt and Derision to the foolish and wicked, and of Grief and shame to the wise among Mankind, and all this in the Space of a few Years."

THOUGHT QUESTIONS:

1. What were some reasons that Americans consumed so much alcohol in the late eighteenth and early nineteenth centuries?

2. What harmful effects did early American leaders fear excessive drinking would pose to the new nation?

3. What health benefits did eighteenth century Americans think alcohol provided?

Thomas Paine, Non-Conformist

What happened in America didn't stay in America.   One controversial man, Thomas Paine, played a key role not only in the American revolt against British role, but in the French Revolution as well.   Paine's pamphlet, *Common Sense,* inspired the patriots in 1776 just as the struggle got under way.   But Paine remains one of the least loved of the nation's founders.   In the twentieth century, President Theodore Roosevelt disdained Paine as a "filthy little atheist."   A radical, who at one point called for governments to guarantee a minimum annual income, Paine feuded with far more beloved figures of his day, like George Washington, and when he died, only six people would attend the funeral of a man infamous for supposedly attacking Christianity.

Born in Norfolk, England in 1737, the future author left school at age 13 to labor as a corset maker.   In 1774, Paine got fired from his government job when he fought for better pay and working conditions for himself and other tax collectors.   Paine also objected to British laws that forced Jews to pay taxes but did not allow them to vote.   The loss of his paycheck drove Paine to sail across the Atlantic in late 1774.

Paine quickly attached himself to the cause of American independence upon landing in his new homeland.   His pamphlet, *Common Sense*, reached at least a half-million people.   "Without the pen of the author of *Common Sense*," fellow revolutionary John Adams wrote, "the sword of Washington would have been raised in vain."

Appointed in 1777 to the Committee for Foreign Affairs by the Continental Congress, Paine earned a reputation as a troublemaker when he revealed that a member of Congress had attempted to personally enrich himself through French wartime aid to the United States.   For his troubles, the committee expelled him in 1779.   His combative personality sometimes fueled by alcohol abuse, Paine nevertheless proved a tireless crusader for admirable causes, becoming a loud critic of slavery.   Restless, Paine moved back to his home country in 1787, where he viewed with admiration the French Revolution, which he praised in a 1791 work, *The Rights of Man.*

In England, many conservatives feared the French revolution might inspire a violent overthrow of the British government and many read Paine's book as a call to arms against King George III.   "What are the present governments of Europe, but a scene of iniquity and oppression?" he wrote.   Paine fled to France just before the British government ordered his arrest.   The British put Paine on trial for sedition in absentia, convicted him, and barred him from ever returning.   English mobs burned Paine in effigy and made bonfires of his books.

The French greeted him as a hero and, in spite of his inability to speak French, he won election to the National Convention.   He put his life in danger, however, by voting against the execution of King Louis.   When a more radical regime headed by Maximilien de Robespierre seized power, the French government ordered the arrest of Paine for treason in December 1793. Paine faced the guillotine, in part because of his British citizenship (France was at war with Britain at the time).

Paine argued that he was an American citizen, but the United States minister to France, Gouverneur Morris, made little effort to help him. It's probable that only Robespierre's timely overthrow and execution spared Paine's life. Paine would be convinced for the rest of his life that George Washington's administration had plotted to have him arrested and killed. During these troubles, Paine authored *The Age of Reason*. The treatise attacked any religious belief at variance with established scientific fact and ridiculed each religion's claim to have a special connection with God. "The Jews have their Moses; the Christians their Jesus Christ, their apostles and saints; and the Turks their Mohomet, as if the way to God were not open to every man alike," he wrote. Paine returned to the United States by 1803, but because of *The Age of Reason*, he was shunned as a heretic and atheist and, when he died in 1809 in Greenwich Village in New York, the local Quakers refused to let him be buried in their graveyard. His remains were sent to England, but it's unclear where they ended up, a quiet, obscure fate for a man who lived so fiercely.

THOUGHT QUESTIONS:

1. What does Paine's career say about the state of free speech in the United States, Great Britain, and France in the late eighteenth and early nineteenth centuries?

2. For what reasons might Thomas Paine be less remembered and revered as an American "Founder" than other figures like George Washington and John Adams?

3. In what ways was Paine ahead of his time, even in an age of revolution?

Chapter 7

The Critical Period, 1781-1789

**Letter, Abigail Adams to Thomas Jefferson,
January 29, 1787**

After the conclusion of the American Revolution, the newly born United States went into a recession. Trade with Great Britain fell off sharply, inflation was rampant, unemployment high, and American currency was nearly worthless and in short supply. States struggled to balance budgets. In addition, the federal government had not paid debts owed to soldiers who served in the Continental Army during the War for Independence or to farmers who were given IOUs during the war after they supplied the armed forces with supplies. In Massachusetts, farmers faced losing their farms because they could not pay their mortgages. The Massachusetts state government approached the crisis with a series of harsh measures including high taxes that were more rigorously collected than in the past. Farmers started arming themselves and interrupting foreclosure hearings in local courthouses. In 1787, Daniel Shays, who had reached the rank of captain during the Revolution War, led armed protestors who staged an assault on the federal arsenal at Springfield, Massachusetts. Authorities eventually suppressed "Shays's Rebellion," but the incident shocked and frightened elites who saw in it the potential for a second American revolution in a decade, this time aimed at wealthy and powerful persons such as themselves. The Shays revolt provided momentum for the drafting and ratification of a new American Constitution from 1787-1789. In her letter to Thomas Jefferson below, Abigail Adams (the wife of future Vice President John Adams and one of his chief political advisors) expresses her contempt for Shays's ragged army and their motives.

My dear sir

. . . With regard to the Tumults in my Native state which you inquire about, I wish I could say that report had exaggerated them. It is too true Sir that they have been carried to so allarming a Height as to stop the Courts of Justice in several Counties. Ignorant, wrestless desperadoes, without conscience or principals, have led a deluded multitude to follow their standard, under pretence of grievances which have no existance but in their immaginations. Some of them were crying out for a paper currency, some for an equal distribution of property, some were for annihilating all debts, others complaning that the Senate was a useless Branch of Government, that the Court of common Pleas was unnecessary, and that the Sitting of the General Court in Boston was a grieveince. By this list you will see, the materials which compose this Rebellion, and the necessity there is of the wisest and most vigorous measures to quell and suppress it.

Instead of that laudible Spirit which you approve, which makes a people watchfull over their Liberties and alert in the defence of them, these Mobish insurgents are for sapping the foundation, and distroying the whole fabrick at once. But as these people make only a small part of the State, when compared to the more Sensible and judicious, and altho they create a just allarm, and give much trouble and uneasiness, I cannot help flattering myself that they will prove Sallutary to the state at large, by leading to an investigation of the causes which have produced these commotions. Luxury and extravagance both in furniture and dress had pervaded all orders of our Countrymen and women, and was hastning fast to Sap their independance by involving every class of citizens in distress, and accumulating debts upon them which they were unable to discharge. Vanity was becoming a more powerfull principal than Patriotism. The lower order of the community were prest for taxes, and tho possest of landed property they were unable to answer the Demand. Whilst those who possesst Money were fearfull of lending, least the mad cry of the Mob should force the Legislature upon a measure very different from the touch of Midas.

. . . A Number of Vollunteers Lawyers Physicians and Merchants from Boston made up a party of Light horse . . . and were fortunate enough to take 3 of their Principal Leaders, Shattucks Parker and Page. Shattucks defended himself and was wounded in his knee with a broadsword. He is in Jail in Boston and will no doubt be made an example of . .

. . . I am Yours &c &c

A Adams

Source: https://founders.archives.gov/documents/Adams/04-07-02-0181

THOUGHT QUESTIONS:

1. How did Abigail Adams's economic status and political connections influence how she viewed Shays's Rebellion?

2. What approaches might the Massachusetts state legislature have taken to prevent Shays's Rebellion?

3. What does this incident say about economic inequality in the early American republic?

The Federalist Papers No. 68:
The Mode of Electing the President
March 14, 1788

*A recent hit musical celebrates Alexander Hamilton as a man of humble immigrant origins who through his vast intelligence and grit helped create the American economy and system of government. The real-life Hamilton's frank elitism and disdain for the common person in spite of his humble origins, however, stands as one of the key paradoxes of his life. An admirer of the aristocratic system of government, Hamilton argued during the Constitutional Convention in Philadelphia in 1787, that those elected to the newly proposed Senate and the presidency should serve for life. Hamilton worried that demagogues could easily sway an ignorant and emotional general public and wanted to guarantee that those he considered the best in American society—the educated and wealthy—would exercise a heavy hand in choosing leaders. "The voice of the people has been said to be the voice of God; and however generally this maxim has been quoted and believed, it is not true in fact," Hamilton said. "The people are turbulent and changing; they seldom judge or determine right. Give therefore to the first class a distinct, permanent share of the government." Hamilton persuaded the convention to avoid the direct election of presidents by the public. Thus was born the Electoral College, a system in which states are awarded electors based on how many representatives each has in the U.S. House of Representatives (determined by population), plus the state's two senators. Under this system, candidates who win enough states can capture the White House, even if most voters reject them. This has happened five times: John Qunicy Adams in 1824, Rutherford B. Hayes in 1876, Benjamin Harrison in 1888, George W. Bush in 2000 and Donald Trump in 2016; all lost the popular vote but captured the presidency. In the 68th installment of the **Federalist Papers**, a series of essays written to boost support for the Constitution, Hamilton argued for the merits of the Electoral College.*

To the People of the State of New York:

THE mode of appointment of the Chief Magistrate of the United States is almost the only part of the system, of any consequence, which has escaped without severe censure, or which has received the slightest mark of approbation from [the Constitution's] opponents.

. . . It was desirable that the sense of the people should operate in the choice of the person to whom so important a trust was to be confided. This end will be answered by committing the right of making it, not to any preestablished body, but to men chosen by the people for the special purpose, and at the particular conjuncture.

It was equally desirable, that the immediate election should be made by men most capable of analyzing the qualities adapted to the station . . . A small number of persons, selected by their fellow-citizens from the general mass, will be most likely to possess the information and discernment requisite to such complicated investigations.

It was also peculiarly desirable to afford as little opportunity as possible to tumult and disorder. This evil was not least to be dreaded in the election of a magistrate, who was to have so important an agency in the administration of the government as the President of the United States. . . .   The choice of SEVERAL, to form an intermediate body of electors, will be much less apt to convulse the community with any extraordinary or violent movements, than the choice of ONE who was himself to be the final object of the public wishes . . . Nothing was more to be desired than that every practicable obstacle should be opposed to cabal, intrigue, and corruption.

The process of election affords a moral certainty, that the office of President will never fall to the lot of any man who is not in an eminent degree endowed with the requisite qualifications. Talents for low intrigue, and the little arts of popularity, may alone suffice to elevate a man to the first honors in a single State; but it will require other talents, and a different kind of merit, to establish him in the esteem and confidence of the whole Union, or of so considerable a portion of it as would be necessary to make him a successful candidate for the distinguished office of President of the United States. It will not be too strong to say, that there will be a constant probability of seeing the station filled by characters pre-eminent for ability and virtue.

Source: *https://www.congress.gov/resources/display/content/The+Federalist+Papers#TheFederalistPapers-68*

THOUGHT QUESTIONS:

1. What biases led Hamilton to conclude that elites will choose presidents more wisely than the general public?

2. Does the Electoral College magnify the influence of individual states in national elections?

3. What does the Electoral College reveal about the view the nation's Founders had of democracy?

Madison Speech Advocating a Bill of Rights June 8, 1789

At the Constitutional Convention, delegates knew that the new government they were creating to replace the Articles of Confederation represented a major transfer of power from the states to the federal government and that this loss of local control would be seen by many in the public as a betrayal of a key principle of the American Revolution. Virginia delegate George Mason adamantly insisted that the document about to be submitted to the states for ratification was badly flawed because it lacked a "Bill of Rights" that guaranteed individual rights. In 1776, Mason had already served on a committee in his home state that drafted a Declaration of Rights later incorporated in the state constitution. Mason's Declaration opened with these words: "That all men are by nature equally free and independent, and have certain inherent rights. . . namely, the enjoyment of life and liberty, with the means of acquiring and possessing property, and pursuing and obtaining happiness and safety." At the Constitutional Convention, Mason argued that the Constitution needed to specify which rights individuals have, as a bulwark against the new government moving in an authoritarian or even tyrannical direction. One of the principal authors of the Constitution, James Madison, argued that limits already placed on government made a declaration of rights unnecessary, and his words carried the day. Madison came to regret this victory, as much of the opposition to the Constitution at the state ratifying conventions stemmed from the lack of a Bill of Rights. After the Constitution was ratified, Madison won election as a member of the newly created House of Representatives, and he introduced a series of amendments to the Constitution that came to be known as "The Bill of Rights." The amendments forbade the federal government from infringing on free speech and freedom of religion, compelling the accused to testify against themselves, and so on. A proposal of Madison's, to allow the Congress or a joint Congressional-Judicial committee to veto state laws, did not pass the Congress. Ten of the Amendments were ratified by the states by December 1791.

. . . I believe that the great mass of the people who opposed [the Constitution], disliked it because it did not contain effectual provision against encroachments on particular rights, and those safeguards which they have been long accustomed to have interposed between them and the magistrate who exercised the sovereign power: nor ought we to consider them safe, while a great number of our fellow citizens think these securities necessary . . . The amendments which have occurred to me, proper to be recommended by congress to the state legislatures are these:

. . . . That [there] be inserted these clauses, to wit, The civil rights of none shall be abridged on account of religious belief or worship, nor shall any national religion be established, nor shall the full and equal rights of conscience be in any manner, or on any pretext infringed.

The people shall not be deprived or abridged of their right to speak, to write, or to publish their sentiments; and the freedom of the press, as one of the great bulwarks of liberty, shall be inviolable. The people shall not be restrained from peaceably assembling and consulting for their common good, nor from applying to the legislature by petitions . . . for redress of their grievances. The right of the people to keep and bear arms shall not be infringed; a well armed, and well regulated militia being the best security of a free country . . .

Excessive bail shall not be required, nor excessive fines imposed, nor cruel and unusual punishments inflicted . . .

The exceptions here or elsewhere in the constitution, made in favor of particular rights, shall not be so construed as to diminish the just importance of other rights retained by the people; or as to enlarge the powers delegated by the constitution; but either as actual limitations of such powers, or as inserted merely for greater caution.

. . . . I wish also, in revising the constitution, we may throw into that section, which interdicts the abuse of certain powers in the state legislatures, some other provisions of equal if not greater importance than those already made. The words, "No state shall pass any bill of attainder, ex post facto law, &c." were wise and proper restrictions in the constitution. I think there is more danger of those powers being abused by the state governments than by the government of the United States. The same may be said of other powers which they possess, if not controuled by the general principle, that laws are unconstitutional which infringe the rights of the community. I should therefore wish to extend this interdiction . . . that no state shall violate the equal right of conscience, freedom of the press, or trial by jury in criminal cases; because it is proper that every government should be disarmed of powers which entrench upon those particular rights.

Source: : Allen Johnson, ed., *Readings in American Constitutional History, 1776-1876* (Boston: Houghton Mifflin Company, 1921).

THOUGHT QUESTIONS:

1. What recent experiences would have made the Revolutionary Generation concerned about threats to civil rights without the inclusion of the Bill of Rights in the U.S. Constitution?

2. Why was George Mason's proposal for a Bill of Rights initially rejected?

3. How do James Madison's proposals during the debate on the Bill of Rights in 1789 reflect a shift in power from the states to the federal government in the late 1780s?

Vignettes

An 18th Century Refugee Crisis

In many ways, the American Revolution was not just a struggle for independence, but also a civil war between those seeking to create a new nation and those who remained loyal to Great Britain, the so-called Tories. About 19,000 Tories served in the British Army during the war. Americans who felt that differences with the British government could be worked out peacefully, who believed that the revolutionaries' concerns were overblown, who recently arrived in the thirteen colonies and had not yet fully adjusted, southern slaves offered freedom in return for service to the crown, and Native Americans who allied with the British government made up the ranks for the Tories. Few were well-off, with most struggling as farmers or working in trades.

Slaves seeking freedom left the southern states as the British retreated from the southern states. Outnumbered, Tories suffered as patriot gangs assaulted them, vandalized their houses, and in some cases murdered them. Tories began to leave the United States in large numbers at the start of the 1780s and eventually, more than 100,000 Tories fled the United States, most departing after the decisive Battle of Yorktown fought on October 19, 1781, that ended conflict between the revolutionary forces and the British military. Most Tories left the United States between 1783-1784.

Some migrated across the Atlantic Ocean to Great Britain, sometimes to colonies in the Caribbean. About half of the American refugees headed north to Canada, to Nova Scotia or Quebec, or became some of the first white inhabitants of the new province of New Brunswick.

Many experienced extreme hardship on their way to their new northern home. New York Loyalists often travelled through territory held by the Oneida Nation, which had allied with the Patriots. The refugees travelled on muddy, poorly maintained roads and, during icy weather, the trip to Quebec and other provinces could take as long as three months. Running out of food, refugees dug for roots, and also ate nuts and even leaves in other to survive. Many arrived in Canada in utter poverty, hungry and seriously ill.

African Americans who had been promised freedom often faced betrayal in Canada. In some cases, authorities arrested former slaves who had fought bravely for the British Army against the rebellious Americans, and these people were sold into slavery or falsely claimed as human property by white Canadians. Some ended up enduring the cruelties of sugar plantations in British-held Caribbean islands.

The British did not anticipate the refugee crisis and were poorly prepared when Tories started pouring over the Canadian border. The British offered aid to children, mothers with infants, and the disabled, who were placed in refugee camps. Food and blankets were often in short supply. The housing units at the hastily constructed camps often exposed the refugees to cold and crowding that accelerated the spread of dangerous diseases such as pneumonia and smallpox.

Authorities expected women and children to work for their aid, and refugees spent their days sewing clothes and blankets, even though they shivered in tattered rags in the wintertime. While many Tories went on to live successful lives and establish thriving communities in Canada, these refugees of the American Revolution often succumbed to the pressures of their unsettled, poverty-stricken lives. Rather than a more secure future, Tories often suffered divorces, depression, and suicide at these camps for the unwanted refuse of war.

THOUGHT QUESTIONS:

1. What were some reasons that some Americans chose to support Great Britain during the revolution?

2. What accounts for the poor treatment of American refugees by the British in Canada?

3. How does the treatment of Tory refugees from the United States after the American Revolution compare to the later American response to refugees from Southeast Asia after the Vietnam War and Syrians fleeing civil war in their country beginning in 2011?

Confronting the Horrors of Slavery

Olaudah Equiano's early life is shrouded in mystery, and his time as a slave in Virginia proved remarkably brief—about a month. But the man who claimed to have been seized by slave traders in the mid-1750s in modern-day Nigeria before being brought to the colonial South wrote a memoir that became one of the earliest, most well-read depictions of human bondage in the eighteenth century and helped inspire an American abolitionist movement still in its infancy.

The exact date is unknown, but Equiano is believed by scholars to have been born around 1745. In his two-volume *The Interesting Narrative of the Life of Olaudah Equiano, or Gustavus Vassa, the African*, he describes himself as the son of an Ibo-speaking chief but said that around the age of 10 slave traders kidnapped him. Equiano's memoir includes one of the most hair-raising accounts of the Middle Passage, the agonizing ship-bound journey slaves endured on the way to bondage in the Western Hemisphere.

"The stench of the [slave ship's] hold while we were on the coast was so intolerably loathsome, that it was dangerous to remain there for any time, and some of us had been permitted to stay on the deck for the fresh air; but now that the whole ship's cargo were confined together, it became absolutely pestilential," he wrote. "The closeness of the place, and the heat of the climate, added to the number in the ship, which was so crowded that each had scarcely room to turn himself, almost suffocated us. This produced copious perspirations, so that the air soon became unfit for respiration, from a variety of loathsome smells, and brought on a sickness among the slaves, of which many died, thus falling victims to the improvident avarice . . . of their purchasers. This wretched situation was again aggravated by . . . the filth of the necessary tubs, into which the children often fell, and were almost suffocated. The shrieks of the women, and the groans of the dying, rendered the whole a scene of horror almost inconceivable."

Equiano also described two slaves who, unable to bear their suffering on their slave ship any longer, jumped over the side of the ship and another who was beaten when he was fished out of the water before drowning. After this harrowing journey, Equiano's ship reached Barbados. No one bought Equiano at the slave market there, so after two weeks he boarded another ship, this time to Virginia. Michael Henry Pascal, a Royal Navy lieutenant, bought him one month later. Pascal renamed his slave Gustavus Vassa. His master took Equiano to England, where the young man educated himself over the next seven years. In 1766, Equiano purchased his freedom, and he became a leading anti-slavery lecturer. He reached a much wider audience in 1789 with the publication of his *Interesting Narrative*.

Equiano's memoir became a bestseller in England, where it went through nine printings while someone printed an unauthorized edition in the United States that was widely read. In his lifetime, defenders of slavery tried to undermine the credibility of Equiano's narrative, claiming that he was a native of the Caribbean and could not have experienced the Middle Passage scenes of horror described in the book. Later scholarship revealed two documents, a baptismal record of 1759 (when he was approximately 14) and a muster roll from the Royal Navy, that indicated Equiano had been born in South Carolina. The reason for the discrepancy is unclear. As the literary scholar Byrcchan Carey suggests, it is possible that prior to writing his memoir, he was not ready to reveal his African origins, and may have provided false information for the baptismal certificate and muster roll. In any case, his description of the Middle Passage fits what historians have discovered about that experience.

The Interesting Narrative, the first detailed slave narrative in American history and the first to describe the slave trade from the slave's perspective, marks an important moment in the evolution of African-American literature in the United States. The book provided rhetorical ammunition for abolitionists as Congress in 1794 passed the Slave Trade Act that prohibited American ships from transporting slaves intended for sale to other countries and New York in 1799 passed its gradual emancipation act that freed the offspring of adult slaves and provided for freedom for all slaves in the state by 1827. Numerous slave narratives would be published between 1789 and the end of the Civil War in 1865, and all sparked skepticism from some white readers.

THOUGHT QUESTIONS:

1. Why would slave narratives play an important role in the debate over abolition?

2. What racial stereotypes might make white audiences reluctant to accept the details of slave narratives in the eighteenth and nineteenth centuries?

3. Do modern depictions of slavery, such as fictional films like *Django Unchained* and movies based on non-fiction sources like *Twelve Years a Slave* help shape race relations today?

Class Conflict and "The Doctor's Riot"

Medical students depend on dissection of corpses to learn about the human body. Until recently, however, the practice provoked highly emotional debate that sometimes exploded into violence. Many saw dissection as blasphemous and a sign of disrespect towards the deceased. Economic resentments in the 1780s, a period of extreme wealth inequality that saw high unemployment, inflation, and homes and farms seized by courts because of delinquent mortgages, only aggravated suspicions regarding where the bodies used by medical schools came from. In New York City, stories circulated that the two local medical schools stole bodies for dissection from so-called potter's fields, cemeteries where the bodies of those whose families were too poor to afford a formal burial were dumped, and the Negroes Burial Ground. A story was printed in February 1788, in a New York newspaper, *The Advertiser*, that the corpse of a white women buried at a local cemetery had been stolen, which only deepened distrust of doctors and medical schools.

There are at least three versions of what provoked what came to be known as "The Doctor's Riot" in New York that exploded on April 16, 1788. According to one account, a group of boys were playing in a patch of grass underneath a window at New York Hospital, a privately-owned institution that trained medical students and where human anatomy classes taught by Dr. Richard Bayley involved dissecting cadavers. The boys supposedly saw a human arm that had been sawn off hanging out of the window to dry so medical students could more closely investigate its internal structure.

Yet another tale depicted one of boys climbing a ladder to the anatomy classroom window out of curiosity and spying ongoing dissections. A doctor or a medical student spotted the boy and responded by waving a detached arm at him. In yet another variation of the tale, a cruel and mischievous student knew the boy on top of the ladder and knew the child's mother had died. He held up a woman's arm, waved it in front of the boy, and told the child that it belonged to his mother. The boy ran to his father and told him the tale. The father went to the local cemetery, opened up his wife's grave and supposedly found it empty.

Whatever the precipitating event, rage spread throughout the neighborhood as rumors spread and multiplied. A mob of working men armed with picks and shovels quickly ransacked New York Hospital. In the autopsy room, according to a letter by William Heth, a Virginia colonel stationed in New York, the assembly found a body still boiling in a kettle for the purpose of removing the flesh, two other bodies cut open, and human genitalia on display in a mocking fashion. The rioters destroyed equipment used for autopsies and buried the full cadavers they found there. They took diseased organs and malformed limbs that had been preserved for educational purposes and burned them on the street. The frenzied crowd marched to the homes of Dr. Bayley and other physicians in the area looking for evidence of misdeeds. They found none, but they seized Bayley and several medical students and were seemingly on the verge of burning them in the bonfire of body parts when they were stopped by the sheriff and New York Mayor James Duane.

Tensions continued to simmer the next day when a multitude gathered to once again comb through doctors' homes, New York Hospital, and Columbia College (now a university), which also had a medical school. Alexander Hamilton, who attended the school before the American Revolution and in five months would become the first Secretary of the Treasury in the newly created federal government, begged the crowd to leave the school's facilities alone, but to no avail. Students anticipating trouble removed cadavers from the school but about 5,000 people, mostly struggling workers and artisans, charged into the school, hurling rocks at students.

A mob also gathered outside the jail where the medical students were held for safekeeping. One rioter got inside the jail. A guard killed the man, which only increased tensions. The state militia was called to the scene. Soon, John Jay, one of the authors of the *Federalist Papers* and the United States Supreme Court's first Chief Justice, and Baron Friedrich Wilhelm Ludolf Gerhard Augustin von Steuben, the man most credited with professionalizing the Continental Army during the Revolutionary War, suffered injuries in the melee. About 20 people died in the riot.

In the aftermath of the riot, citizens' patrols formed to guard cemeteries while family members checked the burial sites of loved ones to make sure that the graves had not been disturbed. Several states also passed stricter anti-grave robbing laws. Similar riots broke out periodically until the 1850s. Historians long depicted such riots as examples of ignorant mobs resisting the advance of science and are compared to uprisings against smallpox inoculations that also happened in the late eighteenth and early nineteenth centuries. The poor results patients got from medical care in the eighteenth and nineteenth century probably did not help doctors' reputations. These acts of resistance, however, were more likely inspired by resentments against economic exploitation and actual cases of involuntary medical experiment upon the poor generally and African Americans in particular—such as the infamous "Tuskegee Experiment" in which doctors gave sugar pills to black farmers seeking treatment for syphilis in order to track the progress of the disease—up until the latter half of the twentieth century. American society did not value black lives or the lives of the poor, so it was not irrational to believe that they would not leave the bodies of these people in peace after death.

THOUGHT QUESTIONS:

1. What role did racial and class tensions play in the "Doctor's Riot"?

2. What factors could have contributed to the poor reputations of doctors at the time of the riot?

3. How do the events surrounding the Doctor's Riots compare to later conspiracy theories regarding the origin of AIDS and attacks on vaccination?

Chapter 8

The Federalist Era,
1789-1800

Letter From George Washington to the Hebrew
Congregation of Newport, Rhode Island

George Washington was a long-time member of the Anglican and Episcopalian Churches, serving as both a vestryman and warden. He was, however, seldom public about his own religious views. Moreover, in his public life, especially as president, he spoke more generally of Providence, rather than God, and adhered to principles of religious freedom. From the beginning of his presidency, he wrote numerous letters to Protestant congregations, Catholic churches, and Hebrew synagogues. The following is a letter he wrote in response to a welcome he received from the Hebrew congregation of Newport, Rhode Island upon his visit there on August 1790. He wrote this response on the same day.

To the Hebrew Congregation in Newport, Rhode Island

[Newport, R.I., 18 August 1790]

Gentlemen.

While I receive, with much satisfaction, your Address replete with expressions of affection and esteem; I rejoice in the opportunity of assuring you, that I shall always retain a grateful remembrance of the cordial welcome I experienced in my visit to Newport, from all classes of Citizens.

The reflection on the days of difficulty and danger which are past is rendered the more sweet, from a consciousness that they are succeeded by days of uncommon prosperity and security. If we have wisdom to make the best use of the advantages with which we are now favored, we cannot fail, under the just administration of a good Government, to become a great and a happy people.

The Citizens of the United States of America have a right to applaud themselves for having given to mankind examples of an enlarged and liberal policy: a policy worthy of imitation. All possess alike liberty of conscience and immunities of citizenship It is now no more that toleration is spoken of, as if it was by the indulgence of one class of people, that another enjoyed the exercise of their inherent natural rights. For happily the Government of the United States, which gives to bigotry no sanction, to persecution no assistance requires only that they who live under its protection should demean themselves as good citizens, in giving it on all occasions their effectual support.

It would be inconsistent with the frankness of my character not to avow that I am pleased with your favorable opinion of my Administration, and fervent wishes for my felicity. May the Children of the Stock of Abraham, who dwell in this land, continue to merit and enjoy the good will of the other Inhabitants; while every one shall sit in safety under his own vine and figtree, and there shall be none to make him afraid. May the father of all mercies scatter light and not darkness in our paths, and make us all in our several vocations useful here, and in his own due time and way everlastingly happy.

Go: Washington

Source: *https://founders.archives.gov/documents/Washington/05-06-02-0135*

THOUGHT QUESTIONS:

1. What do you think George Washington's purpose was in writing the letter?

2. What might this suggest about George Washington's views on civic society and religion?

3. George Washington's reference to "his own vine and figtree" is taken from the Old Testament. Why would he choose those words instead of language from the New Testament? What might Washington be trying to say?

An Act Respecting Fugitives From Justice, and Persons Escaping From the Service of Their Masters (1793)

While there is little specific mention of slavery in the Constitution, it was a contentious issue for the Framers in Philadelphia. The growth of anti-slavery societies in northern states further exacerbated those tensions as sympathetic Northerners aided runaway slaves seeking freedom in those states. Congress responded to the pleas of southern slaveholders with the following act.

SECTION 1. *Be it enacted by the Senate and House of Representatives of the United States of America in Congress assembled,* That whenever the executive authority of any state in the Union, or of either of the territories northwest or south of the river Ohio, shall demand any person as a fugitive from justice, of the executive authority of any such state or territory to which such person shall have fled, and shall moreover produce a copy of an indictment found, or an affidavit made before a magistrate of any state or territory as aforesaid, charging the person so demanded, with having committed treason, felony or other crime, certified as authentic by the governor or chief magistrate of the state or territory from whence the person so charged fled, it shall be the duty of the executive authority of the state or territory to which such person shall have fled, to cause him or her to be arrested and secured, and notice of the arrest to be given to the executive authority making such demand, or to the agent of such authority appointed to receive the fugitive, and to cause the fugitive to be delivered to such agent when he shall appear: But if no such agent shall appear within six months from the time of the arrest, the prisoner may be discharged. And all costs or expenses incurred in the apprehending, securing, and transmitting such fugitive to the state or territory making such demand, shall be paid by such state or territory.

SEC. 2. *And be it further enacted,* That any agent, appointed as aforesaid, who shall receive the fugitive into his custody, shall be empowered to transport him or her to the state or territory from which he or she shall have fled. And if any person or persons shall by force set at liberty, or rescue the fugitive from such agent while transporting, as aforesaid, the person or persons so offending shall, on conviction, be fined not exceeding five hundred dollars, and be imprisoned not exceeding one year.

SEC. 3. *And be it also enacted,* That when a person held to labour in any of the United States, or in either of the territories on the northwest or south of the river Ohio, under the laws thereof, shall escape into any other of the said states or territory, the person to whom such labour or service may be due, his agent or attorney, is hereby empowered to seize or arrest such fugitives from labour, and to take him or her before any judge of the circuit or district courts of the United States, residing or being within the state, or before any magistrate of a county, city or town corporate, wherein such seizure or arrest shall be made, and upon proof to the satisfaction of such judge or magistrate, either by oral testimony or affidavit taken before and certified by a magistrate of any such state or territory, that the person so seized or arrested, doth, under the laws of the state or territory from which he or she fled, owe service or labour to the person claiming him or her, it shall be the duty of such judge or magistrate to give a certificate thereof to such claimant, his agent or attorney, which shall be sufficient warrant for removing the said fugitive from labour, to the state or territory from which he or she fled.

SEC. 4. *And be it further enacted,* That any person who shall knowingly and willingly obstruct or hinder such claimant, his agent or attorney in so seizing or arresting such fugitive from labour, or shall rescue such fugitive from such claimant, his agent or attorney when so arrested pursuant to the authority herein given or declared; or shall harbor or conceal such person after notice that he or she was a fugitive from labour, as aforesaid, shall, for either of the said offences, forfeit and pay the sum of five hundred dollars. Which penalty may be recovered by and for the benefit of such claimant, by action of debt, in any court proper to try the same; saving moreover to the person claiming such labour or service, his right of action for or on account of the said injuries or either of them.

Source: *http://memory.loc.gov/cgi-bin/ampage?collId=llac&fileName=003/llac003.db&recNum=702*

THOUGHT QUESTIONS:

1. What was the primary purpose of this law?

2. What penalty was there for violating the law? Why?

3. What might this suggest about attitudes regarding slaves in the U.S. at that time?

Proclamation Regarding Commerce With Santo Domingo

When war erupted in Europe in the wake of the French Revolution, the United States declared its intention to remain neutral, refusing to observe a 1778 treaty with France that committed United States aid to France. That, along with the Jay Treaty with England and the XYZ Affair, led to tensions between the U.S. and France known as the Quasi-War, an undeclared naval war between the two nations. The U.S. Congress proceeded to cut off all trade between the United States and France, including all French territories or colonies. The following is a subsequent proclamation by President John Adams regarding trade with the French colony Sainte Domingue (also known as Santo Domingo, the present-day nation of Haiti).

BY THE PRESIDENT OF THE UNITED STATES OF AMERICA.
A PROCLAMATION

Whereas by an act of the Congress of the United States passed the 9th day of February last, entitled "An act further to suspend the commercial intercourse between the United States and France and the dependencies thereof," it is provided that at any time after the passing of this act it shall be lawful for the President of the United States, if he shall deem it expedient and consistent with the interests of the United States, by his order to remit and discontinue for the time being the restraints and prohibitions by the said act imposed, either with respect to the French Republic or to any island, port, or place belonging to the said Republic with which a commercial intercourse may safely be renewed, and also to revoke such order whenever, in his opinion, the interest of the United States shall require; and he is authorized to make proclamation thereof accordingly; and

Whereas the arrangements which have been made at St. Domingo for the safety of the commerce of the United States and for the admission of American vessels into certain ports of that island do, in my opinion, render it expedient and for the interest of the United States to renew a commercial intercourse with such ports:

Therefore I, John Adams, President of the United States, by virtue of the powers vested in me by the above-recited act, do hereby remit and discontinue the restraints and prohibitions therein contained within the limits and under the regulations here following, to wit:

1. It shall be lawful for vessels which have departed or may depart from the United States to enter the ports of Cape Francois and Port Republicain, formerly called Port-au-Prince, in the said island of St. Domingo, on and after the 1st day of August next.

2. No vessel shall be cleared for any other port in St. Domingo than Cape Francois and Port Republicain.

3. It shall be lawful for vessels which shall enter the said ports of Cape Francois and Port Republicain after the last day of July next to depart from thence to any other port in said island between Monte Christi on the north and Petit Goave on the west; provided it be done with the consent of the Government of St. Domingo and pursuant to certificates or passports expressing such consent, signed by the consul-general of the United States or consul residing at the port of departure.

4. All vessels sailing in contravention of these regulations will be out of the protection of the United States and be, moreover, liable to capture, seizure, and confiscation.

Given under my hand and the seal of the United States, at Philadelphia the 26th day of June, A. D. 1799, and of the Independence of the said States the twenty-third.

JOHN ADAMS

By the President:
TIMOTHY PICKERING
Secretary of State

Source: *http://avalon.law.yale.edu/18th_century/japroc02.asp*

THOUGHT QUESTIONS:

1. Why might President Adams want to lift trade restrictions with Santo Domingo?

2. What warning does he make to those who choose to trade there?

3. What might this say about the ability of the United States to use economic sanctions to ensure good behavior from other nations?

Vignettes

The Spitting Lyon

The election of 1796 was the first presidential election in U.S. history with political parties playing a major role. Although those political parties, Thomas Jefferson's Democratic-Republicans and Alexander Hamilton's Federalists, were still in their infancy they would quickly come to dominate American politics. Contention between the parties and their leaders exacerbated tensions at the highest levels of government. A microcosm of the broader political dispute was the Lyon-Griswold Affair, a physical altercation between Republican and Federalist members of the House of Representatives early in 1798.

Matthew Lyon, a Republican representative from Vermont, was an Irish immigrant who migrated to Vermont and served in the American Revolution. During the Revolution, he was accused of cowardice (unjustly according to many who served with him) and ordered to carry a wooden sword in an effort to disgrace him. He redeemed his reputation and rose in the newly-formed Republican Party becoming an ardent defender of the common man as one of the most radical Jeffersonians.

Lyon also established a newspaper, with his son as editor, that was used to attack Federalists and their policies. Lyon suggested to some other members of Congress that he could use his printing press to create a political revolution in Federalist-dominated Connecticut. One of the most ardent Federalists from Connecticut, Roger Griswold, overheard Lyon and asked if Lyon planned to bring his wooden sword to Connecticut with him. Angered, Lyon responded by spitting tobacco juice in Griswold's face. Federalists in Congress called for Lyon's expulsion from Congress, but, needing a two-thirds vote for such action, they failed when they convinced only two Republicans to join them.

With the failure of the Federalist attempt to censure Lyon, Griswold took matters into his own hands. On the morning of February 15, 1798, as members of the House were filling the chamber in preparation for the beginning of the day's business, Griswold approached Lyon, who was seated at his desk reading. Before Lyon realized that Griswold had approached him, the Connecticut Federalist said, "you rascal" and began to hit the Vermonter repeatedly with his cane. Lyon tried to grab his own cane but was unable to do so while trying to fend off the blows. He fought his way out of his seat and charged at Griswold, who retreated while continuing to hit Lyon. As the battle neared the fireplace Lyon grabbed a pair of fire tongs with which to fight back. Eventually the two fell to the floor in hand-to-hand combat. All the while, the Speaker of the House, a Federalist, refused pleas to call the session to order so that Griswold would have every opportunity to get satisfaction for Lyon's spitting. He even chastised two Congressmen who pulled Griswold off of Lyon because they pulled him by the feet. Efforts to censure both of the men failed, largely along party line votes.

Within two months Congress received news of the XYZ Affair and that summer Congress passed the Alien and Sedition Acts. While they were certainly a response to the XYZ Affair and the Quasi-War with France, the Sedition Act was clearly aimed at political opponents of the Federalist-controlled government, especially Matthew Lyon and Albert Gallatin. Days before the election in November of 1798, Lyon was jailed for sedition. Voters in Vermont, symbolic of a broader dissatisfaction with the Sedition Act, re-elected Matthew Lyon as he sat in jail.

THOUGHT QUESTIONS:

1. Why might political tensions of the time result in violence like this?

2. How might the Alien and Sedition Acts be related to the Lyon-Griswold Affair? What might the Federalists hope to accomplish?

3. How does this event relate to other political issues of the time period?

A Fever in Philadelphia

In 1793 Philadelphia had a population of 50,000, the largest in America, and was serving as the nation's capital. By that fall, fear and disorder reigned. As one Philadelphian, Samuel Breck, put it, "The wealthy soon fled; the fearless or indifferent remained from choice, the poor from necessity." Between the end of July and the beginning of November, the city faced the nation's first major yellow fever epidemic.

The epidemic began when refugees from Sainte Domingue, fleeing the slave rebellion there, began to arrive in Philadelphia during the summer of 1793, some bringing with them yellow fever. As a small number of cases of yellow fever were reported, the city's leading physician, Benjamin Rush, declared an epidemic and quarantined the refugees. Rush, however, did not realize that yellow fever was spread by mosquitoes (it would be nearly a century before the medical community understood that). As a result, the quarantine did not prevent the spread of yellow fever as mosquitoes carried the fever from refugees to residents of the city.

With the wealthy fleeing the city, Rush worked tirelessly to save those who remained. That said, his efforts probably caused more harm than good as his aggressive treatment included bloodletting as well as administering large amounts of mercury. Rush also asked leaders of the free black community in Philadelphia to assist him, believing that they carried immunities to the fever similar to those they carried for malaria. Absalom Jones and Richard Allen agreed, and Rush trained black nurses in purging and bloodletting. The black community also buried victims when Rush's treatment failed many of them.

Despite the efforts of city leaders, doctors and nurses, and black volunteers, the epidemic raged, reaching a peak in the first weeks of October with at least 1,000 dying each week. On October 12 those fighting the epidemic got help from nature as the city saw its first frost, killing off much of the mosquito population. By the beginning of November, the epidemic had passed. By that time about 5,000 had died, one tenth of the city's population. Benjamin Rush had not only been wrong about a cure for yellow fever, however, he had also been wrong about African-American immunity. Black Philadelphians died at about the same rate as white Philadelphians.

Yet even as they realized the fever was striking them equally, black residents continued to offer their service at great risk only to be condemned by whites who accused them of profiteering. The following January, Jones and Allen published a lengthy defense of their actions with detailed descriptions of the services rendered by black Philadelphians (services that most white people in the city refused to undertake). The hard feelings created by those accusations likely pushed Jones and Allen to lead black members from St. George's Methodist Church over racial segregation. They formed Mother Bethel African Methodist Church, one of the first African-American churches in the United States.

THOUGHT QUESTIONS:

1. What impacts might the yellow fever epidemic have on Philadelphia? On the United States?

2. What does the epidemic tell us about medical knowledge of that time?

3. What does the epidemic tell us about racial attitudes in Philadelphia?

Little Turtle and Indian Resistance

In 1768, in an effort to calm tensions between Native Americans and colonists in the Ohio River Valley, Britain entered into a treaty with the Six Nations of Iroquois known as the Treaty of Fort Stanwix. It recognized British control below the Ohio River and Indian control above it. Some colonists ignored the treaty and began to move into the territory north of the river leading to tension between colonists and Indians. The American Revolution only exacerbated those tensions. With American independence (and Britain's cession of territory north of the river), the United States government entered into a new Treaty of Fort Stanwix with the Six Nations of Iroquois that ceded Ohio to the United States. Since most of the Indians living in the region were not among those Iroquois, they were unhappy about the treaty and resisted.

A Miami Indian, Michinkinikwa, also known as Little Turtle, became well-known for successful raids against American settlements and rose in the esteem of Miami and other Indian leaders in the region. By the beginning of the 1790s he was leading the military forces of a confederation of Indians made up of Miamis, Shawnees, Wyandots, and others. At the same time, the young United States government was intent on quelling Indian unrest in the region to allow for further expansion into the West.

President George Washington sent a force of about 1500 men into the region, which tried to break the resistance by burning Indian villages but in October 1790, Little Turtle led a force that defeated the Americans. The following year President Washington sent an even larger force of 2000 men into the region under the command of General Arthur St. Clair. Once again, Little Turtle led the decisive battle in which St. Clair lost nearly two-thirds of his army. Indian casualties have been estimated at fewer than 70.

After St. Clair's defeat, the United States increased its efforts, appropriating an army of about 5,000 men under the command of General "Mad" Anthony Wayne. Wayne moved his force into Ohio Territory building a line of forts along the way, including one at the location of St. Clair's defeat that he named Fort Recovery, with the assistance of Chickasaw and Choctaw scouts. After Little Turtle failed in an effort to defeat Wayne's forces at Fort Recovery, he suggested that the Indians pursue peace. When others, including Shawnee Chief Blue Jacket refused, Little Turtle stepped back to allow Blue Jacket to assume command. In the ensuing Battle of Fallen Timbers, the Indian confederation was defeated.

The resulting Treaty of Greenville ceded almost all of Ohio to the United States and established relative peace for the next decade. Little Turtle was one of the Native American leaders to sign the treaty at which time he said, "I have been the last to sign this treaty; I will be the last to break it." From 1795 until his death in 1812, Little Turtle worked to maintain peace in the region, keeping most of the Miamis from joining Tecumseh's Confederacy. He also traveled east to study farming techniques and brought that knowledge back to his people. After his death the United States government buried him with full military honors.

THOUGHT QUESTIONS:

1. What does the story of Little Turtle tell us about the collective Native American experience during this time period?

2. Why might Little Turtle have so dramatically changed his attitude from war to peace?

3. Why might the U.S. government bury Little Turtle with full military honors?

Chapter 9

Jeffersonian America, 1801-1815

Thomas Jefferson on Church and State

In October 1801, the Danbury Baptist Association of Danbury, Connecticut wrote a letter to newly elected President Thomas Jefferson. Baptists had a long history of support for religious liberty and separation of church and state. Fearing that the Constitution was not sufficiently clear on the subject they wrote, "Our Sentiments are uniformly on the side of Religious Liberty—That Religion is at all times and places a matter between God and individuals—That no man ought to suffer in name, person, or effects on account of his religious Opinions—That the legitimate Power of civil government extends no further than to punish the man who works ill to his neighbor." They feared that long-held traditions of one religious sect being granted privileges and advantages by legislatures was not sufficiently reigned in by the establishment clause of the Constitution and, therefore, religious groups that did not curry favor with state or federal legislatures may find themselves threatened. Jefferson's response below offers a clear interpretation of the First Amendment with regard to religion, an opinion that was later upheld by the U.S. Supreme Court in 1878.

To messers. Nehemiah Dodge, Ephraim Robbins, & Stephen S. Nelson, a committee of the Danbury Baptist Association in the state of Connecticut.

Gentlemen

The affectionate sentiments of esteem and approbation which you are so good as to express towards me, on behalf of the Danbury Baptist Association, give me the highest satisfaction. My duties dictate a faithful and zealous pursuit of the interests of my constituents, & in proportion as they are persuaded of my fidelity to those duties, the discharge of them becomes more and more pleasing.

Believing with you that religion is a matter which lies solely between Man & his God, that he owes account to none other for his faith or his worship, that the legitimate powers of government reach actions only, & not opinions, I contemplate with sovereign reverence that act of the whole American people which declared that their legislature should "make no law respecting an establishment of religion, or prohibiting the free exercise thereof," thus building a wall of separation between Church & State. Adhering to this expression of the supreme will of the nation in behalf of the rights of conscience, I shall see with sincere satisfaction the progress of those sentiments which tend to restore to man all his natural rights, convinced he has no natural right in opposition to his social duties.

I reciprocate your kind prayers for the protection & blessing of the common father and creator of man, and tender you for yourselves & your religious association, assurances of my high respect & esteem.

Th Jefferson
Jan. 1. 1802.

Source: *https://www.loc.gov/loc/lcib/9806/danpre.html*

THOUGHT QUESTIONS:

1. Why might the Danbury Baptists want Jefferson to make a clear statement regarding separation of church and state?

2. Based on the letter, what was Jefferson's view of religion?

3. What did Jefferson mean by "a wall of separation"?

Thomas Jefferson and Enforcement of the Embargo

When Thomas Jefferson signed the Embargo Act in December 1807, he saw it as the only way to avert war with Britain. He hoped that all Americans would join in supporting the embargo out of a sense of patriotic duty. Almost immediately, it became clear to him that Americans who derived their economic livelihood from trade with Britain were ignoring the embargo and evading enforcement efforts by smuggling. Despite enlisting the Army and Navy in enforcement efforts, smuggling continued, especially overland into Canada. The following proclamation was issued by Jefferson in April 1808 in order to stem smuggling through the Lake Champlain region into Canada.

By the President of the United States,
A Proclamation

Whereas information has been received that sundry persons are combined or combining & confederating together on lake Champlain & the country thereto adjacent for the purposes of forming insurrections against the authority of the laws of the U.S. For opposing the same & obstructing their execution, and that such combinations are too powerful to be suppressed by the ordinary course of judicial proceedings, or by the powers vested in the Marshals by the laws of the U.S.

Now therefore to the end that the authority of the laws may be maintained, & that those concerned directly or indirectly in any insurrection or combination against the same may be duly warned, I have issued this my Proclamation, hereby commanding such insurgents and all concerned in such combinations, instantly & without delay to disperse & retire peaceably to their respective abodes: And I do hereby further require & command all officers having authority civil or military, and all other persons civil or military who shall be found within the vicinage of such insurrections or combinations, to be aiding and assisting by all the means in their power by force of arms or otherwise to quell & subdue such insurrections or combinations, to seize upon all those therein concerned who shall not instantly and without delay disperse & retire to their respective abodes, and to deliver them over to the civil authority of the place to be proceeded against according to law.

In testimony whereof I have caused the seal of the U.S. to be affixed to these presents, and signed the same with my hand. Given at the City of Washn. the 19th. day of April. 1808. and in the year of the sovereignty & independence of the U.S. the 32d.

(signed) TH: JEFFERSON,
By the President
(signed) JAMES MADISON, Secy of State

Source: *https://founders.archives.gov/documents/Jefferson/99-01-02-7861*

THOUGHT QUESTIONS:

1. How did Jefferson view smuggling efforts aimed at evading the embargo?

2. What action did Jefferson call on to stop smuggling?

3. How did Jefferson's proclamation fit with his principles about government power?

Opposition to the War of 1812

*By the beginning of 1812, it became increasingly likely that the United States was headed for war with Britain. Congress had authorized military preparations the previous November and War Hawks, largely from southern and western states (and led by Kentuckian Henry Clay), were gaining greater popular support amid continuing British depredations. Yet there was still significant opposition to the possibility in northern states where so many people relied on commerce for their livelihoods. The following piece from the **New York Evening Post** offers an argument against war with Britain.*

New York Evening Post
January 26, 1812

Look for yourselves, good people all—The administration tell me that the object for which they are going to war with Great Britain, is to secure our commercial rights; to put the trade of the country on a good footing; to enable our merchants to deal with Great Britain on full as favorable terms as they deal with France, or else not deal at all. Such is the declared object for which all further intercourse is to be suspended with Great Britain and her allies, while we proceed to make war upon her and them until we compel her to pay more respect to American commerce: and, as Mr. Stow truly observed in his late excellent speech, the anxiety of members of Congress to effect this object is always the greater in proportion to the distance any honorable member lives from the seaboard. To enable you, good people, to judge for yourselves, I have only to beg of you to turn your eyes to Mr. Gallatin's letter in a succeeding column, stating the amount of the exports of the United States for the last year; the particular country to which these exports were sent, and specifying the amount received from us by each. If you will just cast a glance at this document, you will find of the articles of our own growth or manufactures we in that time carried or sent abroad (in round numbers) no less than $45,294,000 worth. You will next find that out of this sum, all the rest of the world (Great Britain and her allies excepted) took about $7,719,366, and that Great Britain and her allies took the remainder, amounting to $38,575,627. Now, after this, let me ask you what you think of making war upon Great Britain and her allies, for the purpose of benefiting commerce?

Source: http://teachingamericanhistory.org/library/document/they-call-it-a-war-for-commerce/

THOUGHT QUESTIONS:

1. What does the document identify as the reasons America was contemplating war with Britain?

2. What does the author offer as an argument against war?

3. Based on this document, and your reading of the textbook, do you think America was right to go to war with Britain? Why or why not?

Vignettes

Gabriel's Plot

About one week after the Declaration of Independence was adopted by Congress, a child named Gabriel was born. Gabriel was born to slaves on Thomas Prosser's plantation a short distance from Richmond, Virginia. Although he was a slave, he was taught to read and write and learned the skill of blacksmithing. His intelligence and skill made him a valuable slave to Prosser, who could use him as needed on the plantation but also rent his labor to others who might need the services of a blacksmith.

By the time Gabriel was in his twenties Prosser was sending Gabriel into the city of Richmond to seek work. Gabriel was required to provide his master with a set amount of money gained from his work but could keep any extra he might make beyond that amount. While he would have to provide his own food and lodging while in the city, a hard-working and frugal slave in that situation could save enough money to ultimately buy their freedom. Gabriel was one of a number of slaves hiring their own time in cities like Richmond, often working alongside free blacks and poor white workingmen.

The experience of working alongside free men, and in a nation imbued with the ideals of liberty and equality ever since his birth, certainly must have inspired Gabriel to more than laboring to further enrich his master. The examples of successful revolutions in France and Haiti that touted liberty and equality also inspired Gabriel. So in the summer of 1800, with political rhetoric of an election that would sweep the Federalists out of power that year, Gabriel was spurred to action.

He organized a plan to launch a rebellion of more than 1,000 slaves who would kill all whites they encountered except Methodists, Quakers, Frenchmen, and the poor. He and his fellow rebels, organized into militia units, planned to march into Richmond, seize weapons at the armory, and take Governor James Monroe hostage. The caretaker of the armory was an old slave who had agreed to unlock the armory and let Gabriel and his fellow rebels take the weapons.

On the night of August 30, the night appointed for the raid, a torrential downpour hit the area, swelling rivers and washing out bridges. Gabriel postponed the raid, but two of the conspirators grew nervous and told their master of the plan. Conspirators were rounded up as Gabriel fled only to be caught months later in Norfolk, Virginia (he was turned in by another slave who hoped to gain a promised reward for the purpose of buying his own freedom). He was tried and executed, saying before his execution that his actions were no different than George Washington's in fighting against Britain for independence.

Enough information about Gabriel's plot was discovered that it is clear that slaves for hundreds of miles around Richmond in every direction were involved. Gabriel's plot led to widespread fear throughout the South as state governments' strengthened both slave codes and laws regulating free blacks, which had been made less restrictive after the American Revolution. For instance, Virginia would require manumitted slaves to leave the state within one year of being granted freedom.

THOUGHT QUESTIONS:

1. How might Gabriel have planned such a large rebellion that included slaves who lived so far apart?

2. Why might Gabriel have excluded Methodists, Quakers, Frenchmen, and the poor from the targets of his rebellion?

3. Why might states like Virginia strengthen laws regulating free blacks after Gabriel's plot was discovered?

The Code of Handsome Lake

In 1799, an aging Seneca warrior named Handsome Lake appeared near death as years of alcohol abuse seemed to be taking their toll. Rather than die, however, Handsome Lake declared that he had been visited by three men sent by the Creator. He immediately gave up drinking and became a religious leader among the Seneca, having a number of other visions in the ensuing years. Based on his visions, Handsome Lake called for a new societal and religious order that maintained some traditional ideas while dramatically changing others.

Throughout much of his life Handsome Lake had watched the decline of the Seneca and other Iroquois nations from their high point aided by the fur trade. Since his birth in 1735, the growth of the British colonies, and even more so American independence, had led to loss of land and hunting grounds to white settlers desirous of land. By the 1790s the Iroquois nations had been largely relegated to reservations but maintaining control of even that land was precarious. Moreover, they had lost control of their hunting grounds that supplied them with their ability to support themselves (and for Indian men, their identity that was so tied to hunting and warfare).

Besides watching the decline of the Seneca nation, Handsome Lake may have also been influenced by outside forces. About a year before his first vision, a group of Quakers had arrived on the Seneca reservation with the intent of teaching the Indians modern farming methods (the non-proselytizing Quakers were not seeking to convert the Indians but merely to help them). Adoption of those methods could provide Native Americans with a greater ability to survive in, what for them, was a dramatically changing world.

Handsome Lake's ideas, known as *gaiwiio* (or the Good Word), were widely adopted by most Seneca, as well as some closely related Indian nations, and later became written in what became known as the Code of Handsome Lake. He called for a change from the traditional matrilineal, communal society to a patrilineal society centered around the nuclear family. Men would take on the traditional woman's role of farming while women's roles would focus on the home. And they would live in a single-family home rather than the communal longhouse. The relationship between husband and wife was to become sacred with divorce and sexual promiscuity forbidden. Alcohol and spousal and child abuse were also prohibited as part of Handsome Lake's moral code.

At the same time that Handsome Lake adopted what was useful from American society, he also called for strengthening of native traditions and Indian identity. He forbid the sale of Indian lands unless the Reservation could maintain its size with other purchases. He also rejected centralized police power, the private profit motive, and the Christian religion. Religion remained communal, using the Longhouse as the center of communal life, and family farming introduced with the focus on nuclear families was intended to serve the community rather than the individual family.

By accommodating to some white ways while maintaining Indian identity and traditions allowed the Seneca and other Iroquois to survive in a world that was increasingly hostile to Native Americans. Today, thousands of Iroquois in New York and Canada still follow many of the traditions of the Code of Handsome Lake

THOUGHT QUESTIONS:

1. What problems did the Iroquois face when Handsome Lake emerged as a religious leader?

2. How did Handsome Lake try to address those problems with his social and moral code?

3. Why might the Seneca have been willing to accept the help of Quakers when they had lost so much at the hands of white men?

Thomas Jefferson and Sally Hemings

Among the property that Thomas and Martha Wayles Jefferson inherited from the estate of Martha's father in 1774 were a young slave girl named Sally and her mother Elizabeth Hemings, a mulatto slave. It is believed that Sally's father was John Wayles, Martha's father, who had lived as the concubine of the widower for twelve years before his death. With a white father and mulatto mother Sally was "mighty near white" and was reported to bear a striking resemblance to her half-sister Martha, Thomas Jefferson's wife.

In 1782, Martha Jefferson died, devastating Thomas as he was devoted to her, promising her that he would never marry again. Sally likely cared for Jefferson's youngest child, Maria (only four when her mother died), until 1787 when she accompanied Maria to Paris to serve as a personal servant to Jefferson's two daughters while Jefferson served as American ambassador to France. By that time Sally was blossoming into a beautiful teenager who likely reminded Jefferson of his deceased wife. By the time the Jeffersons and Sally returned to the United States, Jefferson and sixteen-year-old Sally, thirty years his junior, had begun a sexual relationship that likely lasted for the rest of Jefferson's life. Over the course of that relationship they had six children (two of whom died in infancy), all of them becoming the slave property of Thomas Jefferson, their father.

There were occasional whispers about the relationship and, in 1802, even a news story written by a Republican newspaper editor, James T. Callender. When Callender died a few days later (he likely drowned after falling into the James River in a drunken stupor), suspicions were stoked. Jefferson never responded to any of the allegations, but his supporters and family members offered strong rebuttals and labeled Callender a disgruntled office-seeker who had been shunned by Jefferson. While similar accusations that Jefferson had an affair with Hemmings surfaced from time-to-time for nearly two hundred years, they had largely been squelched until DNA testing conducted in 1998 left little doubt.

Jefferson freed the remaining two of Sally's living children, Madison and Eston, in his will. The other two had been allowed to leave the plantation as early as 1821 and moved to Washington, D.C. where they passed into white society, likely changing their names, and disappeared to history. Madison and Eston moved to nearby Charlottesville where they rented a house. After Jefferson's daughter Martha allowed Sally to leave (without formally freeing her), Sally lived with her sons in Charlottesville until her death in 1835. Of her children, only Madison lived as an African American for the remainder of his life.

The types of complex family relations as seen in the Hemings example were not uncommon on southern plantations. In Jefferson's case it appears likely that he had deep affection for Sally and their children. That was not always the case with masters and their slave children who were often the result of white masters raping their female slaves. Even in the case of Sally we cannot know how she viewed her "relationship" with Thomas Jefferson. As a slave, her master wielded absolute power over her, and she likely had little ability to refuse his sexual advances.

THOUGHT QUESTIONS:

1. Why might Jefferson have chosen the companionship of a slave rather than a white woman?

2. What happened when a slaveowner like Jefferson had sexual relations with a slave that produced children?

3. How were three of the Hemings children able to live their free lives as whites? Why might they choose that? Why might Madison not choose that?

Chapter 10

The "Era of Good Feelings"

Andrew Jackson Letter to Georgia Governor William Rabun

As President in the 1830's, Andrew Jackson oversaw Indian removal from the southeastern United States. In 1830 Congress passed the Indian Removal Act granting Native Americans from the southeastern U.S. land in Oklahoma in exchange for their lands in Mississippi, Alabama, Georgia, The Carolinas, and Florida. Jackson portrayed the law as a "benevolent policy" with "obvious advantages" for the Native Americans involved. While two of the five major Indian nations there accepted the offer and willingly moved, the others resisted. The Cherokees went so far as to take a case to the U.S. Supreme Court in order to prevent removal. The Court found that the Cherokees were a sovereign nation with a right to its own territory. President Jackson remarked that "The decision of the supreme court has fell still born, and they find that it cannot coerce Georgia to yield to its mandate." In other words, he would not enforce the decision of the Supreme Court and, instead, continued with the policy of Indian removal, finally forcing the Cherokees to migrate to Oklahoma at the point of bayonet.

Below is an earlier letter from a younger General Andrew Jackson regarding Native Americans and their treatment. Andrew Jackson had been sent into Spanish Florida with a military force in pursuit of Indians and runaway slaves who had been using Florida as a base from which to launch raids on American farms and communities along the border. Assisting his force were numbers of friendly Chehaw Indians (members of the Creek nation). While his force was in Florida, the Governor of Georgia sent the state militia, under the command of Obed Wright, to respond to more Indian attacks along the border. Rather than pursue the Indians responsible for the raids, Wright attacked and burned a Chehaw village in retaliation.

The march toward Pensacolla, 7 miles outside of Fort Gadsden
May 7th 1818

Sir,
I have this moment, received by express the letter of Genl. Glascock, a copy of which is enclosed, detailing the base, cowardly and inhuman attack on the old women and men of the Chehaw Villages, whilst the warriers of that village was with [us] fighting the battles of our country against the common enemy, and at a time too when undoubted testimony had been obtained and was in my possession and also, in the possession of General Glascock, of their innocence of the charge of killing Leigh & the other Georgian at Cedar Creek.

That a Governor of a state should assume the rights to make war against an Indian tribe in perfect peace with and under the protection of the United States; is assuming a responsibility, that I trust you will be able to excuse to the government of the United States, to which you will have to answer, and through which I had so recently passed, promising the aged that remained at home my protection and taking the warriers with me as the campaign is as unaccountable as strange—But it is still more strange that their could exist within the U.States as cowardly monster in human shape, that could violate the sanctity of a flag when borne by any person, but more particularly when in the hands of a superannuated Indian chief worn down with age. Such base cowardice and murderous conduct as this mans action affords has not its paralel in history, and shall meet with its merited punishment.

You Sir as Governor of a State within my Military Division have no right to give a military order whilst I am in the field, and this being an open and violent infringement of the treaty with the creek Indians Capt. Wright must be prosecuted and punished for this outrageous murder, & I have ordered him to be arrested and confined in [2] irons until the pleasure of the President of the United States is known upon the subject. If he has left Hartford before my order reaches him, I call upon you as Governor of Georgia to aid in carrying into effect my orders for his arrest and confinement, which I trust will be afforded, and Capt. Wright brought to condign punishment for this unprecedented murder—It is strange that this hero had not followed the trail of the murderers of your citizens, it would have lead to Mickasooky, where we found the bleeding scalps of your Citizens, but there might have been more danger in this; than, attacking a village containing a few superannuated women and men, and a few young women without arms or protectors—This act will to the last ages fix a stain upon the character of Georgia—

I have the honor to be with due respect.
[Comander] Andrew Jackson
Major Genl Comdg

Source: National Archives, Record Group 107, Manuscript 221-78

THOUGHT QUESTIONS:

1. What was Andrew Jackson's complaint to the Governor of Georgia?

2. What response did he suggest?

3. What does this letter suggest about U.S.-Indian relations in the wake of the War of 1812?

Letter from Thomas Jefferson to John Holmes, 1820

As the nation began to grow and expand, there was a general sentiment that slavery would ultimately end. Every state north of Maryland had ended slavery in one way or another, and the Northwest Ordinance prohibited its expansion into that region. Even as slavery expanded into the Deep South (Alabama and Mississippi), many Southerners defended its continued existence as a "necessary evil," suggesting that once it was no longer necessary, it would cease to be used. When, in 1819, Missouri had gained enough population to adopt a territorial constitution and apply for statehood, the decision of Missourians to allow slavery there caused a firestorm of sectional debate elsewhere in the nation. Crisis was averted when Henry Clay managed to accomplish a compromise that allowed the entry of Missouri as a slave state with the northern territory of Massachusetts admitted as the free state of Maine. To settle the issue for the foreseeable future, slavery was prohibited in all other territory of the Louisiana Purchase above the 36-30 line. Below is a letter from Thomas Jefferson to Massachusetts congressman John Holmes (later senator from Maine) regarding Jefferson's views on the compromise and slavery.

Monticello Apr. 22. 20.

I thank you, Dear Sir, for the copy you have been so kind as to send me of the letter to your constituents on the Missouri question. it is a perfect justification to them. I had for a long time ceased to read the newspapers or pay any attention to public affairs, confident they were in good hands, and content to be a passenger in our bark to the shore from which I am not distant. but this momentous question, like a fire bell in the night, awakened and filled me with terror. I considered it at once as the knell of the Union. it is hushed indeed for the moment. but this is a reprieve only, not a final sentence. a geographical line, coinciding with a marked principle, moral and political, once concieved and held up to the angry passions of men, will never be obliterated; and every new irritation will mark it deeper and deeper. I can say with conscious truth that there is not a man on earth who would sacrifice more than I would, to relieve us from this heavy reproach, in any practicable way. the cession of that kind of property, for so it is misnamed, is a bagatelle which would not cost me in a second thought, if, in that way, a general emancipation and expatriation could be effected: and, gradually, and with due sacrifices, I think it might be. but, as it is, we have the wolf by the ear, and we can neither hold him, nor safely let him go. justice is in one scale, and self-preservation in the other. of one thing

I am certain, that as the passage of slaves from one state to another would not make a slave of a single human being who would not be so without it, so their diffusion over a greater surface would make them individually happier and proportionally facilitate the accomplishment of their emancipation, by dividing the burthen on a greater number of co-adjutors. an abstinence too from this act of power would remove the jealousy excited by the undertaking of Congress, to regulate the condition of the different descriptions of men composing a state. this certainly is the exclusive right of every state, which nothing in the constitution has taken from them and given to the general government. could congress, for example say that the Non-freemen of Connecticut, shall be freemen, or that they shall not emigrate into any other state?

I regret that I am now to die in the belief that the useless sacrifice of themselves, by the generation of 1776. to acquire self government and happiness to their country, is to be thrown away by the unwise and unworthy passions of their sons, and that my only consolation is to be that I live not to weep over it. If they would but dispassionately weigh the blessings they will throw away against an abstract principle more likely to be effected by union than by scission, they would pause before they would perpetrate this act of suicide on themselves and of treason against the hopes of the world.

To yourself as the faithful advocate of union I tender the offering of my high esteem and respect.

Th. Jefferson

Source: https://www.loc.gov/exhibits/jefferson/159.html

THOUGHT QUESTIONS:

1. Was Jefferson supportive of the compromise? Why or why not?

2. What does Jefferson think about the continued existence of slavery? Explain.

3. What does Jefferson mean when he says, "we have the wolf by the ear, and we can neither hold him, nor safely let him go"? Does he suggest any ways to solve the problem?

Excerpt of President Monroe's Message to Congress, December 2, 1823

During the first two decades of the nineteenth century, Spanish and, to a lesser extent, Portuguese colonies began to rebel against colonial authority and win their independence. Many of those newly independent nations established republics based on the American model. American leaders, however, were concerned that European powers might try to take advantage of the weakness of those infant republics, which could, ultimately, pose a threat to the United States. As part of his State of the Union address in December 1823, James Monroe outlined American policy, written largely by Secretary of State John Quincy Adams, with regard to those

Latin American republics and any potential European interference with regard to their independence. That policy became known as the Monroe Doctrine of which an excerpt is printed.

. . . At the proposal of the Russian Imperial Government, made through the minister of the Emperor residing here, a full power and instructions have been transmitted to the minister of the United States at St. Petersburg to arrange by amicable negotiation the respective rights and interests of the two nations on the northwest coast of this continent. A similar proposal has been made by His Imperial Majesty to the Government of Great Britain, which has likewise been acceded to. The Government of the United States has been desirous by this friendly proceeding of manifesting the great value which they have invariably attached to the friendship of the Emperor and their solicitude to cultivate the best understanding with his Government. In the discussions to which this interest has given rise and in the arrangements by which they may terminate the occasion has been judged proper for asserting, as a principle in which the rights and interests of the United States are involved, that the American continents, by the free and independent condition which they have assumed and maintain, are henceforth not to be considered as subjects for future colonization by any European powers. . .

It was stated at the commencement of the last session that a great effort was then making in Spain and Portugal to improve the condition of the people of those countries, and that it appeared to be conducted with extraordinary moderation. It need scarcely be remarked that the results have been so far very different from what was then anticipated. Of events in that quarter of the globe, with which we have so much intercourse and from which we derive our origin, we have always been anxious and interested spectators. The citizens of the United States cherish sentiments the most friendly in favor of the liberty and happiness of their fellow-men on that side of the Atlantic. In the wars of the European powers in matters relating to themselves we have never taken any part, nor does it comport with our policy to do so. It is only when our rights are invaded or seriously menaced that we resent injuries or make preparation for our defense. With the movements in this hemisphere we are of necessity more immediately connected, and by causes which must be obvious to all enlightened and impartial observers. The political system of the allied powers is essentially different in this respect from that of America. This difference proceeds from that which exists in their respective Governments; and to the defense of our own, which has been achieved by the loss of so much blood and treasure, and matured by the wisdom of their most enlightened citizens, and under which we have enjoyed unexampled felicity, this whole nation is devoted. We owe it, therefore, to candor and to the amicable relations existing between the United States and those powers to declare that we should consider any attempt on their part to extend their system to any portion of this hemisphere as dangerous to our peace and safety. With the existing colonies or dependencies of any European power we have not interfered and shall not interfere. But with the Governments who have declared their independence and maintain it, and whose independence we have, on great consideration and on just principles, acknowledged, we could not view any interposition for the purpose of oppressing them, or controlling in any other manner their destiny, by any European power in any other light than as the manifestation of an unfriendly disposition toward the United States. In the war between those new Governments and Spain we declared our neutrality at the time of their recognition, and to this we have adhered, and shall continue to adhere, provided no change shall occur which, in the judgement of the competent authorities of this Government, shall make a corresponding change on the part of the United States indispensable to their security.

The late events in Spain and Portugal shew that Europe is still unsettled. Of this important fact no stronger proof can be adduced than that the allied powers should have thought it proper, on any principle satisfactory to themselves, to have interposed by force in the internal concerns of Spain. To what extent such interposition may be carried, on the same principle, is a question in which all independent powers whose governments differ from theirs are interested, even those most remote, and surely none of them more so than the United States. Our policy in regard to Europe, which was adopted at an early stage of the wars which have so long agitated that quarter of the globe, nevertheless remains the same, which is, not to interfere in the internal concerns of any of its powers; to consider the government de facto as the legitimate government for us; to cultivate friendly relations with it, and to preserve those relations by a frank, firm, and manly policy, meeting in all instances the just claims of every power, submitting to injuries from none. But in regard to those continents circumstances are eminently and conspicuously different.

It is impossible that the allied powers should extend their political system to any portion of either continent without endangering our peace and happiness; nor can anyone believe that our southern brethren, if left to themselves, would adopt it of their own accord. It is equally impossible, therefore, that we should behold such interposition in any form with indifference. If we look to the comparative strength and resources of Spain and those new Governments, and their distance from each other, it must be obvious that she can never subdue them. It is still the true policy of the United States to leave the parties to themselves, in hope that other powers will pursue the same course. . . .

Source: National Archives, Record Group 46

THOUGHT QUESTIONS:

1. What is the main concern addressed by President Monroe in the document?

2. What makes President Monroe and Secretary of State Adams believe that European powers will abide by U.S. expectations of the document?

3. Is the policy proposed in the document consistent with American foreign policy since the War of 1812 or does it propose a dramatic change in policy? Explain.

Vignettes

Henry Clay and the Tariff of 1824

For two days, March 30 and 31 of 1824, Henry Clay argued strenuously for passage of a bill that would impose tariff rates (taxes on certain imports) of 35 percent on a number of imports, which included iron, wool, cotton and hemp. After two days, his arguments and effective politicking behind the scenes enabled him to gain passage of that tariff.

The tariff was one part of Clay's proposed economic policy (largely based on Hamiltonian principles), which he called the American System. In order to promote economic growth, Clay wanted the federal government to support the building of infrastructure that would include turnpikes (well-made roads) as well as canals, and, later, railroads. A network of well-made roads, and other means of transportation, would facilitate the growth of a national economy. He also, in 1816, had convinced his fellow Congressmen to re-charter the national bank in order to maintain greater economic stability and as a source of funding entrepreneurial activity. The final part of Clay's plan was the tariff.

Money generated by the tariff could provide funding for infrastructure projects but generating revenue was not Clay's goal in pursuing high tariff rates. It was rather to encourage Americans to buy American-made products (made with American-produced raw materials) as opposed to European made goods. By placing a tax on imports the price of those imports would be artificially raised to allow upstart American producers to compete with established European enterprises. Ultimately, by promoting a wide range of American industries, America would become self-sufficient and would not have to rely on foreign trade at all. Without such government supports, many emerging industries in America may have failed. To critics who worried the tariff would have a negative effect on them (for example, by raising prices), Clay argued, "The sole object of the tariff is to tax the produce of foreign industry with the view of promoting American industry. The tax is exclusively leveled at foreign industry . . . . If it subjects any part of American industry to burthens, that is an effect not intended."

It was clear to most people in America, however, that the tariff would most directly benefit those engaged in the emerging factory system in the northeast. Farmers in the West and, especially, the South would face higher prices for goods while also likely seeing retaliatory tariffs placed on cash crops by European nations, thereby reducing the profits they could make in Europe.

But Clay managed to create an alliance between northern and western congressmen and senators. He convinced many in those regions that failure to protect American industries from foreign competition would leave the nation "doomed to behold our industry languish and decay" and would leave the American economy "overwhelming [under the] influence of foreigners." Clay was clearly playing on a sense of nationalism that emerged in the wake of the War of 1812. His efforts at a similar tariff had failed in 1820, but in 1824, shortly after his two-day speech, the Tariff of 1824 was passed. His eloquence and political skills were certainly instrumental, but Clay also benefitted from dramatic demographic changes going on in America. The North and western Ohio Valley regions had seen dramatic population growth in the decade since the end of the war while population growth in the South had been much more modest. The population increase gave northern and western states increased congressional power. Those additional seats were the most important reason for Clay's success with the tariff.

Passage of the tariff, however, came with some unintended consequences. Clay had appealed to southern patriotism, but to Southerners the tariff benefitted one group of Americans at the expense of others. The federal government was picking winners and losers, and, with increased congressional power due to demographic changes, the North increasingly controlled that government. Just a few years earlier the Missouri Crisis laid bare sectional tensions between a slave South and non-slave North. The Tariff of 1824 further exacerbated those existing tensions. Clay's American System was certainly instrumental in the economic development of the nation but may have also threatened its long-term existence.

THOUGHT QUESTIONS:

1. For Clay, what was the purpose of tariffs? What arguments did he make in favor of the Tariff of 1824?

2. What were the reasons Clay was able to secure passage of the Tariff in 1824?

3. What broader implications did the Tariff of 1824 have for the future of the United States?

Changing Work and Life in New England

During the late 1820s a man named Sam Patch became a noted daredevil, jumping from extreme heights to rivers below. In October 1829, he twice jumped from Goat Island at Niagara Falls into the river, 125 feet below. Just weeks later, on November 13, he tried a similar 125-foot jump into the Genesee River but did not survive the jump. The American fascination with daredevils like Patch coincided with the emergence of the traveling circus in America (the first was established by J.Purdy Brown in 1825). But Sam Patch's decision to engage in dangerous stunts may have had less to do with the crowds his feat generated than it did with his own dissatisfaction with changing ways of life, especially in the northeastern U.S. where Patch grew up.

Sam Patch was the son of Greenleaf and Abigail Patch who married in 1788. The world in which Greenleaf and Abigail grew up was dramatically changing. They were born in Massachusetts at a time when land was increasingly scarce, due to population growth, and less productive, due to years of farming in the region. Land was the primary determinant for independence, but survival on the increasingly smaller farms in the region relied upon some other economic activity to support the family economy, like shoemaking. While Greenleaf's father bankrupted himself trying to extend his landholdings (the same year that Greenleaf was born), twenty-two year old Greenleaf was fortunate enough to marry seventeen-year-old Abigail McIntyre, whose father owned over 100 acres. His new father-in-law built the young couple a shoemaker's cottage and use of the land on which it sat. Greenleaf could farm the land and supplement the family by making shoes and selling them to merchants in larger coastal towns.

By the early 1790s, Greenleaf Patch was a respected member of the community largely because of that land and because of the connections to the community his wife's family afforded the young couple. When Abigail's father died in 1791, Greenleaf was named executor of his estate. All of the land, however, was willed to Abigail's nineteen-year-old brother (who was bound out to a guardian until he reached the age of 21). In the meantime, Greenleaf remained in control of the land as executor. He tried to use that position to ensure the futures of himself and his family but increasingly turned them against him, losing even the small farm and shoemaker's shop when Abigail's brother assumed full control of the estate. Having estranged her family, Greenleaf, Abigail, and their growing family bounced from town to town relying on members of his family and friends, while they supported themselves by renting small farms and making shoes. Greenleaf's efforts for respectability and independence as a farmer became increasingly hard to maintain. By 1805, he was in debt, had his last piece of property repossessed, and had exhausted any help he could hope for from family and friends.

The family disappears from the public record until 1807 when they show up in the fledgling mill town of Pawtucket, Rhode Island. While men could find work in the mills, the mills mainly employed women and children. Men could still find plenty of work in and around Pawtucket. Many engaged in farming while their wives and children supplemented the family economy through labor in the mills. In the case of Greenleaf Patch, however, he apparently did not pursue those opportunities. He drank and lived off the money made by his family. Then, in 1812, he deserted his family. Abigail divorced him in 1818, a year after he had been arrested in Massachusetts for passing counterfeit money.

From the moment the Patches arrived in Pawtucket, however, life within the home had dramatically changed. Up until that time, Abigail had been the subservient wife that patriarchal New England society expected. She apparently submitted to her husband in all things, from leaving the church her family attended to naming their children after his relatives. After arriving in Pawtucket, the family dynamic changed. Abigail and her oldest daughter, Molly, joined a Baptist church (Greenleaf did not). Her daughter also dropped the name Molly and adopted the name Mary, the name of Abigail's oldest sister. Her second daughter, Nabby, joined the church in 1811, as Abby, later calling herself Abigail. The elder Abigail Patch had become the unquestioned head of the family. Her daughters delayed marriage, and, after Mary's husband left her, Mary and her two daughters moved in with Abigail. Mary would live the rest of her life with her mother as would her daughters. None of them ever married again.

The case of Abigail Patch is obviously unique. But the circumstances around her story were felt by many in the northeastern U.S. due to economic and social changes. The economic changes threatened the identity of men built on patriarchy and independence. As women assumed a greater role in the family economy, and a greater ability to support themselves without husbands, some men became dissatisfied with challenges to their positions as the head of their families and to their economic independence. Many struggled within the changing system to maintain as much of the old world as they could. Others, like Greenleaf Patch, may have lost all hope of success because it could never match the ideal of success with which he grew up. Seeing what happened to his father, and his own dim prospects for the future, may also have led Sam Patch to engage in a life of danger, tempting the fates one last time on November 13, 1829.

THOUGHT QUESTIONS:

1. How did the New England economy change from the Revolutionary era to the first decade of the 1800s?

2. Why might land ownership be so important to a man's view of his own independence in the late 1700s? How did changes in the region undermine that sense of independence?

3. How did changing views of women and their roles undermine patriarchy in New England society?

Complexities of Southern Life

In 1790, near Columbia, South Carolina, a slave boy named April was born on the plantation of Robert Ellison. The mulatto slave child was probably the son of either Robert or, more likely, his son William. The family relationship was probably a significant factor in April, at the age of ten, being apprenticed to a cotton gin maker where he would learn that skill as well as blacksmithing. After serving a six-year apprenticeship, he continued to work for the cotton gin maker as a paid laborer. Most of his wages went to his master (by that time, William Ellison), but he was able to keep some of the wages for himself.

Through hard work and frugality April purchased his freedom in 1816, later also purchasing the freedom of his wife and daughter. He relocated to Stateburg, South Carolina and opened his own business making cotton gins where he employed a number of slaves hired out by their masters. After two years in business, April had earned enough money that he purchased two slaves to work alongside those he had hired.

By 1820, his business was thriving as he took steps to solidify his place in society to match his economic success. On June 20 of that year he filed in the county courthouse to legally change his name to William Ellison, Jr., thereby cementing his connections to the white Ellisons. And in 1824, he purchased a bench on the first floor of the local Episcopal church, the first black man to do so, among the wealthier white families in Stateburg.

His goals, however, were not just a successful business and general acceptance among white society. He desired greater wealth—the kind of wealth one could not gain merely by processing cotton but by producing it. He began to acquire land on which to grow cotton and slaves to provide the labor. He died in December 1861 just as the Civil War was beginning. By that time he had acquired over 1000 acres of land and owned 63 slaves. He had also developed a reputation for harsh treatment of those slaves and for selling young slave girls, as they offered less benefit as field hands—they did, however, provide increased revenue for Ellison through their sale, and he became recognized for the practice of slave breeding.

Men like Ellison were a rarity. According to historian Carter G. Woodson's analysis of the 1830 census, in that year only 3,776 African Americans in the United States owned black slaves. African-American slaves owned by black masters represented little more than 0.6 percent of the country's total slave population. Many black slave owners bought family members to protect them from white slave masters and to keep families together.

When the Civil War began, Ellison pledged his support, offering the services of 53 slaves, and converted his farm from cotton to food crops in order to help feed the army. His sons, themselves slaveholders, volunteered to serve in the army. They were, however, denied because of their race.

THOUGHT QUESTIONS:

1. Why might a former slave like Ellison become a slave owner himself?

2. Why might Ellison treat his slaves as harshly as he was known to do? Why might he sell many of his female slaves?

3. What can the story of William Ellison, Jr. tell us about race in the nineteenth century South?

Chapter 11

Andrew Jackson and the "White Man's Republic"

Chief Justice John Marshall,
***Cherokee Nation v. State of Georgia*, 1831**

The ideology of white supremacy and the notion that valuable land that could be exploited for commercial uses was being wasted in the hands of supposedly "savage" Indians led whites to believe they had an inherent right to territory held by Native Americans. In violation of federal treaties signed with the indigenous nations within their borders, the Georgia state government in the 1820s and early 1830s began to remove the Cherokee people from the state at gunpoint and passed a series of laws denying Cherokees their land rights and voiding laws the Cherokee had adopted to govern their territory. The Cherokee challenged the constitutionality of these laws in the federal courts, the case eventually reaching the United States Supreme Court. The Court tried to resolve one of the most vexing legal issues raised by the cases: What exactly was the relationship between native peoples, the federal government and the various states? In **Cherokee Nation v. Georgia***, plus the separate* **Worcester v. Georgia***, the U.S. Supreme Court defined Indian groups as domestic "dependent nations" within the United States that held some rights to self-governance and ruled that the Cherokee still owned their land until they voluntarily surrendered such property. In the* **Worcester** *case, the Court ruled that the federal government held the right to deal with Indian nations, not the states. Unfortunately, the Court's decision to not define Indian nations as "foreign" ultimately weakened their ability to protect themselves from white encroachment upon their territory. In any case, President Andrew Jackson and his successor, Martin Van Buren, ignored these Supreme Court rulings, and the federal government would aid the State of Georgia as it forcibly removed the Cherokee and other indigenous nations from their land.*

This bill is brought by the Cherokee nation, praying an injunction to restrain the state of Georgia from the execution of certain laws of that state, which, as is alleged, go directly to annihilate the Cherokees as a political society, and to seize, for the use of Georgia, the lands of the nation which have been assured to them by the United States in solemn treaties repeatedly made and still in force.

If courts were permitted to indulge their sympathies, a case better calculated to excite them can scarcely be imagined. A people once numerous, powerful, and truly independent, found by our ancestors in the quiet and uncontrolled possession of an ample domain, gradually sinking beneath our superior policy, our arts and our arms, have yielded their lands by successive treaties . . . until they retain no more of their formerly extensive territory than is deemed necessary to their comfortable subsistence. To preserve this remnant, the present application is made. . . .

Has this court jurisdiction of the cause?

The third article of the constitution describes the extent of the judicial power. The second section closes an enumeration of the cases to which it is extended, with "controversies" "between a state or the citizens thereof, and foreign states, citizens, or subjects." . . . Is the Cherokee nation a foreign state in the sense in which that term is used in the constitution?

The counsel for the plaintiffs . . . intended to prove the character of the Cherokees as a state, as a distinct political society, separated from others, capable of managing its own affairs and governing itself, has, in the opinion of a majority of the judges, been completely successful. They have been uniformly treated as a state from the settlement of our country. The numerous treaties made with them by the United States recognize them as a people capable of maintaining the relations of peace and war, of being responsible in their political character for any violation of their engagements, or for any aggression committed on the citizens of the United States by any individual of their community. . . .

A question of much more difficulty remains. Do the Cherokee constitute a foreign state in the sense of the constitution?

The counsel have shown conclusively that they are not a state of the union, and have insisted that individually they are aliens, not owing allegiance to the United States. . . . But the relation of the Indians to the United States is marked by peculiar and cardinal distinctions which exist nowhere else . . .

The court has bestowed its best attention on this question, and, after mature deliberation, the majority is of opinion that an Indian tribe or nation within the United States is not a foreign state in the sense of the constitution, and cannot maintain an action in the courts of the United States.

The motion for an injunction is denied.

Source: Richard Peters, *The Case of the Cherokee Nation Against the State of Georgia Argued and Determined at The Supreme Court of the United States* (Philadelphia: John Gregg North Fourth Street, 1831).

THOUGHT QUESTIONS:

1. What led many whites to believe that they had a right to Native American land?

2. Why did Chief Justice John Marshall declare his sympathies for the Cherokee Nation?

3. What legal issues did the Supreme Court try to resolve in the *Cherokee Nation v. the State of Georgia* case and on what key ground was the case decided?

Washington Irving, *A Tour of the Prairies*
(1832)

*By 1831, Washington Irving had long secured his reputation as one of the most popular and acclaimed American writers, having authored in his youth the comical **A History of New York** (1809) and the widely read story "Rip Van Winkle," a short story about a man who falls into a deep sleep before the American Revolution and awakens 20 years later, astonished by the changes that have taken place in the interim. Irving also penned "The Legend of Sleepy Hollow," a ghost story about a headless horseman. The two short stories saw publication between 1819-1820 and appeared in the book **The Sketch Book of Geoffrey Crayon, Gent**.*

When he was writing, Irving served as an American diplomat and spent more of the years between 1815-1832 in Europe, including a stint as a member of the United States legation from 1826-1829. In some ways, with his long absence from the United States, Irving had become like Rip Van Winkle, and in 1832, he was eager to explore the so-called "frontier": lands west of the Appalachian Mountains increasingly populated by whites, an onslaught that pushed Indians ever farther west. He embarked on an expedition to the territories west of Arkansas set aside for the Indians.

***Irving's A Tour of the Prairies** recounted his adventures travelling through modern-day Oklahoma, a trip during which he met Sam Houston, the former Tennessee governor who had resigned and was living with the Cherokee. Houston would soon move on to Texas where he'd be a leader in the Texas Revolution and serve as president of the Texas Republic and then governor of the state of Texas. Irving's account saw print in 1835.*

HAVING crossed the ford, we soon reached the Osage Agency [trading post], . . . Near . . . was a group of Osages: stately fellows; stern and simple in garb and aspect. They wore no ornaments; their dress consisted merely of blankets, leggings, and moccasons. Their heads were bare; their hair was cropped close, excepting a bristling ridge on the top, like the crest of a helmet, with a long scalp-lock hanging behind. They had fine Roman countenances, and broad deep chests; and, as they generally wore their blankets wrapped round their loins, so as to leave the bust and arms bare, they looked like so many noble bronze figures. The Osages are the finest looking Indians I have ever seen in the West. They have not yielded sufficiently, as yet, to the influence of civilization to lay by their simple Indian garb, or to lose the habits of the hunter and the warrior; and their poverty prevents their indulging in much luxury of apparel.

In contrast to these was a gayly dressed party of Creeks. There is something, at the first glance, quite oriental in the appearance of this tribe. They dress in calico hunting shirts, of various brilliant colors, decorated with bright fringes, and belted with broad girdles, embroidered with beads; they have leggings of dressed deer skins, or of green or scarlet cloth, with embroidered knee-bands and tassels; their moccasons are fancifully wrought and ornamented, and they wear gaudy handkerchiefs tastefully bound round their heads . . .

. . . We had not been long encamped, when our recently engaged attendant, Beatte, the Osage half-breed, made his appearance . . . Beatte was evidently an "old soldier," as to the art of taking care of himself and looking out for emergencies. . . . I thought Beatte seemed to feel his independence, and to consider himself superior to us all, now that we were launching into the wilderness. He maintained a half proud, half sullen look, and great taciturnity, and his first care was to unpack his horses and put them in safe quarters for the night.

. . . While we were holding a parley with him on the slope of the hill, we descried an Osage on horseback issuing out of a skirt of wood about half a mile off, and leading a horse by a halter. The latter was immediately recognized by our hard-winking friend as the steed of which he was in quest.

. . . The youth rode slowly up to us with a frank open air, and signified by means of our interpreter Beatte, that the horse he was leading had wandered to their camp, and he was now on his way to conduct him back to his owner.

I had expected to witness an expression of gratitude on the part of our hard-favored cavalier, but to my surprise the old fellow broke out into a furious passion. He declared that the Indians had carried off his horse in the night, with the intention of bringing him home in the morning, and claiming a reward for finding him; a common practice, as he affirmed, among the Indians. He was, therefore, for tying the young Indian to a tree and giving him a sound lashing . . . Such . . . is too often the administration of law on the frontier, "Lynch's law," as it is technically termed, in which the plaintiff is apt to be witness, jury, judge, and executioner, and the defendant to be convicted and punished on mere presumption . . . When I compared the open, noble countenance and frank demeanor of the young Osage, with the sinister visage and high-handed conduct of the frontiersman, I felt little doubt on whose back a lash would be most meritoriously bestowed.

As for the youthful Osage, we were all prepossessed in his favor . . . Such is the glorious independence of man in a savage state. This youth, with his rifle, his blanket, and his horse, was ready at a moment's warning to rove the world; he carried all his worldly effects with him, and in the absence of artificial wants, possessed the great secret of personal freedom. We of society are slaves, not so much to others as to ourselves; our superfluities are the chains that bind us, impeding every movement of our bodies and thwarting every impulse of our souls.

Source: Washington Irving, *A Tour of the Prairies* (Paris: A. and W. Galignani & Co., 1835).

THOUGHT QUESTIONS:

1. What descriptions of Native Americans in Washington Irving's account might be considered stereotypes?

2. What does this brief passage suggest about cultural diversity among Native American groups?

3. What does Irving see as the differences between white culture and that of Native Americans?

Letter, President Andrew Jackson to U.S. Secretary of War Lewis Cass
December 17, 1832

In 1828, the Congress passed a marked increase in tariffs (taxes on foreign-made goods) on foreign-produced wool, flax, distilled spirits, iron, and hemp, giving aid to those industries in the northern states. This policy dramatically increased the cost of these products in the heavily agricultural South, which depended on imports to buy manufactured products. Many Southerners condemned the import law as "The Tariff of Abominations."

Vice President John C. Calhoun believed the tariff would economically harm South Carolina and also feared that the law represented a growing assertion of federal power, a power that might eventually be used to curb or abolish slavery. In 1828, Calhoun anonymously authored a politically explosive pamphlet, **The Exposition and Protest***, which argued that the Constitution basically represented a treaty between nations and that it was up to each sovereign state, and not the federal courts, to determine whether a federal law violated the Constitution. Calhoun argued that a state could nullify within its borders any national law it deemed unconstitutional. He also said that states had the right to secede if the federal government exceeded its constitutional limits. Opponents to this idea, like Massachusetts Senator Daniel Webster, argued that the nullification theory would create government chaos, with federal laws in effect in some states and not in others, that federal law prevailed over state laws, and that the Founders intended the union to be perpetual and that no state had a right to secede. Such an arrangement, he said, would keep the nation perpetually on the precipice of collapse.*

When Andrew Jackson became president in March 1829, Calhoun expected the new chief executive to oppose the tariff, anticipating that the new chief executive would propose a repeal, but the vice president faced an unpleasant surprise. In order to appease South Carolina, Congress passed lower tariffs in 1832, but the rates were not cut enough to appease Calhoun's allies. In October 1832, the South Carolina legislature authorized the convening of a nullification convention. The convention met in November 1832 and nullified not only the tariff of 1828, but also the duties approved in 1832. The convention approved an Ordinance of Nullification that declared that the state would not collect duties at its ports beginning February 1, 1833. Jackson saw the convention as an act of treason. The president asked the Congress for a "Force Bill" that would empower him to dispatch federal troops into South Carolina to end resistance to the tariff and restore the authority of the executive branch. He asked his Secretary of War, Lewis Cass, to prepare for war to suppress what he saw as an incipient rebellion. Meanwhile, the president backed another bill reducing tariffs over a long duration to levels acceptable to the South Carolina nullifiers, what came to be known as the Compromise Tariff of 1833. In response, South Carolina rescinded its nullification ordinance, but the southern states that formed the Confederacy in 1860-1861 would later use Calhoun's arguments in the **Exposition** *as their justification of secession. Whether or not states have the right to secede would be resolved by the 1861-1865 Civil War.*

Washington, December 17, 1832.
Confidential

My D'r sir,

If I can judge from the signs of the times Nullification, and secession, or in the language of truth, disunion, is gaining strength, we must be prepared to act with promptness, and crush the monster in its cradle before it matures to manhood. We must be prepared for the crisis. The moment that we are informed that the Legislature of So Carolina has passed laws to carry her rebellious ordinance into effect, which I expect tomorrow we must be prepared to act. Tenders of service is coming to me daily and from Newyork, we can send to the bay of charleston with steamers such number of troops as we may please to order, in four days.

We will want three divisions of artillery, each composed of nines, twelves, and Eighteen pounders, one for the East, one for the west, and one for the center divisions. How many of these calibers, are ready for field service. How many musketts with their compleat equipments are ready for service. How many swords and pistols and what quantity of fixed ammunition for dragoons, Brass pieces for the field, how many, and what caliber. At as early a day as possible, I wish a report from the ordinance Department, on this subject, stating with precision, how many peaces of artillery of the caliber, are ready for the field, how many good musketts etc. etc., and at what place in deposit.

Source: https://www.loc.gov/resource/maj.01082_0244_0245/?sp=1&st=text

THOUGHT QUESTIONS:

1. If put into practice, how would John C. Calhoun's theory of nullification affect the United States' ability to govern itself?

2. The Nullification Crisis of 1832 was ostensibly about taxes on imported goods, but what issue was also on the mind of white Southerners at this time?

3. What arguments did Daniel Webster make against Calhoun's *Exposition and Protest?*

Vignettes

A Nation in Eclipse

The solar eclipse that shadowed much of the United States on February 12, 1831, struck many as a portent of earthshaking change. After all, the world seemed convulsed by the spirit of revolution. In Paris, days of rioting the previous July led to the collapse of King Charles X's regime and the installation of his distant cousin, Louis Phillipe, on the throne. Another 1830 revolution led to Belgian independence from the Netherlands, while a third, led by Polish rebels against occupation of their homeland by Russia, failed. Many wondered what the cosmic event of the winter of 1831 might augur.

One Philadelphia newspaper correspondent described an "old shoe black" who, the day before the eclipse, grabbed a stranger and declared, with tears in his eyes, "the world is to be destroyed to-morrow; the sun and the moon are to meet . . . and a great earthquake was to swallow us all!" The day after the eclipse, newspapers reported that preachers delivered sermons with Luke 21:25 as their key text: "And there shall be signs in the sun, and in the moon, and in the stars; and upon the earth distress of nations, with perplexity; the sea and the waves roaring."

Newspapers and almanacs predicted such darkness that workers might have to toil by candlelight during normal daytime hours. According to historian Louis P. Masur, who researched American reaction to the eclipse, the United States House of Representatives considered a motion to adjourn because of the anticipated lack of sunlight. In spite of so many grandiose predictions, however, many Americans did not panic and some Philadelphia residents spent the day ice-skating on the Delaware River, which had frozen solid during an unusually cold winter.

Generally speaking, the eclipse disappointed. The day did not grow as dark as some almanacs and astronomers had suggested. "The darkness being less visible than generally expected," one newspaper wrote, meant that many who had anxiously watched the skies turned away feeling "bamboozled."

Many, however, still saw in the eclipse a powerful metaphor for a restless era of wrenching change. In New York, the Working Man's Party called for universal education, a ban on the death penalty, an abolition of debtors' prisons, direct election of United States senators, and complete separation of church and state. Religious revivals swept Western New York. By 1831 many Americans fought for more humane prisons, better schools, alcohol prohibition, banning prostitution and, most explosively, the abolition of slavery. As the Philadelphia Gazette noted, "An irresistible spirit of reform seems burning with occult but mighty energy among the nations." Just as an eclipse passes and light returns, some hoped that the darkness of human bondage and other social evils would yield to the light of social justice.

THOUGHT QUESTIONS:

1. What social and political conditions made many think that the eclipse of 1831 was a sign of future radical change?

2. What does the public reaction to the eclipse suggest about the public's understanding of science in 1831?

3. How did the public's understanding (or misunderstanding) of science shape reaction to the start of the 1980s AIDS epidemic, the panic over the so-called "Y2K" bug, and climate change?

"Jump Jim Crow"

Nineteenth-and early twentieth-century American satirist Mark Twain, usually significantly ahead of his time on racial politics, once confessed his love for what he called, "the real nigger show – the genuine nigger show, the extravagant nigger show which to me had no peer and whose peer has not yet arrived, in my experience." Twain was referring to "blackface minstrelsy," musical-comedy stage shows in which white performers applied shoe polish or burned corks blended with grease paint to blacken their faces as they crudely imitated African American appearances, speech, music, and dance.

Minstrel performers wore curly wigs, black gloves, flamboyantly shabby, colorful, and ill-fitting clothes and oversized shoes in order to ridicule slaves and free African Americans. In the late 1820s, T.D. "Big Daddy" Rice became a major stage star in New York City with the first of the minstrel shows, which became one of the most popular forms of entertainment for whites throughout the 19th century.

As the minstrel shows spread from New York across the country, new stars associated with the genre such as George Washington Dixon began to feature standard characters with names like "Zip Coon," a pretentious free black, and his frequent companion, a happy, good-natured slave called "Jim Crow." Jim Crow represented a particularly cruel example of Rice's humor. He later said that he based the character on a disabled stableman he once met in the Ohio Country who had an unusual style of dancing that made Rice laugh.

A song, "Jump Jim Crow!" became an expected highlight of minstrel performances. It is not clear how and why, but as Southern states implemented segregation laws in the late 1800s and early 1900s, these codes came to be known as "Jim Crow" laws. Minstrel songs would have a profound effect on American popular music, with composer Stephen Foster penning several classics, such as "The Old Folks at Home" and "Oh! Susanna" in the minstrel style.

In addition to the songs, minstrel shows included not just jokes demeaning black people, but also longer humorous stories, and satirical sketches about abolitionists, politicians, and celebrities. Much of the humor derived from the interactions between the show's host, a dignified character called the "Interlocutor," who asked questions, and two "endmen," called "Mr. Bones" and "Mr. Tambo," who provided usually ignorant and foolish answers.

Whites overwhelmingly made up the ranks of minstrel performers, but African Americans like William Henry Lane realized there was money to be made in minstrel shows and would, like white minstrels, don blackface, becoming black people pretending to be white people pretending to be black people. In other cases, black minstrels advertised their racial identities in order to sell themselves as more "authentic" than white minstrel performers. Black minstrel performers introduced white audiences to African American gospel music, but these programs mostly reinforced racism. The population of the free states in 1860, the last year before the Civil War, was about 99 percent white. Whites in the free states knew few African Americans, so their views of the black population were derived largely from the stereotypes offered on the minstrel stage.

Minstrel show audiences generally came from the white working class. These shows were popular among Irish immigrants, who in the North competed with African Americans for the lowest-paid and least respected jobs. Spectators often shouted out to performers to repeat dances and songs, actors provoking loud applause when they complied. The shows reaffirmed the audiences' sense of superiority to their black job competitors but also allowed them to fantasize about a return to a slower-paced rural past in an age of ever-expanding industrialization.

Minstrelsy turned out to be surprisingly durable. The first Hollywood movie epic, *The Birth of a Nation*, included white actors in blackface offering stereotypical portrayals of slaves and freedmen drawn from the minstrel tradition. The supposed first "talkie" film, *The Jazz Singer*, starred singer Al Jolson playing a minstrel performer. *The Amos 'n' Andy Show* became a popular radio comedy and eventually a music show from 1928 until 1960. A TV version was broadcast on CBS from 1951-1953 until protests from civil rights groups forced its cancellation. Civic clubs continued to hold live minstrel shows as fundraisers well after World War II. Minstrelsy started a cultural pattern in which whites would expropriate, imitate, and profit off of black culture, a pattern repeated in the history of jazz, rock 'n' roll, disco, and (to a lesser extent) hip-hop. For roughly 140 years, minstrelsy reinforced white supremacist ideology and gave permission to white audiences to mock and laugh at their black fellow citizens.

THOUGHT QUESTIONS:

1. What relationship did the rise of minstrelsy have to industrialization and class politics?

2. How did minstrel shows reinforce white racism?

3. What impact did minstrel shows have on the history of American popular culture?

Teaching Children About a Dangerous World: Brer Rabbit Stories

When slave parents told their children bedtime stories, they had a more important mission than just entertaining them. Slave children faced many dangers and their mothers and fathers had to not only protect them from physical harm, but also teach them to value themselves in spite of a dominant culture that insisted that African Americans were mere property, farm animals that could talk.

One way that slave parents imparted a message of self-love was by sharing folk stories that originated in their African homeland. The hero of many of these stories was Brer (Brother) Rabbit, a small creature who survives encounters with bigger, stronger predators like bears, and foxes through brainpower and courage. Slaveowners assumed that their human property was not smart enough to use symbolic language to describe social injustices, but the bullying large creatures clearly represented white society while Rabbit and the other small creatures served as stand-ins for the slaves.

In one story, Brer Rabbit is hopping and skipping down a road when Brer Bear seizes him, telling the little creature that he's hungry and he's going to eat him. Shivering, Rabbit tells Bear that he shouldn't waste his time on such a tiny animal and that Bear should eat something much bigger and tastier, a man. Brer Bear has never seen a man, so Rabbit says he'll show him one. Bear and Rabbit spot an old man and a little girl, but Rabbit convinces Bear that neither was a man and convinced him to be patient. When an adult man with a rifle appears, Rabbit tells Bear he has found the meal of his dreams. Bear runs toward the man, who fires his rifle, the shot hitting the animal's hide. Mockingly, Rabbit asks, "What did he taste like?" as Bear runs away.

Like the American slaveowners, Bear was a consumer of lives, and was driven by self-destructive greed. An indiscriminate killer, Bear nevertheless gives up the meal already in his hand to capture potential prey he's been promised will be larger and tastier. His greed almost leads to Bear's death at the hands of the hunter. In many Brer Rabbit stories, the predatory animals actually die after being tricked, and Rabbit saves himself from a hopeless situation. But even while he is in danger, he never surrenders his sense of right and wrong. Humans kill rabbits too, but Rabbit acts to save a child and a bent-over elderly man. Rabbit almost always thinks quickly, acts morally, and often risks his own life to protect the weak and the disadvantaged.

Slave children hearing these stories learned that whatever advantages the slaveowners had for the moment, the slave community was not helpless. They learned to not be selfish, to always put their community first, and they were given a message that the shortsightedness and selfishness of the dominant white culture of the time would bring about the demise of the slave system. These were stories of hope in what looked like a hopeless time.

White listeners to these tales continued to dismiss them as harmless children's stories. Oblivious to their political and social content, Joel Chandler Harris, an associate editor at the *Atlanta Constitution* newspaper, wrote new versions of the Brer Rabbit stories he heard from African Americans in the area for his newspaper column. In his versions, he added a stereotypical slave named Uncle Remus who told the yarns to a young white child. These stories were collected in a book, *Uncle Remus: His Stories and His Sayings*, which was published in 1880. A much larger white audience discovered Brer Rabbit and continued to misunderstand him. In 1946, Disney Studios released *The Song of the South*, a movie based on Harris's book. The character also served as an inspiration for the cartoon trickster Bugs Bunny.

THOUGHT QUESTIONS:

1. What were the moral lessons slave parents tried to teach their children through the Brer Rabbit stories?

2. What did the Brer Rabbit stories symbolically say about the experience of American slavery?

3. What characteristics helped Brer Rabbit survive in these stories?

Chapter 12

The United States in Transformation, 1830-1850

Frances Trollope on the Erie Canal

Francis Trollope and her children came to the United States from England to participate in an effort to educate African Americans in Tennessee. She did not stay there long because one of her sons became ill. So the family settled in Cincinnati, Ohio, where she hoped to set up one of her sons in business. That also did not work out, and Trollope had concluded that she did not care for Americans anyway. Her book, **The Domestic Manners of the Americans** *(1832), stated her view of the American population, "town and country ..., rich and poor, in the slave states and the free, without subtly: I do not like them, I do not like their principles, I do not like their manners, I do not like their opinions." She returned to England and became a professional writer.*

Before she left, however, Trollope saw much of the United States. She had come to Tennessee by way of New Orleans and the Mississippi River, and she left by working her way to Canada along the East Coast where she passed through Washington, D.C., Philadelphia, and New York City. Despite her revulsion at Americans generally, she did love the landscape and was impressed with the transportation innovations the country offered. The passage here recounts her travel from New York City to Niagara. It provides a nice view of what one experienced in traveling through the United States in the early- to mid-nineteenth century.

On the 30th of May we set off for Niagara [by steamboat, from New York City].... Every mile shows some new and startling effect of the combination of rocks, trees, and water; there is no interval of flat or insipid scenery, from the moment you enter upon the river at New-York, to that of quitting it at Albany, a distance of 180 miles.

...

117

... We arrived there late in the evening, but had no difficulty in finding excellent accommodation.

The first sixteen miles from Albany we travelled in a stage ... but at Schenectady we got on board one of the canal packet-boats for Utica.

... I can hardly imagine any motive of convenience powerful enough to induce me again to imprison myself in a canal-boat under ordinary circumstances. The accommodations being greatly restricted, everybody, from the moment of entering the boat, acts upon a system of unshrinking egotism. The library of a dozen books, the backgammon board, the tiny berths, the shady side of the cabin, are all jostled for....

...

The Erie Canal has cut through much solid rock, and we often passed between magnificent cliffs. The little falls of the Mohawk form a lovely scene; the rocks over which the river runs are more fantastic in form.... As many locks occur at this point, we quitted the boat, that we might the better enjoy the scenery, which is of the wildest description.... We reached Utica at twelve o'clock the following day....

At two, we set off in a very pleasant airy carriage for Trenton Falls, a delightful drive of fourteen miles. These falls have become within the last few years only second in fame to Niagara....

...

We returned to Utica to dinner, and found that we must either wait till the next day for the Rochester coach, or again submit to the packet-boat. Our impatience induced us to prefer the latter, not very wisely, I think, for every annoyance seemed to increase upon us. The Oneida and the Genesee country are both extremely beautiful, but had we not returned by another route we should have known little about it. From the canal nothing is seen to advantage, and very little is seen at all.... We arrived at Rochester, a distance of a hundred and forty miles, on the second morning after leaving Utica, fully determined never to enter a canal boat again, at least not in America.

Rochester is one of the most famous of the cities built on the Jack and Bean-stalk principle. There are many splendid edifices in wood; and certainly more houses, warehouses, factories, and steam-engines than ever were collected together in the same space of time....

Our journey now became wilder every step, the unbroken forest often skirted the road for miles, and the sight of a log hut was an event. Yet the road was, for the greater part of the day, good, running along a natural ridge, just wide enough for it.... When this ridge ceased, the road ceased too, and for the rest of the way to Lockport, we were most painfully jumbled and jolted over logs and through bogs, till every joint was nearly dislocated.

Lockport is, beyond all comparison, the strangest looking place I ever beheld. As fast as half a dozen trees were cut down, a factory was raised up; stumps still contest the ground with pillars, and porticoes are seen to struggle with racks. It looks as if the demon of machinery, having invaded the peaceful realms of nature, had fixed on Lockport as the battleground on which they should strive for mastery. The fiend insists that the streams shall go one way, though the gentle mother had ever led their dancing steps another; nay, the very rocks must fall before him, and take what form he wills. The battle is lost and won. Nature is fairly routed and driven from the field, and the rattling, crackling, hissing, splitting demon has taken possession of Lockport for ever.

We slept there dismally enough. I never felt more out of humour at what the Americans call improvement; it is, in truth, as it now stands, a most hideous place, and gladly did I leave it behind me.

…

At length we reached Niagara. It was the brightest day that June could give; and almost any day would have seemed bright that brought me to the object which, for years, I had languished to look upon.

…

It is not for me to attempt a description of Niagara: I feel I have no powers for it.

Source: Frances Trollope, *Domestic Manners of the Americans,* 2d ed. (2 vols.; London, 1832), 234-256.

THOUGHT QUESTIONS:

1. Although this passage has Erie Canal in its title, Trollope and her companions did not just travel by canal. How many times did she switch modes of transportation and why? What does this switching between canals and steamships, and carriages say about the nature of travel in the United States?

2. How did Trollope portray the manners of the Americans she travelled with on the Erie Canal? What did they do that bothered her?

3. How did Trollope describe the town of Lockport? What does that description say about her assessment of improvement and progress in the United States?

Frederick Law Olmsted on Violence and Cotton Production

Frederick Law Olmsted made a name for himself in the nineteenth century as a landscape architect. He designed Central Park in New York City and Forrest Part in St. Louis, Missouri, among many others. He and his son also designed a number of university campuses, such as Yale University's. Before he took on these jobs, Olmsted worked as a journalist, and he received an assignment to tour the South in the 1850s and report back what he saw.

*Olmsted published his observations in three books, **A Journey Through the Seaboard Slave States**, **A Journey Through Texas**, and **A Journey Through the Backcountry**. He would then combine those observations into an abridgment, **The Cotton Kingdom**, for the English market. In these books, Olmsted portrayed slavery as an inefficient institution that distributed what benefits it produced to a small number of elite inhabitants. The rest of the population lived relatively destitute lives in an economically underdeveloped region. In this passage, Olmsted used a conversation with an Alabama trader to focus on the relationship between violence and cotton production. Although Olmsted remained skeptical of his companion's assertions that overseers frequently (and freely) killed enslaved Southerners, he certainly agreed that there was a connection between violence and productivity.*

Note: This document appears as written in the original source; it contains offensive language.

In a hilly part of Alabama, fifty miles north of the principal cotton-growing districts of that State, I happened to have a tradesman of the vicinity for a travelling companion, when, in passing an unusually large cluster of negro cabins, he called my attention to a rugged range of hills behind them which, he said, was a favourite lurking-ground for run-away negroes. It afforded them numerous coverts for concealment during the day, and at night the slaves of the plantation we were passing would help them to find the necessaries of existence. He had seen folks who had come here to look after niggers from plantations two hundred miles to the south, ward [sic]. "I suppose," said he, "'t would seem kind o' barbarous to you to see a pack of hounds after a human being?"

"Yes, it would."

"Some fellows take as much delight in it as in runnin' a fox. Always seemed to me a kind o' barbarous sport." [A pause.] "It's necessary, though."

"I suppose it is. Slavery is a custom of society which has come to us from a barbarous people, and, naturally, barbarous practices have to be employed to maintain it."

"Yes, I s'pose that's so. But niggers is generally pretty well treated, considering. Some people work their niggers too hard, that's a fact. I know a man at ———; he's a merchant there, and I have had dealings with him; he's got three plantations, and he puts the hardest overseers he can get on them. He's all the time a' buying niggers, and they say around there he works 'em to death. On these small plantations, niggers ain't very often whipped bad; but on them big plantations, they've got to use 'em hard to keep any sort of control over 'em. The overseers have to always go about armed; their life wouldn't be safe, if they didn't. As 't is, they very often get cut pretty bad." (Cutting is knifing; it may be stabbing, in south-western parlance).

He went on to describe what he had seen on some large plantations which he had visited for business purposes—indications, as he thought, in the appearance of "the people," that they were being "worked to death." "These rich men," be said, "are always bidding for the overseer who will make the most cotton; and a great many of the overseers didn't care for anything but to be able to say they've made so many bales in a year. If they make plenty of cotton, the owners never ask how many niggers they kill."

I suggested that this did not seem quite credible; a negro was a valuable piece of property. It would be foolish to use him in such a way.

"Seems they don't think so," he answered." They are always bragging—you must have heard them—how many bales their overseer has made, or how many their plantation has made to a hand. They never think of anything else. You see, if a man did like to have his niggers taken care of, he couldn't bear to be always hearing that all the plantations round had beat his. He'd think the fault was in his overseer. The fellow who can make the most cotton always gets paid the best."

Overseers' wages were ordinarily from $200 to $600, but a real driving overseer would very often get $1,000. Sometimes they'd get $1,200 or $1,500. He heard of $2,000 being paid one fellow. A determined and perfectly relentless man—I can't recall his exact words, which were very expressive—a real devil of an overseer, would get almost any wages he'd ask; because, when it was told round that such a man had made so many bales to the hand, everybody would be trying to get him.

The man who talked in this way was a native Alabamian, ignorant, but apparently of more than ordinarily reflective habits, and he had been so situated as to have unusually good opportunities for observation. In character, if not in detail, I must say that his information was entirely in accordance with the opinions I should have been led to form from the conversations I heard by chance, from time to time, in the richest cotton districts. That his statements as to the bad management of large plantations, in respect to the waste of negro property, were not much exaggerated, I find frequent evidence in southern agricultural journals....

Source: Frederick Law Olmsted, *The Cotton Kingdom: A Traveller's Observations on Cotton and Slavery in the American Slave States*, 2 vols. (New York, 1861), 2: 184-186.

THOUGHT QUESTIONS:

1. The passage begins with a discussion of enslaved runaways? What efforts did planters take to get such people back? How did the tradesman portray this practice? Why would enslaved people run away, based on the evidence presented by the tradesman?

2. What was the difference in the treatment of enslaved African Americans on large and small plantations? What was the role of the overseer on the larger plantations?

3. What was the relationship between overseers' wages and the productivity of enslaved labor, according to both the tradesman and Olmsted?

Harriet H. Robinson on Changing Conditions in Cotton Mills

---

*Harriet Hanson Robinson's widowed mother brought her family to Lowell, Massachusetts, in the 1830s. Robison's mother came to run a boarding house for the "mill girls" that worked in the town's textile factories. Robinson herself started working in the mills in the mid-1830s when she was ten. During her time in Lowell, she performed various jobs, ranging from replacing spindles, to tending spending frames, to drawing-in threads. She also participated in strike activity over low wages and boarding fees. Robinson considered her time at Lowell as a period of opportunity, and she especially emphasized the education she received. Her job left her time to attend school at night, and she found an outlet for writing in the **Lowell Offering**, a local literary magazine produced by the mill workers.*

Those opportunities proved to be fleeting. The passage here recounts her experience as a worker in one of Lowell's cotton factories, the impact of declining working conditions, and the labor force that replaced the original mill girls.

In 1831 Lowell was little more than a factory village. Several corporations were started, and the cotton-mills belonging to them were building. Help was in great demand; and stories were told all over the country of the new factory town, and the high wages that were offered to all classes of work-people,—stories that reached the ears of mechanics' and farmers' sons, and gave new life to lonely and dependent women in distant towns and farmhouses. Into this Yankee El Dorado, these needy people began to pour by the various modes of travel known to those slow old days. The stage-coach and the canal-boat came every day, always filled with new recruits for this army of useful people. The mechanic and machinist came, each with his home-made chest of tools, and oftentimes his wife and little ones. The widow came with her little flock and her scanty housekeeping goods to open a boarding-house or variety store, and so provided a home for her fatherless children. Many farmers' daughters came to earn money to complete their wedding outfit, or buy the bride's share of housekeeping articles.

Women with past histories came, to hide their griefs and their identity, and to earn an honest living in the "sweat of their brow." Single young men came, full of hope and life, to get money for an education, or to lift the mortgage from the home-farm. Troops of young girls came by stages and baggage-wagons, men often being employed to go to other States and to Canada, to collect them at so much a head, and deliver them at the factories.

...

But the early factory girls were not all country girls. There were others also, who had been taught that "work is no disgrace." There were some who came to Lowell solely on ac- count of the social or literary advantages to be found there. They lived in secluded parts of New England, where books were scarce, and there was no cultivated society. They had comfortable homes, and did not perhaps need the money they would earn; but they longed to see this new "City of Spindles," of which they had heard so much from their neighbors and friends, who had gone there to work.

...

Except in rare instances, the rights of the early mill-girls were secure. They were subject to no extortion, if they did extra work they were always paid in full, and their own account of labor done by the piece was always accepted. They kept the figures, and were paid accordingly. This was notably the case with the weavers and drawing-in girls. Though the hours of labor were long, they were not over-worked; they were obliged to tend no more looms and frames than they could easily take care of, and they had plenty of time to sit and rest. I have known a girl to sit idle twenty or thirty minutes at a time. They were not driven, and their work-a-day life was made easy. They were treated with consideration by their employers, and there was a feeling of respectful equality between them. The most favored of the girls were sometimes invited to the houses of the dignitaries of the mills, showing that the line of social division was not rigidly maintained.

...

One of the first strikes of cotton-factory operatives that ever took place in this country was that in Lowell, in October, 1836. When it was announced that the wages were to be cut down, great indignation was felt, and it was decided to strike, en masse....

...

Cutting down the wages was not their only grievance, nor the only cause of this strike. Hitherto the corporations had paid twenty-five cents a week towards the board of each operative, and now it was their purpose to have the girls pay the sum; and this, in addition to the cut in the wages, would make a difference of at least one dollar a week....

....

And after a time, as the wages became more and more reduced, the best portion of the girls left and went to their homes, or to the other employments that were fast opening to women, until there were very few of the old guard left; and thus the status of the factory population of New England gradually became what we know it to be to-day.

...

I should not feel that the whole purpose of this book had been fulfilled unless I added a word in behalf of the factory population of to-day [1898].

...

The hours of labor are now less, it is true; but the operatives are obliged to do a far greater amount of work in a given time. They tend so many looms and frames that they have no time to think. They are always on the jump; and so have no opportunity to improve themselves....

...

The factory population of New England is made up largely of American-born children of foreign parentage,—two-thirds it is estimated....

The cotton-factories themselves are not so agreeable nor so healthful to work in as they used to be. Once they were light, well ventilated, and moderately heated; each factory-building stood detached, with pleasant sunlit windows, cheerful views, and fresh air from all points of the compass. But these buildings are now usually made into a solid mass by connecting "annexes," and often form a hollow square, so that at least one-half of the operatives can have no outlook except upon brick walls, and no fresh air but that which circulates within this confined space.

A year or two ago I revisited the dressing- room where I used to work, and found the heat so intense that I could hardly breathe; and the men who were working there (there were no women in the room) wore the scantiest of clothing, and were covered with perspiration.

Source: Harriet H. Robinson, Loom and Spindle; or, Life among the Early Mill Girls, with a Sketch of the "Lowell Offering" and Some of Its Contributors (New York, 1898), 62-63, 66, 71, 83-84, 86, 202, 205, 207-209.

THOUGHT QUESTIONS:

1. According to Robinson, what was the composition of the original labor force at Lowell? Where did the workers come from and why?

2. How did Robinson describe her working conditions? What issues drove her and her fellow workers to go on strike?

3. How had the working conditions in the mill changed in the time from when Robinson had worked in the mill (1830s) and the time she wrote this account (1898)? What difference stood out most?

Vignettes

Southern Universities and the Defense of Slavery

Beginning in the 1830s, faculty in universities across the South began articulating a defense of slavery that presented the institution as an alternative to the economic changes taking place in the American North and in Europe. Contemporary university faculty have a reputation for advocating social justice causes, but, as historian Alfred Brophy notes, antebellum southern faculty took up the cause of slaveholders and argued that enslavement generally benefited everyone involved.

Academic defenses of slavery had their origins in the work of Thomas R. Dew, a professor of political economy at Virginia's William and Mary University. In the wake of Nat Turner's Rebellion, Virginia held a convention that debated ending slavery (with compensation to masters and the forced deportation of people set free). Dew reviewed the debates for the *Southern Literary Messenger* and argued, among other things, that emancipation would destroy the state's economy (because the plan was too expensive) and was inhumane (because enslaved African Americans were not yet ready for freedom and they would face starvation—or worse—in what he considered the wilds of Africa). Continuing slavery thus represented the only responsible position for the South.

Other faculty extended Dew's arguments. Professors at schools like Washington College (now Washington and Lee), Transylvania University, University of Virginia, Randolph Macon College, William and Mary, Centenary College, Emory College, Mississippi Planter's College, Greensboro Female Academy, and Tuscaloosa Female Seminary echoed his conclusions. They argued that enslavement created conditions for white equality (a necessary foundation for republican government), emphasized racial traits that they believed rendered blacks unfit for freedom, and predicted that emancipation would bring economic ruin.

Surviving evidence indicated that southern college students accepted these ideas. They invited speakers, often political leaders, to campus that delivered orations in defense of slavery. Debating societies often took up issues on racial equality, South Carolina nullification, or whether slavery was evil. More often than not, students voted that the races were not equal, that South Carolina was justified in resorting to nullification, and that slavery was not evil. Nineteenth-century college students, by the way, generally came from wealthy families, and university educations were stepping stones on the way to careers in law and politics. Given the potential influence these students would have later in life, their embrace of these ideas proved to be quite consequential.

The impact of proslavery thought became clear in the 1850s. By then proslavery writers had developed fully-fledged arguments that portrayed slavery as more than just a labor system—it was a social system and one upon which the survival of southern civilization depended. Enslavement, these theorist argued, protected the South from labor unrest and the potential for socialist revolution. Unlike in Europe and the North, southern workers had no expectation for advancement but received (so the argument went) adequate material support. Workers in places like England and the American North suffered material deprivation, and in the North at least those workers could vote—and they might use that power to attack private property. Viewed from this perspective, which was widely accepted among educated Southerners in the 1850s, Lincoln's election threatened this system, and a majority of southern voters opted to secede from the Union in order to save it.

THOUGHT QUESTIONS:

1. Who began to develop the proslavery argument, and what event triggered that work?

2. Did southern college students accept the proslavery argument? How do we know whether they did or not?

3. What was the ultimate outcome of the growing influence of these ideas? Do you believe that these ideas were responsible for secession or were there other factors at play?

Day Labor in Baltimore

In the nineteenth century, wage labor became the standard way of compensating workers in the United States, especially in urban areas. Working for a wage, however, was not generally considered a desirable way to make a living over the long term. Advocates of wage labor generally portrayed it as a stepping-stone to something better—a salaried middle-class job, an established business, or a farm. Yet an increasing number of workers sustained themselves entirely by wage work for their entire life. Doing so was especially difficult and so is studying the people who did it.

Nineteenth-century wage laborers did not have much time to write and thus left few records (workers in craft guilds in places like New York City excepted). Historians, of course, have developed methods to study people who could not (or did not have time to) write. They use census and court records and painstakingly piece together their histories. But these methods also tend not to work for wage workers. They moved frequently from city to city and often disappear from records as rapidly as they appear.

Baltimore provides an exception to this trend. The city's archives contain payrolls for its "mudmachine," a steam-powered contraption that dredged the city's shallow harbor for nine months of the year. The work was hard and unpleasant—workers were always wet and machine pulled up a foul-smelling slime that was used to fill in ground for the rapidly growing city. Pay was low—a little over a dollar a day—but the work was steady for those who could endure it. That stood in sharp contrast to other jobs—many American laborers lived in what we would now call a "gig economy" where they received pay for a particular job (such as unloading a ship) and then had to find another one to piece together regular pay. Outside of the winter months, however, mudmachine work was always available because Baltimore's harbor constantly filled with silt.

Despite the prospect of steady work, most people hired quickly moved on. Over half of the workers hired to work with the mudmachine between 1809 and 1819 remained on the payroll for more than a month. Slightly over a third of those hired stayed for three months or more. Only two percent remained on the payroll for an entire year. Even those who managed to stay on lived a precarious existence. Owen Mullen worked on the mudmachine in 1817 and 1818. He owned a house that fronted fifteen feet of an ally in one of the poorest sections of town, and they appeared to supplement their income by taking in borders. Michael Gorman worked on the mudmachine for five years. He worked steadily in 1815 and 1816, and then appeared sporadically on the payroll in 1817. He returned in 1818 and then dropped off the rolls again in 1819. He owned a house, but he lost it in the 1820s and lived out the last ten years of his life in Baltimore's almshouse.

The early nineteenth century was a period of tremendous economic growth and development. But the work in this new economy was hard and unsteady, and survival in the early American Republic remained a constant struggle.

THOUGHT QUESTIONS:

1. What was the significance of wage labor in the early nineteenth century?

2. What are the challenges historians face in studying the lives of wage workers in the early nineteenth century?

3. What do the experiences of Owen Mullen and Michael Gorman reveal about the nature of wage work in Baltimore?

An Exceptional Couple: The Hardens of Brazoria County, Texas

Tamar Morgan Harden and her husband Samuel lived in Brazoria County, Texas, in the 1830s and 1840s. The were a prosperous couple. They owned a modest amount of land, including a few town lots in the county seat and a hundred-acre farm nearby. They owned four slaves, a number that fell within the average amount of slaves owned by slaveholding households in the antebellum U.S. Yet according to standard historical accounts, this couple should not have existed: because they were a free black, slaveholding, landowning couple in Texas.

Texas maintained an official hostility to free blacks. An 1840 law ordered all such people to leave the republic. Brazoria County, moreover, had one of the largest concentrations of slaves in Texas. In 1850, over seventy percent of the county's population was enslaved. Slaveholders used brutality to maintain control. Phineas Smith, a New York minister who lived in Texas but who failed to acquire any land, reported torture by whipping, arbitrary murders, and the hunting of fugitives with dogs. Smith's account appeared in Theodore Dwight Weld's *American Slavery as It Is* (1839), which was essentially a book of examples for abolitionist lecturers, but his account meshes well with other descriptions of antebellum slavery.

Yet the Hardens' experience differed radically from that of their enslaved neighbors. Samuel Hardin, a free man of color born in North Carolina, came to Texas in the 1820s. His wife, Tamar Morgan, arrived in Texas in 1832, as a slave and managed to purchase her freedom, although no records have survived to determine how she did so. When Texas passed its law ordering free blacks to leave the Republic, sixty-three people, including several slaveowners, signed a petition requesting that the Hardens be allowed to remain in Texas. Samuel, they wrote, had earned "the reputation of being an industrious and orderly citizen, having acquired amount of property in this Country besides supporting his wife and family." His wife was also "industrious and useful citizen." The petition actually sold Tamer short. She provided the economic lifeblood for the Harden household, and her labor created a foundation of property that allowed Samuel to live independently into the late 1850s—years after her death.

Samuel and Tamar married sometime in the late 1830s, but only after Samuel, who, according to court documents, was "somewhat encumbered in his pecuniary affairs," signed a prenuptial agreement allowing both parties retain control of their own property and contracts. Samuel owned property, but Tamar owned more, and she recorded her possessions with the Brazoria County Clerk. She claimed the household furniture, a horse, the household's "stock of cattle and hogs." She held sole proprietorship of a 100-acre farm (Harden's Place) near the county seat. She also owned some lots in town. And she owned four enslaved African Americans: "One negro man named Daniel, aged about forty years, one negro woman named Mahala aged about thirty years, and two children of said Mahala named Margaret and Millery." (Enslaved people in free black households were often family members and not chattel. But this seems not to have been the case here. The Hardens sold Mahala in 1842; there is no record of what happened to other enslaved members of the Harden household.)

Tamar died around 1846, and she left Samuel enough property to provide for him in his old age. The census return for 1850 notes that Samuel was 68 years old and that he owned a 100-acre farm valued at $1,000 along with 1 horse, 2 milch cows, 4 working oxen, 10 head of cattle, and 25 pigs. Two white laborers also lived with him. County court records show how Harden used these resources to support himself as he aged. In 1852, he rented his land—identified as Harden's Place in the records—to one Samuel P. Fowler for eight years. The agreement stipulated that Harden could trade on Fowler's account at any store in Brazoria up to the cost of the rent ($100 annually). A few years later, Harden used his livestock and a share of the crops growing on his land to hire enslaved laborers, the "negro Boy Demps" in 1858 and "the girl Lucy" in 1859, to perform some unspecified work. Harden appears to have died in 1859 or 1860 (he would have been around 78 years old). He did not manifest in the 1860 census.

The example of Tamar Morgan and Samuel Harden shows the complexity of the historical record at the local level. Although the state and community was hostile to free blacks, a sliver of people managed to carve out a place for themselves despite the general climate of hostility. They did so by building up good will with their white, slaveholding neighbors—exactly how they did so is unknown—and by acquiring a foundation of property that allowed themselves to sustain a household. But students should keep in mind that the Hardens were an exception that proved the rule. Almost all African Americans in Brazoria County were enslaved. And none of the other free blacks in the county (who numbered fewer than ten) sustained a household for very long. But the historical record always contains exceptions to general trends and finding them is one of the joys of historical research.

THOUGHT QUESTIONS:

1. According to the text, what sort of treatment did African Americans, both enslaved and free, receive in Texas?

2. How did the Hardens' experience differ from that of other African Americans in antebellum Texas?

3. Why may it be important to highlight exceptional cases in the historical record, like the one found here?

Chapter 13

The Spirit of Reform, 1820-1860

"Declaration of Sentiments and Resolutions"
Woman's Rights Convention, Seneca Falls, 19-20 July 1848

The battle for women's voting rights became a long and winding road, full of disappointing detours. Although women like Abigail Adams in the late eighteenth century argued for giving women a political voice in the United States, the suffrage movement can mark its start at a Waterloo, New York tea party in July 1848. From this humble beginning sprang a serious, sustained campaign for women's suffrage in the United States. The party was attended by several of the leading feminists of the era, including Elizabeth Cady Stanton and Lucretia Mott, who had already gained extensive political experience as anti-slavery crusaders. Stanton and Mott,, as well as the other three attending the party, resolved to organize a women's rights convention to be held in nearby Seneca Falls just six days later, on July 19.

In spite of the short time available to organize, the convention was a success, drawing about 260 women and 40 men, including one of the nation's leading abolitionists, Frederick Douglass. Those in attendance heard a series of dramatic speeches, including one co-written by Stanton and Mott that included "The Declaration of Sentiments." Intentionally, the statement was closely modeled on the Declaration of Independence.

During the two-day convention, the delegates unanimously approved numerous resolutions calling for women to enjoy greater rights in marriage and an end to gender discrimination regarding property and education, but they only narrowly approved a resolution calling for women's suffrage, with some attending afraid that the suffrage was too radical a demand. The convention and the Declaration, however, inspired a grassroots movement. Nevertheless, women would not win suffrage nationally until the ratification of the Nineteenth Amendment, on August 18, 1920.

When, in the course of human events, it becomes necessary for one portion of the family of man to assume among the people of the earth a position different from that which they have hitherto occupied, but one to which the laws of nature and of nature's God entitle them, a decent respect to the opinions of mankind requires that they should declare the causes that impel them to such a course.

We hold these truths to be self-evident: that all men and women are created equal; that they are endowed by their Creator with certain inalienable rights; that among these are life, liberty, and the pursuit of happiness. . . Whenever any form of Government becomes destructive of these ends, it is the right of those who suffer from it to refuse allegiance to it, and to insist upon the institution of a new government, laying its foundation on such principles, and organizing its powers in such form as to them shall seem most likely to effect their safety and happiness. . . . When a long train of abuses and usurpations, pursuing invariably the same object, evinces a design to reduce them under absolute despotism, it is their duty to throw off such government, and to provide new guards for their future security. Such has been the patient sufferance of the women under this government, and such is now the necessity which constrains them to demand the equal station to which they are entitled.

The history of mankind is a history of repeated injuries and usurpations on the part of man toward woman, having in direct object the establishment of an absolute tyranny over her. To prove this, let facts be submitted to a candid world. He has never permitted her to exercise her inalienable right to the elective franchise. He has compelled her to submit to laws, in the formation of which she had no voice. He has withheld from her rights which are given to the most ignorant and degraded men—both natives and foreigners. . . . He has taken from her all right in property, even to the wages she earns. . . . In the covenant of marriage, she is compelled to promise obedience to her husband, he becoming, to all intents and purposes, her master—the law giving him power to deprive her of her liberty, and to administer chastisement. . . . He has monopolized nearly all the profitable employments, and from those she is permitted to follow, she receives but a scanty remuneration. He closes against her all the avenues to wealth and distinction, which he considers most honorable to himself. As a teacher of theology, medicine, or law, she is not known. He has denied her the facilities for obtaining a thorough education—all colleges being closed against her. ... He has endeavored, in every way that he could to destroy her confidence in her own powers, to lessen her self-respect, and to make her willing to lead a dependent and abject life.

Now, in view of this entire disfranchisement of one-half the people of this country, their social and religious degradation ... we insist that they have immediate admission to all the rights and privileges which belong to them as citizens of these United States.

In entering upon the great work before us, we anticipate no small amount of misconception, misrepresentation, and ridicule; but we shall use every instrumentality within our power to effect our object.

Source: Elizabeth Cady, Susan B. Anthony, and M.J. Cage. *A History of Woman Suffrage*, vol. 1 (Rochester, N.Y.: Fowler and Wells, 1889).

THOUGHT QUESTIONS:

1. What were the likely political reasons that Stanton and Mott chose to so closely base their declaration of women's rights on *The Declaration of Independence*?

2. What shortcomings did the *Declaration's* reference to rights given "most ignorant and degraded men—both natives and foreigners" suggest about the early feminists' ability to build support for women's suffrage?

3. What rights were men denying women in the mid-nineteenth century, according to the *Declaration*, and how many of the issues raised are still relevant today?

Civil Disobedience By Henry David Thoreau, 1849

A native of Concord, Massachusetts, Henry David Thoreau's non-conformity often got him in trouble with the authorities. He graduated from Harvard University in 1837 just as a deep depression gripped the country. The slow economy closed off most employment opportunities for him, and when he took a job as a teacher at the Concord Center School, he lasted only two weeks. He resigned because he refused to obey the school system's rules and use corporal punishment against a student.

A socially awkward man with few friends, Thoreau did form an important relationship with Ralph Waldo Emerson, a one-time clergyman and author who became a leader of the "Transcendentalist" movement. Transcendentalists held deep doubts about large institutions such as the church and government, which they saw as threats to individual liberties, and doubted if meaningful change could be achieved through voting. They emphasized feeling over reason. They hoped to "transcend" reliance on scientific reasoning and sought instead the divine spark that transcendentalists believed resided in each person.

*Thoreau became a poet and writer and, searching for self-reliance and independence from materialism, he began a sojourn at Walden Pond in late July 1846. Thoreau went on an errand in Concord and encountered a local tax collector who demanded payment of six years' worth of delinquent poll taxes. Thoreau refused to pay, convinced that his taxes would fund the war the United States was then waging against Mexico. Thoreau saw this war as unprovoked and part of a conspiracy to create new slave states out of territory seized from Mexico. (Thoreau was mistaken: the poll tax did not fund the Mexican War.) He spent a night in jail, but was freed when an unknown person paid the overdue taxes, against his will. The experience inspired an essay he published in 1849 as **Resistance to Civil Government** (most commonly known as **Civil Disobedience**).*

In the essay, Thoreau called for Massachusetts's citizens to not support a state government he sees as supporting the Mexican-American War. He rejected any obligation to respect laws compelling him to act in a way that violated his personal sense of right and wrong. Thoreau argued that no individual owed obedience to a government that committed evil, such as permitting the spread of slavery. An individual only owes obedience to a "higher law," that of morality and justice. This work inspired Mahatma Gandhi's campaign for India's independence from Great Britain in 1948 and Martin Luther King, Jr. during the African-American civil rights struggles of the 1950s and the 1960s.

I heartily accept the motto, "That government is best which governs least"; and I should like to see it acted up to more rapidly and systematically. Carried out, it finally amounts to this, which also I believe- "That government is best which governs not at all"; and when men are prepared for it, that will be the kind of government which they will have. . . . The government . . . which is only the mode which the people have chosen to execute their will, is equally liable to be abused and perverted before the people can act through it. Witness the present Mexican war, the work of comparatively a few individuals using the standing government as their tool; for, in the outset, the people would not have consented to this measure.... But, to speak practically and as a citizen, unlike those who call themselves no-government men, I ask for, not at once no government, but at once a better government. Let every man make known what kind of government would command his respect, and that will be one step toward obtaining it.

After all, the practical reason why, when the power is once in the hands of the people, a majority are permitted, and for a long period continue, to rule is not because they are most likely to be in the right, nor because this seems fairest to the minority, but because they are physically the strongest . . . I think that we should be men first, and subjects afterward. It is not desirable to cultivate a respect for the law, so much as for the right. The only obligation which I have a right to assume is to do at any time what I think right. . . . Law never made men a whit more just; and, by means of their respect for it, even the well-disposed are daily made the agents of injustice . . .

. . . I do not hesitate to say, that those who call themselves Abolitionists should at once effectually withdraw their support, both in person and property, from the government of Massachusetts, and not wait till they constitute a majority of one, before they suffer the right to prevail through them. I think that it is enough if they have God on their side, without waiting for that other one. Moreover, any man more right than his neighbors constitutes a majority of one already. . . . [T]he State never intentionally confronts a man's sense, intellectual or moral, but only his body, his senses. It is not armed with superior wit or honesty, but with superior physical strength. I was not born to be forced. I will breathe after my own fashion. Let us see who is the strongest. . . . The authority of government, even such as I am willing to submit to- for I will cheerfully obey those who know and can do better than I, and in many things even those who neither know nor can do so well- is still an impure one: to be strictly just, it must have the sanction and consent of the governed. It can have no pure right over my person and property but what I concede to it. . . . There will never be a really free and enlightened State until the State comes to recognize the individual as a higher and independent power, from which all its own power and authority are derived, and treats him accordingly.

Source: Henry David Thoreau, *On the duty of civil disobedience*. (New Haven, Conn.: Carl & Margaret Rollins, 1928.)

THOUGHT QUESTIONS:

1. What example does Henry David Thoreau give of how the American government might be acting in defiance of "higher" moral law?

2. Does Thoreau believe that the will of the majority always provides moral authority to a law or to a government?

3. What examples are there in American history of political movements that acted in defiance of what activists saw as immoral laws?

Dorothea Lynde Dix,
Memorial Soliciting a State Hospital for the Protection and Cure of the Insane: Submitted to the General Assembly of North Carolina
November 1848

In the early nineteenth century, many families had to care for mentally ill relatives themselves and often locked them in rooms, tying them to bedposts so they couldn't harm themselves or others. In other cases, the insane were chained to jail walls, where they often suffered from exposure and were underfed. Appalled by this, Dorothea Dix tirelessly fought for humane treatment of the insane.

Born in Hampden, Maine, in 1802, Dix grew up in the care of an abusive alcoholic father and a mentally unstable mother. Wealthy relatives, however, funded Dix's education and helped her establish a private school for girls between ages six and eight. Dix's life changed at age 39 when she taught a women's Sunday school class at an East Cambridge jail and witnessed how officials crammed the mentally ill and the mentally disabled into cells with loud and disorderly drunks and criminals into cold, foul-smelling, cramped spaces with no heat. In 1840-1841, she traveled across Massachusetts to investigate the state's mental health care system, finding that most town and city governments contracted with private individuals subject to no regulations.

She presented a report in 1848 to the Massachusetts state legislature, which persuaded legislators to increase the budget for the state mental hospital in Worcester. Dix proceeded to tour mental health facilities across the country, winning mental health reforms in 14 states in every region of the country. She later lobbied for a bill that would have funded a federal home for the insane poor, but President Franklin Pierce vetoed the bill in 1854, claiming that the federal government was not authorized to provide such charitable care.

I admit that public peace and security are seriously endangered by the non-restraint of the maniacal insane. I consider it in the highest degree improper that they should be allowed to range the towns and country without care or guidance; but this does not justify the public in any State or community, under any circumstances or conditions, in committing the insane to prisons; in a majority of cases the rich may be, or are sent to Hospitals; the poor under the pressure of this calamity, have the same just claim upon the public treasury, as the rich have upon the private purse of their family as they have the need, so have they the right to share the benefits of Hospital treatment. Urgent cases at all times, demand, unusual and ready expenditures in every community.

If County Jails must be resorted to for security against the dangerous propensities of madmen, let such use of prison-rooms and dungeons be but temporary . . . In nearly every jail in North Carolina, have the insane at different times, and in periods varying in duration, been grievous sufferers. In Halifax County, several years since, a maniac was confined in the jail; shut in the dungeon, and chained there. The jail was set on fire by other prisoners: the keeper, as he told me, heard frantic shrieks and cries of the madman, and "might have saved him as well as not, but his noise was a common thing he was used to it, and thought nothing out of the way was the case." The alarm of fire was finally spread; the jailer hastened to the prison: it was now too late; every effort, (and no exertions were spared,) to save the agonized creature, was unavailing. He perished in agony, and amidst tortures no pen can describe. . .

In illustration of the blessing and benefit of Hospital care in cases long and most cruelly neglected, I adduce the following examples recorded by Dr. Hill, and corresponding with many cases under my own immediate observation since 1840. "Two patients," writes the Dr. "were brought to me in 1836, who had been confined in a poor-house between eighteen and twenty years. During this period they had not known liberty. They had been chained day and night to their bedsteads, and kept in a state so filthy that it was sickening to go near them.—They were usually restrained by the strait-waistcoat, and with collars round their necks, the collars being fastened with chains or straps to the upper part of the bedstead, to prevent, it was said their tearing their clothes. The feet were fastened with iron leg-locks and chains. One poor creature was so wholly disabled by this confinement, that it was necessary for the attendants to bear her in their arms from place to place after she was brought to the Hospital; she shortly acquired good habits, and was long usefully employed in the sewing-room . . . Another case was brought in chains, highly excited; five persons attended her; in six days all restraints were removed; and she walked with her nurse, in the patients' gallery. In June, she was discharged from the wards quite cured, and engaged as assistant in the kitchen.

. . . [A] highly respected citizen writes me that a young woman has been sent to the poor-house so violently insane, that it is quite unfit she should remain there. Also a man has in that County, very recently become so violently mad as to be quite unmanageable, and having no Hospital in the State, they have confined him, with, chains and manacles, hand and feet, and do as best they can. A subscription paper has been circulated for the purpose of raising funds to send him to Columbia, S. C. Other painful cases exist in this, as in the counties which I have visited, and from which I have heard; most of which I do not feel at liberty, through their domestic and social position, to designate; but they plead in heart-reaching language for the early establishment of a State Hospital....

Source: *Memorial Soliciting a State Hospital for the Protection and Cure of the Insane: Submitted to the General Assembly of North Carolina, November, 1848* (Raleigh: Seaton Gales: Printer for the State, 1849)

THOUGHT QUESTIONS:

1. What did Dix identify as the primary dangers to patients created by how North Carolina cared for the mentally ill and disabled in the 1840s?

2. What does Dix describe as the difference between how the mentally ill in poor and rich families are treated?

3. How is President Franklin Pierce's veto of a bill creating a federal home for the insane poor reflective of the dominant American philosophy of government in the 19th century?

Vignettes

Against Reform: Slavery's Defenders

In the 1700s, southern whites had defended slavery as a "necessary evil," the only means to provide manual labor to grow the cash crops needed to buoy the region's economy. As slavery came under increasingly fierce criticism from abolitionists in the 1840s and 1850s—in novels such as *Uncle Tom's Cabin* and the speeches and writings of Frederick Douglass, for example—white Southerners shifted to arguing that slavery was a positive good, a benefit not just to whites but also to the slaves themselves. These opponents of reform argued that nature, or God, had uniquely designed Africans and their descendants in the United States to be slaves.

In their native lands, slavery's defenders argued, Africans had never developed anything that could be called a civilization. The dark-skinned people of African descent might not even be fully human, according to some pro-slavery advocates. John Van Evrie, a New York doctor who authored numerous pamphlets for the Democratic Party, wrote "it is a palpable and unavoidable fact that Negroes are a different species." American scientists like Samuel George Morton of Pennsylvania tried to "scientifically" prove that African Americans, Native Americans, and other so-called races represented different species. In the 1840s, Morton, a Philadelphia physician, amassed one of the largest human skull collections in the world, including specimens from Native Americans, Africans and African Americans, and Europeans and their descendants in the Americas. Assuming that brain size was an indicator of intelligence, Morton measured and compared the brain cases of skulls from these different racial groups.

Morton started with a faulty scientific premise. There is no proven correlation between brain size and intellect. Using sloppy and inconsistent measurement techniques, Morton simply confirmed his pre-existing prejudices and announced that Europeans had larger brain cases than Native Americans and that Native Americans had larger ones than those of African descent. Morton claimed he had proven the permanent intellectual inferiority of Africans and, thus, that they were suited for little other than manual labor under the control of whites.

Virginia author George Fitzhugh undoubtedly ranked as one of the most extreme defenders of slavery in the South. The Virginia lawyer and self-trained sociologist insisted in his inflammatory 1857 book *Cannibals All! Or Slaves Without Masters* that "the negro slaves of the South are the happiest and, in one sense, the freest people in the world" because all of the responsibility for their housing, feeding and medical care rested with their owners. Slave plantations, he argued, represented far more humane institutions than northern factories, where owners routinely abandoned sick, injured and/or elderly workers to hunger, homelessness and ill health. Unlike slaveowners, Fitzhugh wrote, factory owners saw workers as costs on a balance sheet, and not as members of the family.

Even more controversially, Fitzhugh suggested that northern white workers might be better off as slaves toiling for kindly plantation owners than living at the mercy of heartless capitalists. If Fitzhugh intended to win over Northerners to the idea that slavery was humane, this claim badly backfired. Instead, *Cannibals All!* and his 1854 work *Sociology for the South, or the Failure of Free Society* convinced some Northerners that southern slaveowners intended to spread involuntary servitude everywhere in the Union, even where it had long been abolished. Nevertheless, by the 1850s white Southerners generally agreed, along with some of their northern peers, that African Americans stood literally as a breed apart. "Few or none of us seriously adhere to the theory of the unity of the races," declared a newspaper, the *Democratic Review.* "The whole state of science at this moment seems to indicate that there are several races of man on the earth, with entirely different capacities, physical and mental."

THOUGHT QUESTIONS:

1. Why did Southerners likely feel the need to make new arguments to defend slavery in the two decades before the Civil War?

2. What arguments did Samuel Morton and George Fitzhugh make to rationalize the enslavement of African Americans?

3. How did George Fitzhugh use slavery as supposedly practiced in the American South to attack northern industrial capitalism?

"The Five Points": Crime in Early Nineteenth-Century New York

The internationally famous English novelist Charles Dickens spent his career writing about cities, crime, and poverty in books like *Oliver Twist* published in segments between 1837-1839, but even this close observer felt shock when he toured New York City with its "Five Points" neighborhood in lower Manhattan. He compared the Five Points unfavorably to the poorest, most violent neighborhoods in the English port city of Liverpool, a place where "hideous tenements . . . take their name from robbery and murder." The Five Points, he said, served as home to "all that is loathsome, drooping, and decayed . . . reeking everywhere with dirt and filth."

Located near Broadway at the intersection that gave the slum its name, the Five Points rose on the crossroads of Orange, Cross and Anthony Streets. Early on in the nineteenth century, well-off investors tore down artisans' homes there and replaced them with flimsier wood structures crammed with renters, early versions of the low-income tenements that would dot the Gotham landscape late in the century.

The Five Points' bad reputation derived in part from the racist and ethnocentric attitudes of New York elites towards the districts' inhabitants. The neighborhood had served as the first free African-American settlement in the emerging metropolis, and by the early 1800s only African-American tenants occupied many buildings. Many were recently freed slaves, and they labored as domestic servants, barbers, chimney sweeps, and rag pickers or picked up whatever temporary jobs became available. Seasonally employed tradesmen sometimes pooled their incomes to rent small boardinghouses occupied by five or more workers at a time.

By the mid-nineteenth century working class Irish immigrants, often pushed out of gentrifying neighborhoods that had become too expensive to live in, also called the Points home. The crowding only got worse by the 1820s and 1830s, with thirty or more residents crammed into two- or three-story buildings. White elites sneered at the racially mixed neighborhood, one wealthy man expressing disgust at the "vilest rabble, black and white mixt together."

The overcrowding facilitated disease outbreaks, such as an 1820 epidemic that killed 296 in the Five Points near Bancker Street. The wealthy did not respond by demanding an improvement of housing or increased wages, but the affluent Bancker family did demand that the now-infamous street get a new name. Thus, in 1826, the street was renamed "Madison Avenue," famous in the mid-twentieth century as the capital of the American advertising industry

The city government left streets in The Five Points poorly paved and provided only irregular public sanitation while law enforcement there at times became invisible. Saloons, houses of prostitution, and gambling dens stood alongside numerous breweries, tailor shops, shoemaking businesses, and multiple African-American churches. Pickpockets, muggers, and warring street gangs with names like the Forty Thieves, the Shirt Tails, and the Plug Uglies filled the streets, along with children who begged for money, food, or work.

"Clothed in rags, filthy in the extreme, both in person and in language, it is humiliating to be compelled to recognize them as a part and portion of the human family," said an 1849 police report describing the youths who filled the streets in the daytime. "Consisting mainly of small girls, one looks in vain for a single attribute of innocent childhood in their impertinent and persevering demands . . ." The police report despaired over citizens who gave small amounts of money to these impoverished children, warning that whatever "may be their gains during the day, the amount is almost ever spent during the night, in visiting the galleries of the minor theatres, or in the lowest dens of drunkenness and disease which abound in the 'Five Points,' and its vicinity . . ."

With seamstresses and other women working "respectable" jobs earning wages that brought them only hunger, some turned to prostitution, and the Five Points became known as a center of the sex trade. The numerous brothels outraged not only moralists, but also racists who deplored that white and black women plied their trade side-by-side, servicing customers of both races.

An 1834 riot broke out in the Five Points neighborhood partly in response to the anti-slavery evangelizing of prominent abolitionists Arthur and Lewis Tappan. Rumors spread among the Irish immigrants in the area that the Tappans had ordered their daughters to marry black men and that Arthur Tappan himself had divorced and married a black woman. Irish workers already competed with African Americans for the same low-wage jobs and feared that the Tappans were on a "race mixing" campaign to destroy their community. During the riot, whites lit candles and placed them in windows so mobs would leave them alone while black homes were looted and burned. African Americans in the street were beaten. Mobs hurled rocks at Arthur Tappan's store. The Five Points would also become the epicenter of New York City's 1863 racially-fueled Draft Riots, depicted in the 2002 film *Gangs of New York*. Irish immigrants erupted in violence as they faced being drafted to fight a war they feared would end slavery and bring black job competitors to New York City

The term "slum," which originally referred to a packed, dingy, and poorly-lit room, entered the American vocabulary in the 1840s, probably in reference to places like The Five Points. As part of the Age of Reform, religious evangelists, such as the members of the Episcopalian group the Ladies' Home Missionary Society, made saving souls in The Five Points a priority. To many such evangelicals, spreading the Gospel proved more urgent than addressing the racism and greed in such neighborhoods like The Five Points.

THOUGHT QUESTIONS:

1. What do conditions in The Five Points neighborhood in New York suggest about the condition of the working class in nineteenth-century America?

2. How did racial and class politics shape New York City's neglect of The Five Points?

3. What factors created the tensions between the Irish and African Americans in The Five Points?

Joseph Smith: American Prophet

The drastic social and economic changes of the early nineteenth century spawned the creation of numerous prophecy-centered, conservative religious movements. These movements sought to restore what they considered traditional values in an era of materialism, increasing urbanization, and the radical reform movements that demanded, among other things, an end to slavery.

The Church of Jesus Christ of Latter-day Saints, now better known as the Mormon Church, stands as one of the most distinctly American prophecy-shaped religious movements born at this time. Joseph Smith, Jr. was the son of a notably unsuccessful Vermont Baptist, who moved his family to a series of rented farms in a vain search for opportunity. The Smiths ended up in Palmyra, New York in 1820, where they faced eviction. Smith's family had never been intensely religious before, but hardships led Smith's mother and some of his sisters to start attending an evangelical Presbyterian church. Around this time, Smith said he received two visions featuring, first, a pillar of light and, then, God himself warning Smith away from existing religions and telling him to await further instructions. In 1827, Smith said, an angel called Moroni appeared to him and directed him to mysterious buried gold plates inscribed in a language unknown to the young man.

Through the help of this angel, Smith claimed, he translated these plates into English, words that became known as *The Book of Mormon*. His followers then established a new faith. The revelations Smith received found an audience among those uncomfortable with many of the era's social changes, such as the increased role played by women in Baptist and other churches. Smith preached that God had established men as the authority in each family as long as they respected women and children. He also claimed that some Native Americans descended from the so-called Lost Tribes of Israel—ten tribes from the ancient kingdom who lost their separate identity after conquest by the ancient Assyrian Empire. Smith said members of these tribes had traveled to the Americas and were preached to by Jesus after his crucifixion.

Smith's revelation stirred opposition from traditional Christians who objected to his claims of having received direct revelation from God, his insistence that his new sect was the only authentic version of Christianity, and the denomination's embrace of polygamy (allowing male members of the church to marry multiple women in the fashion of the Old Testament patriarchs).

Smith's flock faced hostility due to its unconventional beliefs. They migrated from New York to Ohio and then attempted to set up central headquarters in Independence, Missouri. Smith believed that this location was near where the Biblical Adam and Eve dwelled after their expulsion from the Garden of Eden. Smith taught that Jesus would gather the faithful there when Christ returned to earth. However, non-Mormons resented the presence of Smith and his followers. After skirmishes in which Mormons and non-Mormons exchanged gunfire, Governor Lilburn Boggs issued an executive order in which he declared that, "the Mormons must be treated as enemies, and must be exterminated or driven from the State if necessary."

The Mormons, as they came to be known, fled next to Illinois where they again found trouble. They established the village of Nauvoo, which drew converts from France, Germany, and thousands of recently baptized believers from the port city of Liverpool, England, where the new faith had found a receptive audience. Within five years, the town grew to a population of 12,000, almost the same size as Chicago at the time, and the Nauvoo economically prospered as well.

Like other non-Mormons (which Smith called "Gentiles") before them, residents of nearby Warsaw and Carthage saw Smith as a heretic, and they worried that Nauvoo would eclipse their communities economically and that it would soon dominate trade along that part of the Mississippi River. Smith also raised fears that he planned to establish a theocracy—a dictatorial government in which church and state are blended—when he created a Mormon militia and began to parade around in a colorful, self-designed military uniform. Recalling Boggs' "extermination order," Smith saw the church's army as a means of self-defense.

Mormons totally controlled Nauvoo's government, and the village's laws derived from church doctrine. Smith declared that the consumption of alcohol was a sin. No saloons, therefore, were allowed to open in Nauvoo. More controversial was Smith's 1843 announcement that God had revealed to him that the Lord desired the men of the church to have many wives and that their blessings in heaven would increase with the number of children they had. Before his death, Smith would have 27 wives. No official announcement of the revelation was made until the 1850s, but stories spread across the state of the Mormon "plural marriages." Tensions only increased when Boggs was a target of an attempted assassination. Many concluded Smith was behind the attempted murder and the destruction of the printing press at the *Nauvoo Expositor,* a newspaper that criticized Smith in its only edition.

Illinois Governor Thomas Ford ordered Smith to surrender to authorities in Carthage to face rioting charges. Smith and his brother Hyrum eventually surrendered. Late on the afternoon of June 27, 1844, a mob surrounded the Carthage jail. Breaking into the jail, assailants shot into the second-floor cell containing Joseph and Hyrum. Hyrum died in the cell from the gunfire. After being hit, Smith fell from a window to the street below, but he was propped up against a curb and shot again by a firing squad. About sixty men participated in the mob killing, and nine were eventually indicted, but courts convicted no one for the deed. The remaining Mormons again made a hurried exodus, finally settling in Utah.

In next half century, the Mormons established school systems, factories, mines, mills, and over 200 towns and cities in Utah, including Salt Lake City. After the church renounced plural marriage in 1890, Utah was admitted to the Union as the 45th state in 1896. By the second decade of the twenty-first century there were 15 million Mormons, more than half living outside of the United States.

THOUGHT QUESTIONS:

1. What social conditions contributed to the rise of Mormonism?

2. What provoked the fears non-Mormons held about Mormons?

3. What similarity is there between the reactions to the Church of Jesus Christ of Latter-Day Saints and the treatment of Jews, Catholics, and Muslims in American history?

Chapter 14

America Expands, 1840-1848

John O'Sullivan on Texas Annexation (1845)

*John O'Sullivan edited the **United States Democratic Review**, a publication associated with some of the more radical strains of Jacksonian thought. A university educated lawyer and son of an Irish immigrant, O'Sullivan made a name for himself by advocating America as an example of democracy to the world. "[F]reedom of conscience, freedom of person, freedom of trade and business pursuits, universality of freedom and equality," he wrote in 1837. "This is our high destiny, and in nature's eternal, inevitable decree of cause and effect we must accomplish it."*

In the selection here, O'Sullivan defended Texas annexation and coined the phrase that made him famous—manifest destiny. He also predicted the American acquisition of Texas, something that would not happen for another three years. His argument remains a powerful melding of expansionist land hunger with American democratic ideas.

It is time now for opposition to the Annexation of Texas to cease…. It is time for the common duty of Patriotism to the Country to succeed;—or if this claim will not be recognized, it is at least time for common sense to acquiesce with decent grace in the inevitable and irrevocable.

Texas is now ours. Already, before these words are written, her Convention has undoubtedly ratified the acceptance, by her Congress, of our proffered invitation into the Union…. It is time then that all should cease to treat her as alien….

Why … [are we] in favor of now elevating this question … out of the lower region of our past party dissensions, up to its proper level of a high and broad nationality, it surely is to be found ... in the manner in which other nations have undertaken to intrude themselves . . . in a spirit of hostile interference . . . for the avowed object of thwarting our policy and hampering our power, limiting our greatness and checking the fulfillment of our manifest destiny to overspread the continent allotted by Providence for the free development of our yearly multiplying millions. This we have seen done by England, our old rival and enemy; and by France, strangely coupled with her against us....

It is wholly untrue ... that the Annexation has been a measure of spoliation, unrightful and unrighteous—of military conquest under forms of peace and law—of territorial aggrandizement at the expense of justice.... The independence of Texas was complete and absolute. It was an independence, not only in fact but of right....

Texas has been absorbed into the Union in the inevitable fulfillment of the general law which is rolling our population westward; the connexion of which with that ratio of growth of population which is destined within a hundred years to swell our numbers to the enormous population of two hundred and fifty millions (if not more), is too evident to leave us in doubt of the manifest design of Providence in regard to the occupation of this continent.

California will, probably, next fall away.... Imbecile and distracted, Mexico never can exert any real government authority over such a country.... The Anglo-Saxon foot is already on its borders. Already the advance guard of the irresistible army of Anglo-Saxon emigration has begun to pour down upon it, armed with the plough and the rifle, and marking its trail with schools and colleges, courts and representative halls, mills and meeting-houses. A population will soon be in actual occupation of California, over which it will be idle for Mexico to dream of dominion. They will necessarily become independent. All this without the agency of our government, without responsibility of our people—in the natural flow of events.... And they will have a right to independence—to self-government—to the possession of the homes conquered from the wilderness by their own labors and dangers, sufferings and sacrifices.... Whether they will then attach themselves to our Union or not, is not to be predicted with certainty. Unless the projected railroad across the continent to the Pacific be carried into effect, perhaps they may not; though even in that case, the day is not distant when the Empires of the Atlantic and the Pacific would again flow together....

Source: John O'Sullivan, "Annexation," *United States Democratic Review* 17 (1845): 5–10.

THOUGHT QUESTIONS:

1. Why did O'Sullivan believe that nations such as England and France wanted to block the United States's annexation of Texas?

2. What relationships did O'Sullivan see between expansion, population growth, and divine providence?

3. Why did O'Sullivan predict that California would soon break away from Mexico? What does that prediction reveal about patterns of American expansion in the mid-nineteenth-century?

Walter Colton on the California Gold Rush

A native New Englander, Walter Colton served as **alcalde** *(judge) of Monterey, during the American occupation of California. He had been serving as a navy chaplain when his commanding officer appointed him to the post. Colton's new job positioned him to witness the events of the California Gold Rush in 1849-1850.*

The selections here, taken from Colton's book, **Three Years in California***, recount the flood of people that came to the new territory looking for gold. Colton also notes the diversity of the immigrants—they came from all over the world. Colton also noted the racial tensions that would come characterize labor relations in the American Far West.*

My messenger ... has returned [to Monterey] with specimens of the gold.... The excitement produced was intense; and many were soon busy in their hasty preparations for a departure to the mines. The family who had kept house for me caught the moving infection. Husband and wife were both packing up; the blacksmith dropped his hammer, the carpenter his plane, the mason his trowel, the farmer his sickle, the baker his loaf, and the tapster his bottle. All were off for the mines....

....

Some fifty thousand persons are drifting up and down these slopes of the great Sierra, of every hue, language, and clime, tumultuous and confused as a flock of wild geese taking wing at the crack of a gun.... All are in quest of gold; and, with eyes dilated to the circle of the moon, rush this way and that, as some new discovery, or fictitious tale of success may suggest. Some are with tents, and some without; some have provisions, and some are on their last ration; some are carrying crowbars; some pickaxes and spades; some washbowls and cradles; some hammers and drills, and powder enough to blow up the rock of Gibraltar—if they can but get under it....

...

Much has been said of the amounts of gold taken from the mines by Sonoranians [Mexicans], Chilians, and Peruvians, and carried out of the country. As a general fact, this apprehension and alarm is without any sound basis. Not one pound of gold in ten, gathered by these foreigners, is shipped off to their credit: it is spent in the country for provisions, clothing, and in the hazards of the gaming-table. It falls into the hands of those who command the avenues of commerce, and ultimately reaches our own mints. I have been in a camp of five hundred Sonoranians, who had not gold enough to buy a month's provisions—all had gone, through their improvident habits, to the capacious pockets of the Americans. To drive them out of California, or interdict their operations, is to abstract that amount of labor from the mines, and curtail proportionably the proceeds. If gold, slumbering in the river banks and mountains of California, be more valuable to us than when stamped into eagles and incorporated into our national currency, then drive out the Sonoranians: but if you would have it here and not there, let those diggers alone. When gold shall begin to fail, or require capital and machinery, you will want these hardy men to quarry the rocks and feed your stampers…. They will become the hewers of wood and drawers of water to American capital and enterprise….

…

The causes which exclude slavery from California lie within a nut-shell. All here are diggers, and free white diggers wont dig with slaves. They know they must dig themselves: they have come out here for that purpose, and they wont degrade their calling by associating it with slave-labor: self-preservation is the first law of nature. They have nothing to do with slavery in the abstract, or as it exists in other communities; not one in ten cares a button for its abolition, nor the Wilmot proviso either: all they look at is their own position; they must themselves swing the pick, and they wont swing it by the side of negro slaves. That is their feeling, their determination, and the upshot of the whole business…. You may call it pride, or what you will, but there it is—deep as the foundations of our nature, and unchangeable as the laws of its divine Author.

Source: Walter Colton, *Three Years in California* (New York, 1850), 256-247, 314, 367-368, 374-375.

THOUGHT QUESTIONS:

1. How did the discovery of gold affect Colton's community? How does he describe the people who came to mine gold?

2. Why did Colton oppose excluding the Sonoranians from the mines? Why did he reject the argument that they drained the community of resources, and what role did he expect them to play in California's future?

3. Why did California's miners reject slavery? Were they motivated by abolitionist sentiment?

Fiske William Hooker, On Life in Texas

Fiske William Hooker, a native Northerner, travelled to Texas to settle on land he had purchased from a land company. Upon his arrival, he learned he had been swindled, and his money was lost. Hooker decided to make the best of the situation and write a travel account of his time in Texas. He left Texas before its war for independence.

The selection focuses on Hooker's assessment of Texas's agricultural potential. He also provided some insight into racial relations in the American settlements in Texas.

Early in the month of March I reached New Orleans from the Northern States, on my way to Texas.

There was a vessel at that time preparing to sail for Brazoria, a place on the river Brazos; and I took passage on board....

... There was also a very intelligent man from Alabama, who had several negroes with him.... [H]e had learnt ... that slaves cannot be held in the Mexican territory, and had taken measures ... to evade the general law of abolition, which does so much honor to the patriots of that republic. He had obtained their attested signatures to articles of indenture, by which they bound themselves to serve him for ninety-nine years....

....

These regions [the Texas Gulf Coast] ... whose soil is generally rich, and often of almost incalculable fertility, present superior attractions to colonists. No forests are to be cleared away; and yet, in many places, there is sufficient wood for ... the climate. How many attractions does this splendid country appear at first sight to offer to a settler from our cold and Northern States! No rocky and barren ledges..., no steep acclivities..., no provision to be made for the housing of cattle; no raising, cutting, curing, removing, stowing, or feeding out of winter fodder... The whole business of raising cattle is of course reduced, as it was in the land of Canaan, to the simple operation of letting them take care of themselves.... Tillage is also reduced almost to its simplest form: for cotton is packed as soon as picked, and immediately transported to market; and as to the grain necessary for the colonist's use, although the scarcity of mills is at present a great inconvenience, the planting is often effected without preparing the ground, and the rearing always without hoeing. Vegetables are generally still more easily procured, and that in superabundance: for after having been once sowed, many kinds of useful kitchen plants and roots propagate themselves....

....

.... The caravans are often exposed to the attacks of Indians, who sometimes rob and even kill the owners. They therefore always go armed; and the conductor of one of these expeditions, accompanied by his servants, makes a formidable appearance. A great part of the attendants being Mexicans, however, they are probably more threatening than effective, at least if the common opinion of our countrymen who live among them is to be regarded, for they hold them in great contempt....[T]he Mexicans, although not very inferior in size, appear like a timid and inefficient race; and Indians are generally shot down without hesitation, whenever they present a fair mark, by any colonist who feels that acrimony against them which is apt to arise out of a sense of exposure to their attacks or ambushes. When they wander singly or in small parties far in the settlements, however, or when they are known to belong to certain tribes, they are not usually treated with unfriendliness, for then they are not expected to do injury....

The common wages given to Mexican servants are four dollars a month; but out of this contract abuses of a shameful nature too often arise. While a servant is in debt to his employer, the customs of the country allow the treatment of the former as a slave. He must continue the servant of that master until the debt is cancelled. Now the Mexicans being an ignorant, and apparently a harmless sort of people, sometimes incautiously receive supplies of cloths and other articles from their employers without counting the amount; and as the latter usually charge exorbitant prices—for instance, a dollar a yard for common muslin—the poor fellow is in danger of being in debt a considerable sum over and above his wages. After this it is frequently easy to postpone for a long time his discharge....

...

... At some of these houses, as in many of those in Texas generally, we found one or more negroes, held as slaves, although the laws of Mexico forbid it. The blacks are ignorant, the whites are generally in favor of slavery and ready to sustain the master in his usurped authority: the province is so distant from the capital, and had been for some time so little attended to by the government, that the laws on this subject were ineffectual.

Negroes are even publicly sold....

Source: [Fiske William Hooker,] *A Visit to Texas, Being the Journal of a Traveller through Those Parts Most Interesting to American Settlers with Descriptions of Scenery, Habits, etc., etc.,*2d ed. (New York, 1836), 1-2, 14-15, 177-178, 187.

THOUGHT QUESTIONS:

1. Hooker noted that slaveholding was common in Texas. How did Texas settlers evade the Mexican law? How often did they seem to do so?

2. How did Hooker describe the agricultural potential of Texas? How did farming there compare with farming in the North?

3. How did Hooker describe race relations in colonial Texas? How did the treatment of Mexicans and Native Americans differ from that of enslaved African Americans?

Vignettes

Lessons from the Mexican War

Although overshadowed in the public conscience by the Civil War, the Mexican War anticipated many of the issues raised by twentieth-century conflicts. Two stand out. First, Whigs and Democrats debated the extent of presidential war powers. Second, opponents of the war struggled to find a balance between criticism of the war and the appearance of disloyalty.

President Polk and his supporters portrayed the war as an act of self defense, claiming that Mexican troops attacked American ones on U.S. soil. Yet that incident occurred after months of provocative troop movements by U.S. forces, and Mexico did not respond until U.S. forces had moved more than 100 miles into territory it claimed and blocked access to the Rio Grande River. Polk's use of the military created a set of circumstances that made war very likely, perhaps inevitable. This behavior raised a constitutional issue. Could the president, as commander-and-chief, use troops in ways certain to provoke a war? Did such actions impinge on Congress's power to declare war? Opponents of the war thought the president had no such power—but they could not figure out how to check those exercises. Similar problems would confront Congress in the twentieth century, as its members struggled with American Wars in Asia and the Middle East. Placing limits on the president's commander-in-chief powers has proved to be exceedingly difficult.

Another problem that emerged centered on how to oppose the conflict in Congress. Abraham Lincoln's effort to do so proved unsuccessful, and he nearly destroyed his political career. Lincoln, then a first-term House member, introduced the so-called "Spot Resolutions" to compel Polk to prove that the "spot" where the war began was on U.S. soil. He failed. Supporters of the war ridiculed him (by calling him "spotty"), and he lost support at home. Lincoln served only one term in the House.

More than a decade later, Lincoln's position on the war still haunted him. Stephen Douglas made sure to remind voters when Lincoln ran against him for the Senate in 1858. Lincoln, "thought that war was unconstitutional, unnecessary, and unjust," Douglas said at one debate. The war "was not commenced on the right spot." According to Douglas, Lincoln believed Mexico was right, and he chose it over his own country. "It is one thing to be opposed to the declaration of a war, another and very different thing to take sides with the enemy against your own country after the war has been commenced." Lincoln lost that election as well, although he would later defeat Douglas to win the presidency.

The charge against Lincoln, however, showed the political utility of equating opposition to a war with disloyalty. And this charge has shown its usefulness over and over again. Supporters of World War I used it against their enemies, as did supporters of the Vietnam War, and the wars in Afghanistan and Iraq. But opposition such as Lincoln's also represented a fundamental feature of American democracy. Nations sometimes make the wrong choice, and people in office should try to hold them accountable, even if that means destroying their political careers.

THOUGHT QUESTIONS:

1. In what ways did the war with Mexico raise issues that are relevant to contemporary politics?

2. What was the potential constitutional problem with Polk's use of the military before the beginning of the Mexican War?

3. Why did Lincoln's position on the Mexican War cause so many problems for him in the 1840s and 1850s?

A Wife and Mother Succeeds in the California Gold Rush

As word of the discovery of gold in California spread eastward, people reacted in much the same way as people did in Walter Colton's Monterey. They dropped everything and struck out for the mines in the hope that they would become rich. Luzena Stanley Wilson's husband was one of them. In the 1880s, Wilson recounted her experiences of traveling to California and settling in the state with her husband and children. Her narrative illustrated the hardships of the overland trail as well as the economic opportunities California presented to people selling services to miners. In here narrative, Wilson presents herself as the main character—she never provides the names of her husband and children—whose determination kept the family going. The most interesting aspect of her story was not her description of the Overland Trail, but rather the ways in which she turned the domestic duties assigned to women—cooking and housekeeping—into major money-making enterprises in Gold-Rush Era California.

Immediately upon hearing of the gold discovery, Wilson's husband decided to head for California. Wilson insisted that she and the couple's two toddlers come along, lest they be left forever in Missouri. Within a few days, they had packed up everything they thought they needed and hit the Overland Trail. They were not the only ones. "Our train consisted only of six wagons," she later wrote, "but we were never alone. Ahead, as far as the eye could reach, a thin cloud of dust marked the route of the trains, and behind us, like the trail of a great serpent, it extended to the edge of civilization." The Wilsons were unusual among the travelers, since their group contained women and children. Indeed, one group heading to California refused to travel with them because they though Luzena and the kids would slow them down.

Traveling the Overland Trail, in Wilson's telling, generally proved to be dull. Life consisted of breaking camp in the morning, walking throughout the day, and striking camp in the evening or after dark. That process then repeated on the next day and the day after that—for three months. There were moments of excitement. Crossing rivers was difficult and dangerous. And Wilson reported a sense of terror when she encountered Native Americans. They surrounded her party shortly after they set out on the trail. She had heard stories all her life about their savagery, but the ones she met just wanted to trade. A three-day trek across the desert near the end of her journey also proved harrowing. All along the route, she saw signs of groups that failed—broken wagons, dried bones, and the like. She even encountered members of the group that had rejected them months earlier. Their mules had died, and they had run out of water. They were turning back, but she helped them by giving them some of her water.

Once in California, she quickly discovered that miners flush with gold would pay her to cook for them. They craved food prepared by women, but their camps were mostly filled with men. She could charge five dollars or more for something that would cost far less than one dollar in Missouri. She and her husband opened a hotel in Sacramento, but the town flooded, and they lost everything. The couple then borrowed enough money to move to Nevada City, and Wilson started another hotel, "and I shortly after took my husband into partnership." The establishment prospered, Wilson reported hosting "from seventy-five to two hundred boarders at twenty-five dollars a week." Wilson earned enough to pay back what they had borrowed. Then a fire destroyed the town. The couple then bought some land in the Vaca Valley, took up farming, and became permanent residents of California.

THOUGHT QUESTIONS:

1. How did Wilson's husband react when he heard about the discovery of gold in California? How did Wilson react and how quickly did they move?

2. How did Wilson describe life on the Overland Trail? What as the significance of her being a women among the travelers?

3. Why did Wilson manage to turn cooking and housekeeping into a way to make significant money in California? What does the reaction of the miners to her reveal about the number of women in early California?

Jose Maria Rodríguez: The Persistence of Mexican Landowners

When she settled in the Vaca Valley, Luzena Stanley Wilson reported that her nearest neighbors were Mexicans. One of them, Manuel Vaca, once owned the land that she and her family had settled. He left quite an impression. Wilson described him as "lord of the soil" who greeted her family "with all the ceremony and courtesy of a Spanish grandee." Over time, however, landowners like Vaca lost their land. "Mexican ... slothfulness and procrastination," Wilson wrote, "undermine[d] their financial stability, and they succumbed to the strategy and acuteness of the American trader." Wilson's account contained a great deal of racial and ethnic chauvinism, but she did describe a pattern of land loss that many Mexicans experienced in the wake of American expansion.

Yet Wilson did not describe a universal experience: Texas's Jose Maria Rodríguez and his family remained established and politically powerful well after the United States annexed the state. Rodríguez's family lived in San Antonio when the Texas Revolution broke out, when Jose was just a boy. Although they had lived in the area longer than their Anglo neighbors, Rodríguez's family sided with the Texans. Jose's father fought in the war and later opened a store in San Antonio.

When he was thirteen, Rodríguez attended a French-speaking school in New Orleans. He returned to San Antonio a few years later to work in his father's store. In 1854, when he was in his mid-twenties, Rodríguez entered politics and won election as an alderman. He later served as tax assessor and collector for Bexar County and then as an interpreter at Texas's secession convention. Rodríguez eventually moved to Laredo where he would serve as Webb County judge for thirty-four years. He also maintained his family land holdings and business interests (cattle ranching especially) until his death in the early twentieth century.

Rodríguez explicitly countered arguments similar to those made by Luzena Stanley Wilson about California's Mexican population. Speaking of Laredo and Webb County, Rodríguez said:

> The affairs of the City and County have always been in the hands of the Spanish speaking people, and the manner in which the affairs of that city and County have been managed is a complete answer to the proposition that the Spanish people cannot govern themselves under a Republican form of government.

By way of example, he noted that Laredo sent three companies to fight for the Confederacy during the Civil War. Webb County also built two courthouses and two jails during Rodríguez's tenure as judge, and they did so without incurring any debt. "That is a fairly good showing where 75 per cent of the County are of Mexican parentage and speak the Spanish language." Of course, there were a few Americans who "would rant at public meetings and declare that this was an American country and the Mexicans ought to be run out." But they did not get very far. "The Spanish families of the first class who live in Webb County, have been there over 150 years, and it hardly seems reasonable to suppose that they would voluntarily leave to please the strangers."

Thus a few families, those with resources and the ability to forge alliances with their new neighbors, managed to retain their wealth and power after the United States incorporated their territory. Their ability to do so, however, rested squarely on their relative economic privilege. Rodríguez observed that "humble and hardworking Mexican laborers" had much more difficult time. "I know of no class of men who are paid less for what they do than these poor men." Rodríguez's experience proved significantly different, and he remained quite aware of the class differences between him, and poorer Mexicans. But his experience also differed starkly from the one described by California's Luzena Stanley Wilson.

THOUGHT QUESTIONS:

1. How did the experience of Manuel Vaca and Jose Maria Rodríguez differ from one another?

2. How would you describe Rodríguez's educational and professional accomplishments?

3. How does Rodríguez describe citizenship in Laredo? How does this differ from other descriptions of citizenship during this period of U.S. history?

Chapter 15

Expansion, Slavery, and Secession: The Road to Civil War

Alexander Stephens, "Corner-Stone" Speech (1861)

After the Civil War, many southern writers and politicians argued that secession had very little to do with slavery. The conflict stemmed from an aggressive North's failure to respect its constitutional obligations and the sovereignty of the southern states. This line of argument allowed post-war southern intellectuals to portray the war as a noble, if lost, cause devoted to preserving a distinct, locally governed, deeply Christian civilization.

This speech, delivered on the eve of the Civil War by Alexander Stephens, Vice President of the newly created Confederate States of America, complicated that view. Stephens explained what he considered to be the Confederacy's improvements on the Constitution of the United States. Although he paid homage to the ideas of states' rights—noting limitations on national commerce power—Stephens emphasized that the real merit of the new government sat squarely on its support for slavery.

The new constitution has put at rest, forever, all the agitating questions relating to our peculiar institution—African slavery as it exists amongst us—the proper status of the negro in our form of civilization. This was the immediate cause of the late rupture and present revolution. Jefferson in his forecast, had anticipated this, as the "rock upon which the old Union would split." He was right. What was conjecture with him, is now a realized fact. But whether he fully comprehended the great truth upon which that rock stood and stands, may be doubted. The prevailing ideas entertained by him and most of the leading statesmen at the time of the formation of the old constitution, were that the enslavement of the African was in violation of the laws of nature; that it was wrong in principle, socially, morally, and politically....

Those ideas, however, were fundamentally wrong. They rested upon the assumption of the equality of races....

Our new government is founded upon exactly the opposite idea; its foundations are laid, its corner-stone rests upon the great truth, that the negro is not equal to the white man; that slavery—subordination to the superior race—is his natural and normal condition. [Applause.]

This, our new government, is the first, in the history of the world, based upon this great physical, philosophical, and moral truth. This truth has been slow in the process of its development, like all other truths in the various departments of science.... Those at the North, who still cling to these errors, with a zeal above knowledge, we justly denominate fanatics. All fanaticism springs from an aberration of the mind—from a defect in reasoning.... They assume that the negro is equal, and hence conclude that he is entitled to equal privileges and rights with the white man. If their premises were correct, their conclusions would be logical and just—but their premise being wrong, their whole argument fails.... They were attempting to make things equal which the Creator had made unequal.

In the conflict thus far, success has been on our side, complete throughout the length and breadth of the Confederate States. It is upon this, as I have stated, our social fabric is firmly planted; and I cannot permit myself to doubt the ultimate success of a full recognition of this principle throughout the civilized and enlightened world.

As I have stated, the truth of this principle may be slow in development, as all truths are and ever have been, in the various branches of science. It was so with the principles announced by Galileo—it was so with Adam Smith and his principles of political economy.... May we not, therefore, look with confidence to the ultimate universal acknowledgment of the truths upon which our system rests? It is the first government ever instituted upon the principles in strict conformity to nature, and the ordination of Providence, in furnishing the materials of human society. Many governments have been founded upon the principle of the subordination and serfdom of certain classes of the same race; such were and are in violation of the laws of nature. Our system commits no such violation of nature's laws. With us, all of the white race, however high or low, rich or poor, are equal in the eye of the law. Not so with the negro. Subordination is his place. He, by nature, or by the curse against Canaan, is fitted for that condition which he occupies in our system....

Source: Alexander Stephens, "Speech Delivered on the 21st of March, 1861, in Savannah, Known as the 'Corner-Stone' Reported in the Savannah Republican, in Henry Cleveland, ed., *Alexander Stephens in Public and Private, with Letters and Speeches, before, during, and after the War* (Philadelphia, 1866), 721-723.

THOUGHT QUESTIONS:

1. How did Alexander Stephens portray the ideas about slavery contained in the original constitution?

2. How did the Confederate Constitution differ from the older one, and what did Stephens mean when he discussed the corner-stone of the new government?

3. Many critics of slavery argued that it was a backward institution and fundamentally out of step with modern society. Did Stephens agree? How did he describe slavery?

Harriet Jacobs on Racial Prejudice in the North

Writing under the name of Linda Brent, Harriet Jacobs wrote one of the most powerful slave narratives of the nineteenth century. Her **Incidents in the Life of a Slave Girl** *recounted her experience as an enslaved woman who worked as a house servant before she escaped to the North. When she reached the age of fifteen, her master stalked her in a tireless effort to get her into bed—it was very important to him that she go willingly. He followed her around. He wrote her lurid letters when he learned she could read. Linda finally responded by sleeping with different white man and having children by him. She cited this experience as evidence of slavery's power to corrupt those who lived under it.*

An overlooked part of **Incidents**, *however, focused on Linda's experiences in the North, where she worked as a nanny (or, nurse, in her words). Although she was not a slave, she did not truly experience freedom until she left the United States. This passage recounts some of her travel with the Bruce family, who employed her after her escape from slavery.*

We went to Albany in the steamboat Knickerbocker. When the gong sounded for tea, Mrs. Bruce said, "Linda, it is late, and you and baby had better come to the table with me." I replied, "I know it is time baby had her supper, but I had rather not go with you, if you please. I am afraid of being insulted." "O no, not if you are with me," she said. I saw several white nurses go with their ladies, and I ventured to do the same. We were at the extreme end of the table. I was no sooner seated, than a gruff voice said, "Get up! You know you are not allowed to sit here." I looked up, and, to my astonishment and indignation, saw that the speaker was a colored man. If his office required him to enforce the by-laws of the boat, he might, at least, have done it politely. I replied, "I shall not get up, unless the captain comes and takes me up." No cup of tea was offered me, but Mrs. Bruce handed me hers and called for another. I looked to see whether the other nurses were treated in a similar manner. They were all properly waited on....

....

We reached Rockaway before dark, and put up at the Pavilion.... Thirty or forty nurses were there, of a great variety of nations.... I was the only nurse tinged with the blood of Africa.... I took little Mary and followed the other nurses. Supper was served in a long hall. A young man...pointed me to a seat at the lower end of it.... I sat down and took the child in my lap. Whereupon the young man came to me and said, in the blandest manner possible, "Will you please to seat the little girl in the chair, and stand behind it and feed her? After they have done, you will be shown to the kitchen, where you will have a good supper."

This was the climax! I found it hard to preserve my self-control, when I looked round, and saw women who were nurses, as I was, and only one shade lighter in complexion, eyeing me with a defiant look, as if my presence were a contamination. However, I said nothing. I quietly took the child in my arms, went to our room, and refused to go to the table again. Mr. Bruce ordered meals to be sent to the room for little Mary and I. This answered for a few days; but the waiters of the establishment were white, and they soon began to complain, saying they were not hired to wait on negroes....

....

We sailed from New York, and arrived in Liverpool.... We proceeded directly to London.... For the first time in my life I was in a place where I was treated according to my deportment, without reference to my complexion. I felt as if a great millstone had been lifted from my breast. Ensconced in a pleasant room, with my dear little charge, I laid my head on my pillow, for the first time, with the delightful consciousness of pure, unadulterated freedom.

....

We next went to Steventon, in Berkshire. It was a small town, said to be the poorest in the county. I saw men working in the fields for six shillings, and seven shillings, a week, and women for sixpence, and sevenpence, a day, out of which they boarded themselves. Of course they lived in the most primitive manner; it could not be otherwise, where a woman's wages for an entire day were not sufficient to buy a pound of meat. They paid very low rents, and their clothes were made of the cheapest fabrics, though much better than could have been procured in the United States for the same money. I had heard much about the oppression of the poor in Europe. The people I saw around me were, many of them, among the poorest poor. But when I visited them in their little thatched cottages, I felt that the condition of even the meanest and most ignorant among them was vastly superior to the condition of the most favored slaves in America.... The father, when he closed his cottage door, felt safe with his family around him. No master or overseer could come and take from him his wife, or his daughter.... The relations of husband and wife, parent and child, were too sacred for the richest noble in the land to violate with impunity.

Source: Linda Brent [Harriet Jacobs], *Incidents in the Life of a Slavery Girl*, ed. L. Maria Child (Boston, 1861), 264-266, 275-277.

THOUGHT QUESTIONS:

1. Alexander Stephens argued in his Corner-Stone Speech that northern society had embraced racial equality. How does this selection by Harriet Jacobs complicate that argument?

2. How did the other nurses and servants treat Harriet Jacobs, and what does that treatment reveal about race relations in the pre-Civil War North?

3. What aspect of her trip to England did Harriet Jacobs consider to be most significant?

Stephen Douglass on Racial Equality (1858)

In the summer of 1858, Stephen Douglas ran for reelection to the United States Senate, where he had represented Illinois. Douglas by the mid-1850s had emerged as the North's most prominent Democratic politician, but his status came with a great deal of controversy. In 1854, Douglas engineered the Missouri Compromise's repeal and replacement with popular sovereignty. His action delighted Southerners who hoped to bring another slave state into the Union. Many Northerners were horrified—and they flocked to the new Republican Party, which opposed the extension of slavery. Then in 1857, Douglas opposed the admission of Kansas as a slave state, alienating many Southerners.

When he ran for reelection, Douglas faced Abraham Lincoln, an obscure and generally unsuccessful politician, who had joined the new Republican Party. Douglas's tactic in this election was to paint Lincoln and the Republicans as extremists. He did so by playing racial politics and portraying Lincoln as an advocate of racial equality.

I must now bestow a few words upon Mr. Lincoln's main objection to the Dred Scott decision.... [W]hy? Because he says that that decision deprives the negro of the benefits of that clause of the Constitution of the United States which entitles the citizens of each State to all the privileges and immunities of citizens of the several States. Well, it is very true that the decision does have that effect. By deciding that a negro is not a citizen, of course it denies to him the rights and privileges awarded to citizens of the United States. It is this that Mr. Lincoln will not submit to.... I have not the slightest idea but that he conscientiously believes that a negro ought to enjoy and exercise all the rights and privileges given to white men; but I do not agree with him.... I believe that this Government of ours was founded on the white basis. I believe that it was established by white men, by men of European birth, or descended of European races, for the benefit of white men and their posterity in all time to come. I do not believe that it was the design or intention of the signers of the Declaration of Independence or the framers of the Constitution to include negroes, Indians, or other inferior races, with white men, as citizens.... Our fathers...from the time they planted foot on the American continent, not only those who landed at Jamestown, but at Plymouth Rock, ... pursued the policy of confining civil and political rights to the white race, and excluding the negro in all cases. Still, Mr. Lincoln conscientiously believes that it is his duty to advocate negro citizenship. He wants to give the negro the privilege of citizenship.... In other words, he is willing to give the negro an equality under the law.... He says that, by the Declaration of Independence, therefore, all kinds of men, negroes included, were created equal and endowed by their Creator with certain inalienable rights, and, further, that the right of the negro to be on an equality with the white man is a divine right, conferred by the Almighty.... In order to accomplish this, the first thing that would have to be done, in this State would be to blot out of our State Constitution that clause which prohibits negroes from coming into this State and making it an African colony, and permit them to come and spread over these charming prairies until in midday they shall look black as night.... He wants them to vote.... He is going to bring negroes here, and give them the right of citizenship, the right of voting, and the right of holding office and sitting on juries; and what else? Why, he would permit them to marry, would he not? And if he gives them that right, I suppose he will let them marry whom they please, provided they marry their equals. If the divine law declares that the white man is the equal of the negro woman, that they are on a perfect equality, I suppose he admits the right of the negro woman to marry the white man....

Well, I confess to you, my fellow-citizens, that I am utterly opposed to that system of Abolition philosophy. I do not believe that the signers of the Declaration of Independence had any reference to negroes when they used the expression that all men were created equal, or that they had any reference to the Chinese or Coolies, the Indians, the Japanese, or any other inferior race. They were speaking of the white race, the European race on this continent, and their descendants, and emigrants who should come here. They were speaking only of the white race, and never dreamed that their language would be construed to include the negro....

Source: Stephen A. Douglas, Speech on the Occasion of Hist Public Reception at Chicago, July 9, 1858, in *Political Debates between Abraham Lincoln and Stephen A. Douglas in the Celebrated Campaign of 1858 in Illinois, including the Preceding Speeches of Each at Chicago and Springfield, etc., also the Two Great Speeches of Abraham Lincoln in Ohio in 1859* (Cleveland, OH, 1894), 46-48.

THOUGHT QUESTIONS:

1. Alexander Stephens argued that the Framers believed in racial equality. Did Douglas agree? How did he portray the Framers' attitude toward race?

2. Why did Douglas believe Lincoln rejected the *Dred Scott* decision, and what position did he accuse Lincoln of advocating?

3. What did Douglas say would happen in Illinois if Lincoln got his way? Does this argument provide more support for the ones made by Alexander Stephens or Harriet Jacobs?

Vignettes

Two Marriages That Led to *Dred Scott*

More than one-hundred-and-fifty years have passed since the Supreme Court ruled in *Dred Scott v. Sanford*, but it remains one of the most reviled legal rulings in American history. The case played a key role in the string of events that led to the Civil War, but its origins lay in the decisions of two couples—Dred Scott and Harriet Robinson and Irene Emerson and Calvin C. Chafee—to marry.

Sometime in the mid-1830s, Dred and Harriet Scott met and married at Fort Snelling, a frontier army base located in present-day Minnesota. Although the post sat in territory closed to slavery by the Missouri Compromise, Dred's owner, army surgeon Dr. John Emerson, brought him along anyway. Officers often brought enslaved people to wait on them—slaveowning provided a way to mark the social distance between enlisted men and officers in the small posts along the frontier.

Dred Scott was not the only enslaved person at Fort Snelling. Harriet Robinson, an enslaved woman claimed by Lawrence Taliaferro, had been living at the post a few years along with a few other enslaved people. Soon after he arrived, Dred and Harriet wed and seemed to live as if they were free. Taliaferro, the local justice of the peace, married them in a civil ceremony, which were not generally available to enslaved people. Records also indicated that they maintained their own household, and Emerson at times left the couple at Fort Snelling when he served at other posts. But Emerson never gave up his claims of ownership. In fact, he purchased Harriet from Taliaferro, and he ultimately moved the couple to St. Louis.

After Emerson died, Dred and Harriet Scott sued his widow, Irene Emerson, for their freedom. They may have been worried that their family, which now included two daughters, would be sold and split to settle Emerson's estate. And Missouri law gave them a strong case. They had resided for years in free territory—and Dred had lived with Emerson in Illinois as well as at Fort Snelling. Missouri's courts since the 1820s had produced a steady stream of rulings that held even brief stays (anything more than a necessary delay, in fact) could create a freedom claim. At least one person freed by the court had resided at Fort Snelling.

When Dred and Harriet's case, *Scott v. Emerson*, came before the Missouri Supreme Court in 1852, however, the judges reversed course and refused to free the couple. "Time are not now what they were when the previous decisions were made," the Court said. Abolition sentiment had poisoned relations between the North and the South, and slaveholding states had to defend themselves. Missouri's judges would make their stand here. The Court also issued its ruling in a way that only involved state law, which meant the Scotts had no option to appeal to the United States Supreme Court. The Scotts' prospect for freedom thus looked dim.

But then another marriage took place, opening a new avenue to continue the suit. Emerson's widow, Irene married Calvin C. Chafee. Chafee, an antislavery politician and part of Massachusetts's delegation in the House of Representative, did not approve of slaveholding. So Irene transferred control of the Scotts to her brother, John F.A. Sanford. Because Sanford lived in New York, the Scotts could sue him for their freedom. Under the Constitution, citizens from different states could sue each other in the federal courts, which provided a neutral forum. The Scotts thus claimed citizenship in Missouri and sued Sanford.

Ultimately, the United States Supreme Court ruled against the Scotts. The Supreme Court used their case to rule that no black person, free or enslaved, could be a citizen of the United States and to find the Missouri Compromise unconstitutional. The case helped set the stage for Abraham Lincoln's rise to prominence and intensified the tensions that led to the Civil War. But this case might have never come about had it not been for the marriage of an enslaved couple in free territory and the marriage of a slaveholding wife and an antislavery husband.

THOUGHT QUESTIONS:

1. How did the Dred and Harriet Scott's experiences at Fort Snelling differ from the ways in which slavery is generally portrayed in the textbook?

2. Why did Dred and Harriet believe that they had a claim to freedom under Missouri law? Why did the state Supreme Court change the law it finally ruled in their case?

3. What was the significance of Irene Emerson's marriage to Calvin Chafee for Dred and Harriet Scott's case? Does the example provided her provide any insight into the capacity of ordinary people to alter the course of history?

Harriet Beecher Stowe's Achievement

Harriet Beecher Stowe's novel, *Uncle Tom's Cabin* (1852), succeeded where much abolitionist writing had failed in the decades before the Civil War. Her book moved a mass audience of northern readers to sympathize with the sufferings of enslaved blacks in the South.

Abolitionist writing generally reached an audience of readers already converted to the cause. Their accounts contained lurid depictions of violence that non-abolitionist readers found off putting. A single example should suffice. In her contribution to *American Slavery as It Is* (1839)—essentially a book of examples for abolitionist lecturers—Angelina Grimké described the treatment of house servants in her native South Carolina. House servants, she wrote, often could not reenter the residence for days after being whipped. "The putrid flesh of their lacerated backs" produced a "smell ... too horrible to be endured."

Stowe drew upon much of this material for *Uncle Tom's Cabin*, but she told her story in a manner that emphasized the inner character of her subjects rather than the brutalization of their bodies. She introduced Tom, one of the novel's main characters, by having Mr. Shelby, his original owner, describe what defined him. "Tom is a good, steady, sensible, pious fellow." He was a sincere Christian, and Shelby "trusted him ... with everything I have,—money, house, horses." Shelby even sent him to Cincinnati on business, knowing that he would not run away. The novel the goes on to show how slavery destroyed this good man.

One of the sources Stowe used to develop Uncle Tom was Josiah Henson's *The Life of Josiah Henson, Formerly a Slave, Now an Inhabitant of Canada* (1849). Henson, born enslaved in Maryland, converted to Christianity and served his master dutifully—to the point that he refused to run away when sent into free territory (although he later did so when he and his family faced the prospect of being sold into the Deep South). Stowe used aspects of Henson's narrative to highlight the essential decency of Uncle Tom and to underscore the destructive power of enslavement.

Henson's narrative, which emphasized many of the same points as did Stowe, opened with an horrific incident of violence, separation, and corruption:

> I was born.... The only incident I can remember ... was the appearance of my father ... with his head bloody and his back lacerated.... His right ear had been cut off ... and he had received a hundred lashes on his back. He had beaten the overseer for a brutal assault [i.e., rape] on my mother, and this was his punishment. Furious at such treatment, my father became a different man, and was so morose, disobedient, and intractable, that Mr. N. determined to sell him.... [N] either my mother nor I, ever heard of him again. He was naturally ... a man of amiable temper ... but it is not strange that he should be essentially changed by such cruelty and injustice under the sanction of law.

In contrast, Stowe's fictional narrative proceeded for seventeen chapters before showing any violence—and that was an act of self-defense by runaways confronting slave-hunters on northern soil. Before she got to that point, however, Stowe spent a great deal of time exploring the slave trade and developing her characters by narrating their reactions to it. Stowe took her time and delivered a scathing indictment of slavery. She stated her point early in the book:

> So long as the law considers all these human beings, with beating hearts and living affections, only as so many things belonging to a master,—so long as the failure, or misfortune, or imprudence, or death of the kindest owner, may cause them any day to exchange a life of kind protection and indulgence for one of hopeless misery and toil.

She then developed that point by investing in the emotional world of her main characters—Uncle Tom, a dutiful Christian man sold into slavery by a well meaning, but financially pressed owner, and Eliza, a Christian mother driven to run away to save her son from being sold by that same owner. By proceeding in this way, Stowe drew northern readers through abolitionist arguments in a manner that elicited sympathy for the plight of enslaved Americans.

THOUGHT QUESTIONS:

1. What features limited the reach of abolitionist literature to northern readers?

2. How did Harriet Beecher Stowe use abolitionist literature, and how did her approach differ from that of other antislavery writers?

3. How did Stowe's approach to writing *Uncle Tom's Cabin* make her argument more appealing to northern readers? What did she argue?

Whiteness in Antebellum America

"I believe," Stephen Douglas said over and over again in his debates with Abraham Lincoln in 1858, "that this Government of ours was founded on the white basis." He meant that the government "was established...for the benefit of white men and their posterity in all time to come." The Framers, he thought, never intended "to include negroes, Indians, or other inferior races, with white men, as citizens."

Many readers today (rightly) recoil at such language—just as Lincoln did when he heard it. But Douglas exposed a key dynamic of American politics. He used phrases like "white basis," "white men," "European birth," and "European races" to connote a common identity, which gave the people who claimed it access to privileges denied to others. Although awareness of color differences was nothing new in the United States, whiteness offered a way to navigate ethnic tensions in the pre-Civil War North.

Nineteenth-century Americans often emphasized ethnic differences among people who would later identify themselves as whites—and usually that emphasis implied (or asserted) the superiority of some groups over others. John O'Sullivan, a Democratic proponent of Manifest Destiny and the Mexican War, illustrated the point when he remarked in 1845 on a group of Americans rushing toward California. "Already the advance guard of the irresistible army of Anglo-Saxon emigration has begun to pour down upon it, armed with the plough and the rifle, and marking its trail with schools and colleges, courts and representative halls, mills and meeting-houses." The term Anglo-Saxon did not merely mean white—it meant English and Protestant. And Sullivan explicitly portrayed those identities as better than Mexican and Catholic. Sullivan also wrote on the eve of a surge immigration, which brought large numbers of German and Irish Catholics to the United States.

Irish immigrants drew a great deal of hostility for a variety of reasons. Upper-class Americans despised them for their poverty (the Irish came to the United States to escape famine at home). Yet employers hired them because the Irish would accept lower wages than native-born workers. Native-born workers resented the Irish because the newcomers undercut them in the labor market. Protestant Americans found the Irish's Catholicism to be problematic. Irish Catholics would put their fidelity to the Pope over their allegiance to the Constitution. All of these currents fed into the nativism—calls for the exclusion or subordination of newly arrived ethnic and religious groups—that roiled politics in the American North in the 1840s and 1850s.

White identity provided both immigrants and native-born politicians a way through this morass. For the Irish, whiteness gave them a claim against economic and political exclusion. Whites had a right to compete for all jobs to which they were qualified. Whites had a right to live where they wanted, assuming they had the money to do so. Whites had the right to vote and hold office. All of those privileges were up for grabs to Irish in the mid-nineteenth century. For native-born politicians, like Stephen Douglas, whiteness provided a common ground to build coalitions. "European races" (different ethnic groups) were a diverse lot, but they all shared a common trait. They were white, and as such, they were entitled to better treatment than people of color. Banding together against advocates of racial equality, which was how Douglas misleadingly portrayed Lincoln, ensured that those privileges would be protected.

The white identity that Douglas invoked, however, was never universally accepted. Crowds occasionally heckled him for criticizing racial equality. And the identity itself proved to be especially malleable. Lincoln had his own version of whiteness, which assumed whites to be superior but did not call for the enslavement or exclusion of African Americans. A few non-whites also bought into the concept. Norman Assing, a Chinese immigrant who became a naturalized citizen in South Carolina before he moved to California in the 1850s, criticized the new state's governor for calling for the exclusion and subordination of Chinese immigrants:

> [W]e ... remind you that when your nation was a wilderness, and the nation from which you sprung barbarous, we exercised most of the arts and virtues of civilized life.... [W]e are not the degraded race you would make us. We came amongst you as mechanics or traders, and following every honorable business of life.... As far as regards the color and complexion of our race, we are perfectly aware that our population have been a little more tan than yours.

Assing went on to assert that Chinese immigrants were "as much allied to the African race and the red man as you are yourself." His plea failed, and the Chinese faced exclusion on the West Coast. Most other non-white leaders advocated equality, not hierarchy. But many whites exhibited a growing comfort with a system of racial hierarchy at the core of a democratic republic.

THOUGHT QUESTIONS:

1. What political benefit did Douglas gain when he emphasized that the United States was created for the benefit of white men? How did the identity of whiteness differ from other identities (like Anglo-Saxon)?

2. What benefit did groups like the Irish, or perhaps the Chinese, hope to gain by identifying as white (or tan)?

3. In what ways did people contest the identity of whiteness in the pre-Civil War period?

Chapter 16

The American Civil War, 1861-1865

Sam R. Watkins Recounts the Battle of Shiloh

Private (later Corporal) Sam R. Watkins served the entirety of the Civil War with the First Tennessee Regiment. Twenty years later, he wrote a memoir of his experience as a private soldier, who did all of the fighting and marching and digging in exchange for very little glory. His surprisingly light-hearted account describes the terror of battle, the boredom of camp life, the stench of hospitals, and the morale of soldiers under different generals. White male Confederate soldiers died in horrific numbers during the Civil War (one died for every five who served), and the experience of Watkins's regiment confirm that statistic. At its height, his regiment numbered around 3,200 men, but when the army surrendered, only 65 remained. Not all of those men died. Many deserted, languished in hospitals, or had become separated from their units in the chaotic days at the end of the war. But the deaths of the men he served alongside appear regularly throughout his memoir.

The selection that follows recounts Watkins's experience in the Battle of Shiloh, which was his first major engagement. Shiloh was also one of the first battles that illustrated the level of violence the Civil War would unleash.

This was the first big battle in which our regiment had ever been engaged. I do not pretend to tell of what command distinguished itself; of heroes; of blood and wounds; of shrieks and groans; of brilliant charges; of cannon captured, etc. I was but a private soldier, and if I happened to look to see if I could find out anything, "Eyes right, guide center," was the order. "Close up, guide right, halt, forward, right oblique, left oblique, halt, forward, guide center, eyes right, dress up promptly in the rear, steady, double quick, charge bayonets, fire at will," is about all that a private soldier ever knows of a battle....

I had heard and read of battlefields, seen pictures of battlefields, of horses and men, of cannon and wagons, all jumbled together, while the ground was strewn with dead and dying and wounded, but I must confess that I never realized the "pomp and circumstance" of the thing called glorious war until I saw this[.] Men were lying in every conceivable position; the dead lying with their eyes wide open, the wounded begging piteously for help, and some waving their hats and shouting to us to go forward. It all seemed to me a dream ; I seemed to be in a sort of haze, when siz, siz, siz, the minnie balls from the Yankee line began to whistle around our ears....

Down would drop first one fellow and then another, either killed or wounded, when we were ordered to charge bayonets. I had been feeling mean all the morning as if I had stolen a sheep, but when the order to charge was given, I got happy. I felt happier than a fellow does when he professes religion at a big Methodist camp-meeting. I shouted. It was fun then. Everybody looked happy. We were crowding them. One more charge, then their lines waver and break. They retreat in wild confusion. We were jubilant; we were triumphant. Officers could not curb the men to keep in line. Discharge after discharge was poured into the retreating line. The Federal dead and wounded covered the ground.

When in the very midst of our victory, here comes an order to halt. What! halt after to-day's victory? Sidney Johnson killed, General Gladden killed, and a host of generals and other brave men killed, and the whole Yankee army in full retreat.

These four letters, h-a-l-t, O, how harsh they did break upon our ears. The victory was complete, but the word "halt" turned victory into defeat.

The soldiers had passed through the Yankee camps and saw all the good things that they had to eat in their sutlers' stores and officers' marquees, and it was but a short time before every soldier was rummaging to see what he could find.

The harvest was great and the laborers were not few.

The negro boys, who were with their young masters as servants, got rich. Greenbacks were plentiful, good clothes were plentiful, rations were not in demand. The boys were in clover.

This was Sunday.

On Monday the tide was reversed.

Now, those Yankees were whipped, fairly whipped, and according to all the rules of war they ought to have retreated.

But they didn't. Flushed with their victories at Fort Henry and Fort Donelson and the capture of Nashville, and the whole State of Tennessee having fallen into their hands, victory was again to perch upon their banners, for Buell's army, by forced marches, had come to Grant's assistance at the eleventh hour.

Gunboats and transports were busily crossing Buell's army all of Sunday night. We could hear their boats ringing their bells, and hear the puff of smoke and steam from their boilers. Our regiment was the advance outpost, and we saw the skirmish line of the Federals advancing and then their main line and then their artillery. We made a good fight on Monday morning, and I was taken by surprise when the order came for us to retreat instead of advance. But as I said before, reader, a private soldier is but an automaton, and knows nothing of what is going on among the generals, and I am only giving the chronicles of little things and events that came under my own observation as I saw them then and remember them now. Should you desire to find out more about the battle, I refer you to history.

Source: Sam R. Watkins, *"Co. Aytch": Maury Grays, the First Tennessee Regiment: Or, a Side Show of the Big Show,* 2d ed. (Chattanooga, TN, 1900), 31, 33-34.

THOUGHT QUESTIONS:

1. What did Watkins claim to see in the battle? How does he describe his attitude?

2. What surprised Watkins on the first day of fighting? What does that say about his point of view as a private soldier in the war?

3. How did things change on the second day of fighting?

Abraham Lincoln on Ending Slavery, August 1862

*By the summer of 1862, the Civil War had developed into a bloody stalemate. Prospects for a Union victory looked increasingly bleak. President Lincoln faced mounting calls to move against slavery as a way to break southern resistance. He also felt pressure to keep slaveholding border states loyal to the Union by not pushing for emancipation. In this document, Lincoln responded to an open letter by Horace Greeley, Republican editor of the influential **New York Tribune**. Greeley accused Lincoln of pursuing a policy that appeased "certain fossil politicians hailing from the Border States." Appeasing them meant that Lincoln had become "strangely and dangerously remiss in…your official …duty with regard to the emancipating provisions of the New Confiscation Act." That law freed enslaved people loyal to the Union and placed them in service to the Union. But Lincoln seemed in no rush to enforce it. "We complain that the Union cause has suffered…from mistaken deference to Rebel Slavery." A few days later, Lincoln responded and outlined his thinking on slavery's role in the war effort. A few weeks after Lincoln wrote this letter, he gave notice to the South that he intended to issue the Emancipation Proclamation.*

I have just read yours of the 19th. addressed to myself through THE N. Y. TRIBUNE.... As to the policy I "seem to be pursuing," as you say, I have not meant to leave any one in doubt.

I would save the Union. I would save it the shortest way under the Constitution. The sooner the national authority can be restored; the nearer the Union will be "the Union as it was." If there be those who would not save the Union, unless they could at the same time *save* slavery, I do not agree with them. If there be those who would not save the Union unless they could at the same time *destroy* slavery, I do not agree with them. My paramount object in this struggle is to save the Union, and is *not* either to save or to destroy slavery. If I could save the Union without freeing *any* slave I would do it, and if I could save it by freeing *all* the slaves I would do it; and if I could save it by freeing some and leaving others alone I would also do that. What I do about Slavery, and the colored race, I do because I believe it helps to save the Union; and what I forbear, I forbear because I do not believe it would help to save the Union.... I have here stated my purpose according to my view of *official* duty; and I intend no modification of my oft-expressed *personal* wish that all men everywhere could be free.

Source: "President Lincoln's Letter," *New-York Daily Tribune*, August 25, 1862, 4.

THOUGHT QUESTIONS:

1. What is Lincoln's main goal in the Civil War?

2. How does Lincoln describe his official stance toward slavery?

3. Why would Lincoln close with a statement about his "personal wish" that slavery end? Was he telegraphing the emancipation proclamation or just deflecting potential criticism?

Louisa May Alcott: Civil War Nurse

*Louisa May Alcott, best known as the author of **Little Women** (1868), grew up among the New England intelligentsia. Her father had moved the family from Pennsylvania to Boston to establish a school with experimental teaching methods. The school failed, but the family became associated with the transcendelist movement. Alcott thus received an education from Ralph Waldo Emerson and Henry David Thoreau, among others. She also embraced numerous reform movements. She was an abolitionist and wrote proudly of her caring for an African-American toddler that the nurses she worked with scorned. She also described herself as "a women's rights woman."*

*Unwilling to marry and tired of teaching for a living, Alcott worked as a nurse in Washington, D.C., caring for wounded soldiers, a job many women took during the Civil War. Her letters home became the source for her semi-fictional book, **Hospital Sketches** (1863). In it, she recounts the suffering of soldiers as they waited to recuperate (or die) and sometimes bumbling but well-meaning efforts of the hospital's staff. The passage that follows recounts the main character's first day on the job. The soldiers she aided had just come from the Battle of Fredericksburg, which had been a bloody loss for the Union.*

I progressed by slow stages up stairs and down, till the main hall was reached, and I paused to take breath and a survey. There they were! "our brave boys," as the papers justly call them, for cowards could hardly have been so riddled with shot and shell, so torn and shattered, nor have borne suffering for which we have no name, with an uncomplaining fortitude, which made one glad to cherish each as a brother. In they came, some on stretchers, some in men's arms, some feebly staggering along propped on rude crutches, and one lay stark and still with covered face, as a comrade gave his name to be recorded before they carried him away to the dead house. All was hurry and confusion; the hall was full of these wrecks of humanity, for the most exhausted could not reach a bed till duly ticketed and registered; the walls were lined with rows of such as could sit, the floor covered with the more disabled....

The sight of several stretchers, each with its legless, armless, or desperately wounded occupant, entering my ward, admonished me that I was there to work, not to wonder or weep; so I corked up my feelings, and returned to the path of duty, which was rather " a hard road to travel " just then.... Miss Blank tore me from my refuge behind piles of one-sleeved shirts, odd socks, bandages and lint; put basin, sponge, towels, and a block of brown soap into my hands, with these appalling directions:

"Come, my dear, begin to wash as fast as you can. Tell them to take off socks, coats and shirts, scrub them well, put on clean shirts, and the attendants will finish them off, and lay them in bed."

If she had requested me to shave them all, or dance a hornpipe on the stove funnel, I should have been less staggered; but to scrub some dozen lords of creation at a moment's notice, was really—really—. However, there was no time for nonsense, and, having resolved when I came to do everything I was bid, I drowned my scruples in my wash-bowl, clutched my soap manfully, and, assuming a business-like air; made a dab at the first dirty specimen I saw, bent on performing my task *vi et armis* [with force and arms] if necessary....

....

"I say, Mrs. !" called a voice behind me ; and, turning, I saw a rough Michigander, with an arm blown off at the shoulder, and two or three bullets still in him—as he afterwards mentioned, as carelessly as if gentlemen were in the habit of carrying such trifles about with them. I went to him, and, while administering a dose of soap and water, he whispered, irefully:

"That red-headed devil, over yonder; is a reb, damn him! You'll agree to that, I'll bet? He's got shot of a foot, or he'd a cut like the rest of the lot. Don't you wash him, nor feed him, but jest let him holler till he's tired. It's a blasted shame to fetch them fellers in here, along side of us...."

I regret to say that I did not deliver a moral sermon upon the duty of forgiving our enemies, and the sin of profanity, then and there; but, being a red-hot Abolitionist, stared fixedly at the tall rebel, who was a copperhead, in every sense of the word, and privately resolved to put soap in his eyes, rub his nose the wrong way, and excoriate his cuticle generally, if I had the washing of him.

My amiable intentions, however, were frustrated; for, when I approached, with as Christian an expression as my principles would allow, and asked the question—"Shall I try to make you more comfortable, sir ?" all I got for my pains was a gruff—

"No ; I'll do it myself."

"Here's your Southern chivalry, with a witness," thought I, dumping the basin down before him.... He was a disappointment in all respects... for he was neither fiendish, romantic, pathetic, or anything interesting; but a long, fat man, with a head like a burning bush, and a perfectly expressionless face: so I could hate him without the slightest drawback, and ignored his existence from that day forth.

Source: L.M. Alcott, *Hospital Sketches* (Boston, 1863), 33-35, 37-39.

THOUGHT QUESTIONS:

1. What does the condition of the soldiers encountered by the main character reveal about the nature of combat during the Civil War?

2. What does the main character's reaction to being ordered to wash the soldiers reveal about gender roles and her sense of duty?

3. How does the main character view Southerners? And why did she not act as she thought she would around them?

Vignettes

The Civil War and the "Good Death"

In 1864, Confederate Private James Robert Montgomery wrote his final letter to his father in Mississippi. "I write to you because I know you would be delighted to read a word from your dying son." Shrapnel had destroyed Montgomery's shoulder during the Battle of Spotsylvania, and he expected to be dead within a matter of days. He was correct. One of his friends recounted the moment of the soldier's passing for the Montgomery family. "I have never witnessed such an exhibition of fortitude and Christian resignation as he showed. In this sad bereavement you will have the greatest of comforts in knowing that he had made his peace with god and was resigned to his fate."

Civil War soldiers wrote letters describing their comrades' last moments often. Before the war, death usually took the elderly or involved a lingering sickness that permitted time for families to spend time together at the last moments of life. The war changed that. It took the young (Montgomery was twenty-six when he died). And it came suddenly. Four days passed between Montgomery's last letter and his death—much too short a time for anyone to travel between Virginia and Mississippi. Disease, which ran rampant in military camps and killed far more soldiers than fighting did, often took soldiers in a matter of days. Many soldiers died more quickly. Bullets killed them instantly in the field. Artillery shelling and sharpshooters arbitrarily killed soldiers even when they were not fighting.

These letters gave families something the war took from them: assurance that their loved one had experienced a "good death." Pre-war rituals surrounding death gave families an opportunity to assess whether a person was ready to die. In the deeply Protestant culture of the Civil War Era U.S., a "good death" implied that a person had expressed faith in God and could confidently expect salvation. Montgomery's friend made this point when he noted that James had "made his peace with god" and was ready to die. Soldiers recounted their fallen comrades' last days in great detail. They often reported that soldiers who had died instantly in the fighting had gone into battle with a sense of impending death—and that they had made themselves spiritually ready. These rituals also helped soldiers try to give meaning to the unprecedented levels of death that surrounded them, to help them fight against a gnawing sense that they faced nothing but senseless slaughter on American battlefields.

THOUGHT QUESTIONS:

1. How did the Civil War disrupt rituals surrounding death and dying in the mid-nineteenth-century U.S.?

2. Why did soldiers write letters with detailed descriptions of a comrades' death and send them to his family?

3. Why was it important to family members that their loved one had experienced a "good death"?

Who Freed the Slaves?

Racial slavery in the United States ended with the American Civil War. The emancipation of four million people ranks as one of the most significant moments in U.S. History. Yet determining who should receive credit for this development underscores the complex interplay between social groups and institutions that drive historical change in the United States.

Enslaved African Americans formed one such group. As southern white men left home to join the military and as Union forces pushed into the South, control of the enslaved population loosened. Numerous southern blacks responded by taking their own freedom and bolting for Union lines. In some areas, enslaved communities took management of their plantations, focusing on food crops rather than cotton. Wartime resistance by black Southerners had effectively rendered slavery a dead institution by 1863.

That resistance became possible, however, only because of the military conflict between the North and the South. Union forces placed enormous pressure on the South as the war dragged on. Although Union incursions loosened enslavers' hold on the South's black population, that pressure was insufficient on its own to produce emancipation. Yet combined with the tenacious defense of the Confederacy under the leadership of commanders like Robert E. Lee, which prolonged the war and increased the death toll, that pressure made emancipation appear to be a necessary war aim. And the enlistment and combat deployment of African-America soldiers personified the war's transformation into a struggle for freedom.

Yet the Union's ability to articulate (much less pursue) that struggle rested on the deft political maneuvering of President Abraham Lincoln. American public opinion remained divided over the war's ultimate goals. At one extreme, slaveholding Unionists from the border states demanded an outcome that did not result in emancipation. On the other extreme, Radical Republicans, like Horace Greeley, insisted that emancipation be a war aim from the earliest days of the war. Lincoln, at various times, needed support from both sides as well as from numerous factions that held positions that fell between the two poles. Lincoln navigated the Union's politics in a way that slowly, but steadily, moved a majority of northern voters to accept emancipation as an outcome.

Victory on the battlefield, however, may have also been insufficient to secure slavery's demise. Lincoln worried about this and pushed for the ratification of the Thirteenth Amendment, which would incorporate emancipation into the Constitution. The work here lay in Congress and especially in the House of Representatives where enough opposition to emancipation remained to kill the amendment. Floor leaders like James Ashley, a radical Republican from Ohio, thus expended a great deal of energy mobilizing allies and working with people who were generally his political enemies to convince enough opponents to switch sides or skip the votes. He succeeded in the end, although he may have resorted to bribing a few lame duck members to get the amendment through the House.

(The historical record is murky on that point, but contemporaries suspected as much, and the most recent historian of the amendment's passage thinks that bribery was likely.)

In the end, however, the answer to the question "who freed the slaves" is many people. Enslaved men and women who used the war as an opportunity to take their freedom were responsible. So were the soldiers and military commanders—northern and southern, black and white—who contributed in different ways to undermining slavery. And Union politicians used the ebb and flow of the war to move toward and finally to achieve a decisive and official emancipation. Such questions, of course, never yield one answer because major historical developments always grow out of multiple causes.

THOUGHT QUESTIONS:

1. What role did enslaved African Americans play in ending slavery?

2. What role did military forces, both northern and southern, play in creating the conditions that made emancipation possible?

3. How did Abraham Lincoln and Congress help bring about emancipation in the United States?

The Santee Sioux Uprising (1862)

In October 1862, a military court convened by General John Pope—recently reassigned to Minnesota after his defeat at the Second Battle of Bull Run—ordered the hanging of 303 Santee Sioux Indians. The execution orders formed part of the Lincoln Administration's response to the Santee Sioux Uprising that had erupted in the summer of that year. The events surrounding the uprising provide a microcosm into the continued deterioration of U.S.-Native American relations and foreshadowed the brutal repression of Indian resistance that would characterize the post-Civil War era.

Resistance among the Santee Sioux had its origins in the failure of the cash-strapped federal government, which was then struggling to pay for the Civil War, to meet its treaty obligations. The U.S. had agreed to pay annuities in exchange for land cessions made in the 1850s. Those treaties also encouraged farming, but the nomadic Sioux remained divided about whether to embrace the practice and had trouble growing enough food. Federal annuities made up the shortfall. Then the money stopped coming, and the Santee Sioux faced starvation. Indian agents denied requests for emergency funds, and one trader told the Sioux "to eat grass or their own dung."

Tensions mounted. Sioux warriors raided white settlements, which seemed to have plenty of food. In August, a confrontation between raiders and settlers over stolen eggs left five whites dead, and Sioux leaders opted to go to war immediately rather than wait for the military to mobilize its inevitable response. Sioux warriors carried out attacks throughout the Minnesota Valley in an ill-fated attempt to drive out white settlers. With authorization from Lincoln, General Pope promised "to exterminate the Sioux if I have the power to do so." He ordered his subordinates to kill or capture them, noting that "[t] hey are to be treated as maniacs or wild beasts." By September, the Santee Sioux had been defeated. Most of them had been captured, and Pope's court had indiscriminately sentenced 303 of the prisoners to death.

Lincoln thought Pope went too far. He reduced the number of death sentences to 38 (who were hanged en mass). But the government also suspended annuities and removed 1,300 Santee Sioux to the desolate Crow Creek reservation in present-day South Dakota where hundreds succumbed to starvation or disease.

The Santee Sioux Uprising marked an intensification of violence in Indian Country. Sioux leaders understood their resort to war as a last-ditch effort to slow the deterioration of their way of life. Lincoln claimed to be striking a balance. He explained to the Senate that he reduced the number of executions to keep the U.S. from acting "with so much severity as to be real cruelty." At the same time, he perceived a necessity to use enough force to discourage another uprising.

And there were other uprisings. Even before the Santee Sioux's resistance, members of the Five Civilized Tribes fought among themselves over which side to support during the Civil War. Some factions within some of the tribes sided with the Confederacy. Lincoln held all the tribes responsible and sent troops into Indian Territory. By war's end fighting had left the lands of the Five Civilized tribes desolate. In present-day Colorado, gold strikes attracted settlers, and tensions with the region's Native American population increased. Settlers broke that resistance in November 1864 when a Colorado militia attacked a camp displaying a white flag at a place called Sand Creek. The ensuing massacre—elderly men, women, and children formed the majority of the camp's occupants— marked the last major outbreak of violence in Civil-War-Era Indian Country. By then, the Civil War was grinding toward its end, but the wars for control of Indian Country were just beginning.

THOUGHT QUESTIONS:

1. Why did the Santee Sioux go to war with the United States in 1862?

2. How did Abraham Lincoln and his military commanders react to the Sioux uprising?

3. What else was happening in Indian Country during the Civil War Years?

Chapter 17

A Broken Promise of Freedom: Reconstruction, 1863-1877

An executive order issued as a military measure in the middle of the Civil War, Abraham Lincoln's Emancipation Proclamation stands as one of the most important civil rights measures in American history. On September 22, 1862, Lincoln issued the proclamation, which declared the freedom of all slaves in states or portions of states still in rebellion against the United States government as of January 1, 1863.

Confederate states ignored the deadline. Due to Lincoln's order, and Confederate inaction, the Civil War transformed into a war of liberation. The Emancipation Proclamation also made it politically impossible for England and France, which had depended on slave-grown southern cotton for their textile industries before the war, to politically, economically, and diplomatically support the Confederate States of America. By the 1860s, the British and French public opposed slavery. With the Emancipation Proclamation Lincoln made it clear that slavery would die if the Union won the war. Siding with the Confederacy was allying with forced servitude. The British-French-Confederate axis against the Union never materialized.

The Emancipation Proclamation did not free the slaves owned by those loyal to the Union, and provided for the return of escaped slaves owned by Union loyalists. There were still four slaves states in the Union—Kentucky, Missouri, Delaware, and Maryland—and Lincoln did not want to provoke those states into seceding by being perceived as an outright abolitionist. When the proclamation became public, Lincoln still supported the concept of "colonization" in which freed slaves would be sent to Africa upon emancipation. Lincoln did not yet embrace the concept of racial equality and was not convinced that African Americans could compete successfully with whites as freed people. However, he would evolve toward a position of supporting at least limited African-American citizenship and voting rights by the end of the war, and he would spend his last months backing an amendment to the United States Constitution that forever banned slavery in all American states and territories. As he put it, "If slavery is not wrong, nothing is wrong,"

By the President of the United States of America.
A Proclamation.

I, Abraham Lincoln, President of the United States of America, and Commander-in-Chief of the Army and Navy thereof, do hereby proclaim and declare that hereafter, as heretofore, the war will be prosecuted for the object of practically restoring the constitutional relation between the United States, and each of the States, and the people thereof, in which States that relation is, or may be, suspended or disturbed. That it is my purpose, upon the next meeting of Congress to again recommend the adoption of a practical measure tendering pecuniary aid to the free acceptance or rejection of all slave States, so called, the people whereof may not then be in rebellion against the United States and which States may then have voluntarily adopted, or thereafter may voluntarily adopt, immediate or gradual abolishment of slavery within their respective limits; and that the effort to colonize persons of African descent, with their consent, upon this continent, or elsewhere, with the previously obtained consent of the Governments existing there, will be continued.

That on the first day of January in the year of our Lord, one thousand eight hundred and sixty-three, all persons held as slaves within any State, or designated part of a State, the people whereof shall then be in rebellion against the United States shall be then, thenceforward, and forever free; and the executive government of the United States, including the military and naval authority thereof, will recognize and maintain the freedom of such persons, and will do no act or acts to repress such persons, or any of them, in any efforts they may make for their actual freedom.

That the executive will, on the first day of January aforesaid, by proclamation, designate the States, and part of States, if any, in which the people thereof respectively, shall then be in rebellion against the United States; and the fact that any State, or the people thereof shall, on that day be, in good faith represented in the Congress of the United States, by members chosen thereto, at elections wherein a majority of the qualified voters of such State shall have participated, shall, in the absence of strong countervailing testimony, be deemed conclusive evidence that such State and the people thereof, are not then in rebellion against the United States.

. . . All officers or persons in the military or naval service of the United States are prohibited from employing any of the forces under their respective commands for the purpose of returning fugitives from service or labor, who may have escaped from any persons to whom such service or labor is claimed to be due, and any officer who shall be found guilty by a court martial of violating this article shall be dismissed from the service.

. . . All slaves of persons who shall hereafter be engaged in rebellion against the government of the United States, or who shall in any way give aid or comfort thereto, escaping from such persons and taking refuge within the lines of the army; and all slaves captured from such persons or deserted by them and coming under the control of the government of the United States; and all slaves of such persons found on (or) being within any place occupied by rebel forces and afterwards occupied by the forces of the United States, shall be deemed captives of war, and shall be forever free of their servitude and not again held as slaves.

. . . [N]o slave escaping into any State, Territory, or the District of Columbia, from any other State, shall be delivered up, or in any way impeded or hindered of his liberty, except for crime, or some offence against the laws, unless the person claiming said fugitive shall first make oath that the person to whom the labor or service of such fugitive is alleged to be due is his lawful owner, and has not borne arms against the United States in the present rebellion, nor in any way given aid and comfort thereto . . .

. . . [T]he executive will in due time recommend that all citizens of the United States who shall have remained loyal thereto throughout the rebellion, shall (upon the restoration of the constitutional relation between the United States, and their respective States, and people, if that relation shall have been suspended or disturbed) be compensated for all losses by acts of the United States, including the loss of slaves.

In witness whereof, I have hereunto set my hand, and caused the seal of the United States to be affixed.

Done at the City of Washington this twenty-second day of September, in the year of our Lord, one thousand, eight hundred and sixty-two, and of the Independence of the United States the eighty seventh.

[Signed:] Abraham Lincoln
By the President
[Signed:] William H. Seward
Secretary of State

Source: https://www.archives.gov/exhibits/american_originals_iv/sections/transcript_preliminary_emancipation.html

THOUGHT QUESTIONS:

1. What effects did the Emancipation Proclamation have on the course of the Civil War?

2. President Abraham Lincoln was trying to reach which audiences with his proclamation?

3. How did the Emancipation Proclamation reflect Lincoln's attitudes towards slavery and race relations midway through the Civil War?

General William Tecumseh Sherman,
Special Field Order No. 15

One of the chief obstacles freedmen faced after Lincoln issued the Emancipation Proclamation and the states ratified the 13th Amendment abolishing slavery was their utter poverty. Most freedmen had little or no financial resources after a lifetime of work and did not own land. This financial reality meant that although they were no longer human property, the freedmen would for the most part have to depend on their former masters for their livelihoods. This unequal financial relationship gave the white landowners the power to set the terms by which freedmen they employed worked and immense leverage as they tried to control them politically.

With the exception of Union General William Tecumseh Sherman, no major figure in the Reconstruction period—presidents Abraham Lincoln and Andrew Johnson or the United State Congress—made any attempt to deal with the former slaves' lack of financial resources. As the Civil War ground to its conclusion, freedmen faced cold, hunger, and retaliation from bitter whites in the crumbling Confederacy who blamed the former slaves for the South's rapidly approaching defeat. The freedmen followed Union troops, such as those commended by Sherman, seeking protection and food. Still fighting the Confederate Army, Sherman felt overwhelmed by the additional task of protecting and caring for the freedmen.

Sherman led a force of 60,000 troops and conquered Confederate territory from Tennessee to, in September 1864, the city of Atlanta. Sherman had no interest in providing social services to the impoverished freed slaves and wanted to focus on winning the war. He came up with an innovative solution. On January 16, 1865, Sherman announced Special Order No. 15. The Union Army seized land that had been abandoned by owners who had supported the Confederacy in the Georgia Sea Islands, the South Carolina low country, and part of northern Florida's Atlantic Coast. Under Sherman's order, the land was redistributed to freedmen. Freedmen families could apply for use of 40 acres. Upon request, the military also loaned each family a mule

As of June 1865, 40,000 freedmen had started successfully farming on 400,000 acres of what came to be known as "Sherman land." Andrew Johnson, a former slave owner who became president upon Lincoln's assassination, however, saw Sherman's initiative as a dangerous experiment in socialism and as promoting the equality of the races. Johnson reversed Special Order No. 15 and ordered the land returned to the previous white owners. Sherman's directive became yet one more example of freedom promised and the taken away from African Americans in the South during the Reconstruction Era.

The islands from Charleston, south, the abandoned rice fields along the rivers for thirty miles back from the sea, and the country bordering the St. Johns River, Florida, are reserved and set apart for the settlement of the negroes now made free by the acts of war and the proclamation of the President of the United States.

. . . At Beaufort, Hilton Head, Savannah, Fernandina, St. Augustine and Jacksonville, the blacks may remain in their chosen or accustomed vocations—but on the islands, and in the settlements hereafter to be established, no white person whatever, unless military officers and soldiers detailed for duty, will be permitted to reside; and the sole and exclusive management of affairs will be left to the freed people themselves, subject only to the United States military authority and the acts of Congress. By the laws of war, and orders of the President of the United States, the negro is free and must be dealt with as such. He cannot be subjected to conscription or forced military service, save by the written orders of the highest military authority of the Department, under such regulations as the President or Congress may prescribe. Domestic servants, blacksmiths, carpenters and other mechanics, will be free to select their own work and residence, but the young and able-bodied negroes must be encouraged to enlist as soldiers in the service of the United States, to contribute their share towards maintaining their own freedom, and securing their rights as citizens of the United States . . .

Whenever three respectable negroes, heads of families, shall desire to settle on land, and shall have selected for that purpose an island or a locality clearly defined, within the limits above designated, the Inspector of Settlements and Plantations will himself, or by such subordinate officer as he may appoint, give them a license to settle such island or district, and afford them such assistance as he can to enable them to establish a peaceable agricultural settlement. The three parties named will subdivide the land, under the supervision of the Inspector, among themselves and such others as may choose to settle near them, so that each family shall have a plot of not more than (40) forty acres of tillable ground, and when it borders on some water channel, with not more than 800 feet water front, in the possession of which land the military authorities will afford them protection, until such time as they can protect themselves, or until Congress shall regulate their title. The Quartermaster may, on the requisition of the Inspector of Settlements and Plantations, place at the disposal of the Inspector, one or more of the captured steamers, to ply between the settlements and one or more of the commercial points heretofore named in orders, to afford the settlers the opportunity to supply their necessary wants, and to sell the products of their land and labor . . .

BY ORDER OF MAJOR GENERAL W. T. SHERMAN:

Source: Special Field Orders, No. 15, Headquarters Military Division of the Mississippi, 16 Jan. 1865, Orders & Circulars, ser. 44, Adjutant General's Office, Record Group 94, National Archives.

THOUGHT QUESTIONS:

1. In what ways might African-American poverty limit their freedom after they were emancipated as slaves?

2. On what grounds might the army justify seizing land from owners who supported the Confederacy and by what legal challenges might this seizure be challenged?

3. What inspired President Andrew Johnson to reverse Sherman's Special Field Order No. 15 and what might that suggest about his attitude towards the freedmen?

Blanche K. Bruce
Speech in the Senate on The Mississippi Elections
March 31 1876

After African Americans were granted citizenship by the 14th Amendment, ratified in 1868, and states were banned from denying the right to vote based on race, color and previous servitude under the 15th Amendment, ratified in 1870, Republicans briefly ruled states across the old Confederacy. Beginning in 1871, however, white so-called "Redeemer" Democrats began regaining control of the region. The Redeemers accused Republicans of spending too much money, raising taxes too high, embezzling government funds, and of having handed the region over to corrupt and incompetent "negro rule." As Reconstruction wound to a close between 1875-1877, Redeemer campaigns became more openly racist and violent. In Mississippi, Redeemers launched a campaign of terror against Republicans in 1875. The "Mississippi Plan" utilized armed gangs, strategic murders, threats, and bribes to prevent African Americans from voting. In one black majority county there, not a single African American voted. Democrats raided Republican Party meetings. Some African Americans were forced at gunpoint to vote for Democrats. In other counties, Redeemers altered Republican ballots or ballot boxes were stuffed. In September, thugs attacked a Republican Party-sponsored barbecue in Clinton, sparking an exchange of gunfire. Armed Redeemers combed the area, gunning down African Americans indiscriminately. "They just hunted the whole country clean out, just every [African American] man they could see they were shooting at him just the same as birds," said one witness. Estimates of the number killed in the "Clinton Massacre" range from 30-50 with children numbering among the victims. A massacre of blacks in Vicksburg may have claimed as many as 80 lives. The Democrats won the November statewide elections in a landslide, with the new legislature impeaching the Republican lieutenant governor and forcing Governor Adelbert Ames to resign or face a similar fate the following year. In March of 1876, Senator Blanche K. Bruce, who in 1874 became Mississippi's first (and so far only) African-American Senator, condemned the state's 1875 elections as an undemocratic travesty.

The conduct of the late election in Mississippi affected not merely the fortunes of partisans—as the same were necessarily involved in the defeat or success of the respective parties to the contest—but put in question and jeopardy the sacred rights of the citizen
. . . The evidence in hand and accessible will show beyond peradventure that in many parts of the State corrupt and violent influences were brought to bear upon the registrars of voters, thus materially affecting the character of the voting or poll lists; upon the inspectors of election, prejudicially and unfairly thereby changing the number of votes cast; and, finally, threats and violence were practiced directly upon the masses of voters in such measures and strength as to produce grave apprehensions for their personal safety and as to deter them from the exercise of their political franchises.

It will not accord with the laws of nature or history to brand colored people a race of cowards. On more than one historic field, beginning in 1776 and coming down to this centennial year of the Republic, they have attested in blood their courage as well as a love of liberty—I ask Senators to believe that no consideration of fear or personal danger has kept us quiet and forbearing under the provocations and wrongs that have so sorely tried our souls. But feeling kindly toward our white fellow-citizens, appreciating the good purposes and politics of the better classes, and, above all, abhorring a war of races, we determined to wait until such time as an appeal to the good sense and justice of the American people could be made.

. . . The unanimity with which the colored voters act with a party is not referable to any race prejudice on their part. On the contrary. They invite the political cooperation of their white brethren, and vote as a unit . . . They deprecate the establishment of the color line by the opposition, not only because the act is unwise and wrong in principle, but because it isolates them from the white men of the South, and forces them, in sheer self-protection and against their inclination, to act seemingly upon the basis of a race prejudice that they neither respect nor entertain. As a class they are free from prejudices, and have no uncharitable suspicions against their white fellow-citizens, whether native born or settlers from the Northern States. They not only recognize the equality of citizenship and the right of every man to hold, without proscription any position of honor and trust to which the confidence of the people may elevate him; but owing nothing to race, birth, or surroundings, they, above all other classes in the community, are interested to see prejudices drop out of both politics and the business of the country, and success in life proceed only upon the integrity and merit of the man who seeks it. . . .

I have confidence, not only in this country and her institutions, but in the endurance, capacity, and destiny of my people. We will, as opportunity offers and ability serves, seek our places, sometimes in the field of letters, arts, sciences, and the professions. More frequently mechanical pursuits will attract and elicit our efforts; more still of my people will find employment and livelihood as the cultivators of the soil. The bulk of this people—by surroundings, habits, adaptation, and choice—will continue to find their homes in the South, and constitute the masses of its yeomanry. We will there probably, of our own volition and more abundantly than in the past, produce the great staples that will contribute to the basis of foreign exchange, aid in giving the nation a balance of trade, and minister to the wants and comfort and build up the prosperity of the whole land. Whatever our ultimate position in the composite civilization of the Republic and whatever varying fortunes attend our career, we will not forget our instincts for freedom nor our love of country.

Source: *Congressional Record*, 44th Congress, 1st Session, March 31, 1876.

THOUGHT QUESTIONS:

1. In the 1870s, what accusations did Redeemer Democrats level against Republicans in the South?

2. What methods did Redeemers use to suppress the Republican vote in the South?

3. What explanation did Senator Blanche Bruce give for why African Americans in the former Confederacy almost unanimously supported the Republican Party in the Reconstruction Era?

Vignettes

Lincoln in Richmond

Just before he died, Abraham Lincoln got a glimpse of the new world he had created. The Union Army had captured Richmond, Virginia, the now former capital of the Confederacy, a sure sign that the end finally neared for the Civil War. Welcoming any chance to get out of Washington, D.C., Lincoln on April 4, 1865 travelled to Richmond with his son Tad who celebrated his 12th birthday that same day. Lincoln wanted to inspect this slice of the South he knew he had changed forever.

Guarded by a small number of sailors, Lincoln and his son walked through an urban hellscape, with fires still raging from the recently concluded battle for control of the city. Richmond's African Americans knew about Lincoln's Emancipation Proclamation that had declared an end to slavery in the rebel states, and they also knew that the Confederate surrender in Richmond meant that they had won freedom.

They immediately asserted themselves. When word spread that "the President" was strolling through Richmond's chaotic streets, some freedmen thought it was Jefferson Davis, the dethroned Confederate president. They thought he had been arrested for treason and was being marched to prison. "Hang him! Hang him!" they began chanting. When the former slaves came face-to-face with the presidential visiting party, however, they soon realized they had met not their chief oppressor, but a man they hailed as their liberator.

A Boston reporter covering the president's trip informed a freedwoman about the visitor's identity. "That's President Lincoln?" the woman asked and upon confirming the news, she began leaping in the air and shouting, "Glory!" even as a larger group of African Americans gathered and cheered. The president may not have realized the full personal impact of the Emancipation Proclamation on millions of black lives until that moment, but it must have become clear as he walked through a crowd showering him with praise and greeting him with the words, "God bless you."

An elderly freedman removed his hat and bowed to the president, saying through tears, "May the good Lord bless you." Lincoln shattered centuries-old racial rules that demanded whites always assume a position of superiority. The president removed his famous stovepipe hat and quietly bowed back. Lincoln capped off the day by visiting the executive mansion Davis had used as Confederate president and eased into his counterpoint's easy chair. "I wonder if I could get a drink of water," Lincoln simply asked.

The next week he would publicly embrace limited black suffrage for the first time and soon thereafter faced his fatal rendezvous with a bitter, Confederate-sympathizing actor, John Wilkes Booth, who would murder the president at Ford's Theater the evening of April 14, 1865.

THOUGHT QUESTIONS:

1. What do the freedmen's reactions at the time of Lincoln's visit to Richmond suggest about their feelings about their new status and towards their old masters?

2. Based on his reaction to the freedmen he encountered in Richmond, what might have been Lincoln's attitudes towards African Americans and how did they vary from the norms of the time?

3. What emotions might have inspired Lincoln to want to visit the former capital of the Confederacy as the Union approached victory in the Civil War?

A Celebration of Freedom:
Juneteenth

On June 19, 1865, more than two months after Robert E. Lee, commander of the Army of Northern Virginia, surrendered to the Union Army's commanding officer, Ulysses S. Grant, thus effectively ending the Civil War, another northern officer, General Gordon Granger, came ashore in Galveston, Texas. Granger announced to those assembled that the United States Army's General Order No. 3 had taken effect and had the force of law in Texas. The order read in part, "The people of Texas are informed that, in accordance with a proclamation from the Executive of the United States, all slaves are free. This involves an absolute equality of personal rights and rights of property between former masters and slaves, and the connection heretofore existing between them becomes that between employer and hired labor."

News of Abraham Lincoln's Emancipation Proclamation declaring free all slaves in states or parts of states in rebellion as of January 1, 1863, and of the Confederate armed surrender, reached Texas before Granger arrived. The now former slaveowners in Texas, however, kept freedmen toiling as if they remained legal property. The crack of the whip could still be heard in the East Texas cotton fields in the weeks following Lee's encounter with Grant. Granger's arrival not only proclaimed black freedom in the Lone Star State, it also marked the military's enforcement of the emancipation order in Texas.

Approximately 50,000 federal troops would occupy Texas in the months after Granger read his decree. One army report issued in October1865 noted that in more remote parts of the state whites "still claim and control [slaves] as property, and in two or three instances recently bought and sold them." African Americans who insisted on acting as free people met with violence, with one state government committee claiming that between 1865 and 1868, whites killed approximately 400 African Americans. That number is almost certainly a serious underestimate. Meanwhile, whites punished freedmen who celebrated their new status. Historian Randolph Campbell notes that a slave patrol lashed 100 freedmen in Crockett for publicly expressing joy over emancipation while elsewhere a former master fired pistol shots between a freedman's feet when the just-liberated man jumped in the air at news of Granger's order.

Nevertheless, the state's freedmen embraced June 19th, the date of Granger's proclamation, as a black July 4th, a day to celebrate freedom. The day came to be known as "Juneteenth." It was first marked in1866, and it became a major black holiday following a massive parade held by freedmen in Austin in 1867. African Americans marked Juneteenth with family gatherings, feasts, parades, and spirituals. The tradition spread from its Texas birthplace to the neighboring states of Arkansas and Louisiana. As African Americans migrated from the South across the country, it came to be observed in most states. Juneteenth now inspires barbecues, parties, and other gatherings from San Francisco to Minneapolis to Washington, D.C.

During the 1950s through the 1970s, younger African Americans for a time shunned Juneteenth. Some disdained its association with slavery and saw the celebrations as backwards-looking at a time civil rights activists wanted to focus on the fight for a better tomorrow. Juneteenth enjoyed a rebirth, however, when Houston Democrat Al Edwards successfully steered a bill through the Texas Legislature declaring Juneteenth a state holiday in 1979. Texas held its first official state Juneteenth observance in 1980.

Now, Juneteenth is recognized in the District of Columbia and all but five of the fifty states. Repeated efforts have been made to designate June 19 as a national holiday, including an intense lobbying campaign by 90-year-old Opal Lee of Fort Worth who in 2017 lobbied Congress and tried to get action on the matter from President Barack Obama before he left office. So far these efforts have fallen short. America's other "Independence Day" remains widely celebrated, but is not yet on the federal calendar.

THOUGHT QUESTIONS:

1. How did Texas slaveowners maintain human bondage in the months following the Confederacy's defeat in the Civil War?

2. Why did Juneteenth become controversial in the Civil Rights Era that followed World War II?

3. In spite of its nationwide popularity, why do you think that Juneteenth has not yet become an official national holiday?

The Legacy of Newton Knight
and "The Free State of Jones"

Clearly, the United States was a divided nation at the time of the Civil War, enough so that eleven slave states seceded from the Union and fought a bloody war to separate from the Union. The Confederate States of America, however, also badly fractured during its four-year struggle against the Union. Obviously, the four million slaves languishing in the Confederacy did not support the secessionists' cause. In addition, poor whites across the Confederate states increasingly resented having their crops and livestock seized to support the southern war effort and fighting and dying to preserve the enormous wealth of the major slaveowners.

Numerous parts of the Confederate States of America supported the Union during the war. West Virginia broke off from the rest of the Virginia Commonwealth in order to back the federal government. Other anti-CSA strongholds included Eastern Tennessee, parts of Northwestern Alabama, and Northwestern Arkansas. The Hill Country in Central Texas fought against secessionists, as did many in North Central Texas and the "Big Thicket" country in the eastern part of the state. The Confederate Army fiercely battled not only the Union troops, but anti-Confederates from their own region, even as the Confederate ranks dwindled due to an estimated 100,000 or so desertions.

Due to a recent Hollywood movie one of those deserters—Newton Knight—has become famous. Born in 1837 in Jones County, Mississippi, a swampy region thick with trees in which poor farmers struggled to eke out a living, Knight raised livestock and cultivated grain. The extremely wealthy plantation owners who ran Mississippi could not be found here. Knight's father, a Baptist preacher, saw slavery as sinful, and others in the county shared the elder Knight's attitude. In the 1860 election, Jones County voters overwhelmingly supported an anti-secession candidate.

Although he opposed secession, Knight enlisted in the Confederate Army. Scholars disagree why, but some believe that he might have because he probably would have been drafted anyway. Knight and many other soldiers from the "Piney Woods" section of Mississippi, however, grew disgusted by the high cost in human life caused by a war that benefitted only the rich, and their anger deepened as incompetent officers delivered them into unnecessary danger. After months of being poorly fed, Knight and others from the Piney Woods deserted after the Second Battle of Corinth, October 3-4, 1862, a Confederate defeat in which more than 4,000 of the southern forces died, suffered wounds, or were captured.

Returning home to Jones County, Knight saw first-hand the devastating impact of a Confederate tax that allowed the southern military to seize farm animals, crops, or any other supplies it needed from farmers without compensation. Meanwhile, as poor farmers began to suffer hunger, slaveowners with 20 or more slaves had been granted a draft exemption by the Confederate Congress.

The Confederate Army captured Knight in the first months of 1863, but by the end of the year, after another Confederate defeat at Battle of Vicksburg, Jones went absent without leave again. He probably fatally shot a Confederate officer dispatched to round up deserters. In 1864, Jones and more than 120 fellow deserters and escaped slaves formed a militia that battled Confederate troops. Hiding in the swamps, they seceded from Mississippi and declared the territory they controlled "The Free State of Jones."

An enduring myth of Reconstruction is that after the war, when slavery had been abolished and citizenship and voting rights had been granted African Americans, the Union Army imposed "Negro" rule on the South. In fact, although just emancipated African Americans made more than 60 percent percent of the Southern Republican Party, white Southerners who opposed secession during the war, like Knight, made up a significant part of the Republican governing coalition during Reconstruction.

Mississippi remained as divided, along lines of race and class, after the war. Some struggling white farmers made common cause with freedmen during the period. Although he was already married to a white woman, Knight lived with a freedwoman named Rachel. The couple eventually had five children and raised four children who had been fathered by several of Rachel's former masters. At a time when the local Democratic Party used terrorism to suppress black political participation, Knight led a militia that provided physical safety for African-American voters and forced landowners to release African Americans illegally kept in slavery.

When the Democrats regained control of the state through Ku Klux Klan violence, Jones and his interracial family relocated to Jasper County in Southeastern Mississippi, not far from the Alabama border. Knight outlived his many enemies, passing away—perhaps from a heart attack—at the age of 84 in 1922. His headstone bears the inscription, "He Lived for Others."

Knight's family grew into a sizeable tribe in the post-war years. Rachel died in 1889. One year later, the state of Mississippi passed a law banning interracial marriage. (Former Confederate states began passing such "anti-miscegenation" laws during Reconstruction, starting with Tennessee in 1870. Such laws aimed at driving a deeper wedge between blacks and whites in an era of segregation.) Not quite fitting into the black community, and shunned by most whites because of their mixed-race heritage, some of the Knight children began marrying cousins. Light-skinned Knights moved, hid their family past, and married white spouses or married other mixed-race individuals. In 1890, the state of Mississippi passed a law banning interracial marriage. Authorities arrested Knight's light-skinned descendant, Davis Knight, when he married a white woman in 1948 when a resentful relative exposed his mixed-race heritage.

The Mississippi Supreme Court reversed Davis's conviction in 1948, saying that the prosecution had been unable to prove the racial identity of Davis' ancestor Rachel so long after she died. The film *The Free State of Jones*, based on the story of Newton Knight and his descendant Davis and starring Matthew McConaughey in the title role, was released in 2016 to mixed reviews.

THOUGHT QUESTIONS:

1. How did economic inequality possibly contribute to the Confederacy's defeat in the Civil War?

2. What does the Newton Knight story indicate about the makeup of the Reconstruction Era Republican Party in the South?

3. What motives possibly inspired anti-miscegenation laws (statutes banning interracial marriage) beginning during Reconstruction?